IMAGES
of America

WEST ASHLEY

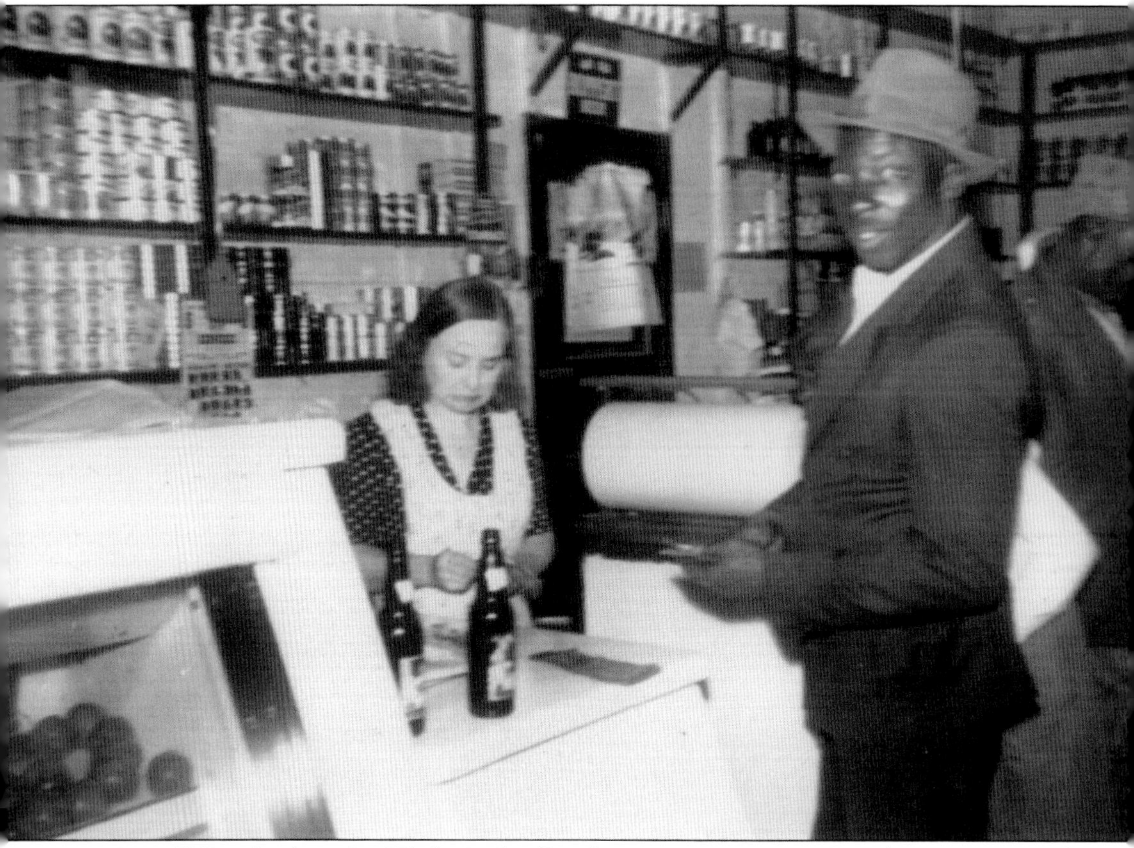

Grace E. Bootle, the wife of Philip Luther Bootle, serves a customer at Bootle's Grocery. Bootle's Grocery was located on the corner of Wappoo Road and Savannah Highway, an active intersection that included the Charleston County Market, Dupont Crossing, Corbett's Packaging, and Whaley's Gas Station. St. Andrew's Parish High School was located about a quarter mile down Wappoo Road on the left. In a time where society struggled with the social pressure of segregation, the Bootle family was known for serving everyone at their establishments. In 1961, Luther's brother, US District Court Judge William Augustus Bootle, ruled to integrate the University of Georgia. (Courtesy of P. Luther Bootle Jr., Ina Bootle.)

ON THE COVER: The front steps of St. Andrew's Parish High School was a popular location for school photographs and the site for this group photograph of the St. Andrew's Chapter of the Future Homemakers of America. Alumni of this school hold fond memories of their time there. They speak with great affection about their principal, teachers, coaches, and classmates. In the beginning, the school was small and everyone knew everyone. *West Ashley* introduces the reader to the time when life in St. Andrew's Parish changed from agrarian to suburban and the future homemakers were active building the community. (Courtesy of P. Luther Bootle Jr., Ina Bootle.)

IMAGES
of America

WEST ASHLEY

Donna F. Jacobs

ARCADIA
PUBLISHING

ISBN 978-0-7385-9120-9

Published by Arcadia Publishing
Charleston, South Carolina

Printed in the United States of America

Library of Congress Control Number: 2011935545

For all general information, please contact Arcadia Publishing:
Telephone 843-853-2070
Fax 843-853-0044
E-mail sales@arcadiapublishing.com
For customer service and orders:
Toll-Free 1-888-313-2665

Visit us on the Internet at www.arcadiapublishing.com

This book is dedicated to the photographers who captured place and time in photographs so we could remember and to the storytellers who kept the history alive so it could be written down.

Contents

Acknowledgments

Do you remember the time when it was popular to gather on the front porch, under a tree, at the local diner, or on the bench at the gas station and tell stories—some taller than others? We passed along our sense of time and being by way of our oral histories. Researching this book afforded me the pleasure of rekindling this tradition. I am forever indebted to the many people who gave so generously of their time, photographs, stories, and scrapbooks in order for me to understand St. Andrew's Parish. During my journey, I met many amazing folks, ate some delicious coffee cake, reminisced about barbecue, the odor of cabbage past its prime in the field, school revues, church gatherings, and movies at the Ashley Theater and the Magnolia Drive-In, met some of the "Parish Girls," found Virginia's chili recipe, and chased Roy Hart. Many times, the stories became personal and out of the scope of this book, but the perspectives I gained were invaluable. The names in parentheses with the captions are just a few of the people I met in the community of St. Andrew's Parish. Everyone told me wonderful stories. I honor you all with this book.

Introduction

The story of West Ashley can be a story of bridges, a story of exploration, a story of a plantation society, a story of war, a story of slavery, or a story of spirit, for it was here along the west bank of the Ashley River that the British colonists landed in 1670. It was here that a society was destroyed and rebuilt and it was here that we live with a spirit of community that redefines and refines itself with every generation.

In 1943, the Exchange Club of St. Andrew's Parish prepared a brochure to celebrate the progress in the Parish. The section of the brochure titled, "Its Historical Past—Its Progressive Present and Its Glorious Future" set the tone for a communal spirit by referring to the Parish as a hallowed spot. The Church Act of 1706 divided the four counties of South Carolina into parishes, including St. Andrew's Parish. Less than 40 years prior, the original colonists had arrived after a tumultuous trip from England via Barbados and Bermuda. They named the settlement Albemarle Point in honor of the oldest Lords Proprietor, George Duke of Albemarle. Colonization was not without its trials and tribulations; however, the development of a plantation structure and a transportation system contributed to the Parish's prosperity as Charles Towne grew into a market for the young colonies and the old world. Eventually, a bridge was needed to augment the ferry traffic that connected the Parish to the Charles Towne settlement growing out from Oyster Point. In 1808, the Charleston Bridge Company was granted a charter to construct such a bridge and a road that would continue south to Rantowles Creek. The road has gone by many names, including the Shell Road, Atlantic Coastal Highway, Savannah Highway, and Highway 17. The bridge served the area until the Civil War when Colonel Bull ordered it burned in anticipation of an assault by General Sherman and his troops on the city of Charleston. Once again, the Ashley River separated St. Andrew's Parish from Charleston.

The Civil War rearranged the entire societal structure of Charleston and effectively destroyed every aspect of the plantation way of life. The plantations along the west bank of the Ashley River were now in ruins and St. Andrew's Parish declined in both prosperity and population. The discovery of phosphate reserves coincident with development of the fertilizer manufacturing industry provided a source of revitalization for the greater Charleston area late in the 19th century; however, it destroyed the social and political impact of the Parish. It did provide some financial recovery for the landowners where phosphate was mined and the freed slaves could now earn wages for working in the mines. Mary Mathews Just was one of these laborers. In 1888, she used her newly earned money to purchase land, formerly part of the Hillsborough Plantation, which would become the town of Maryville, one of several African American towns that formed after the end of the Civil War.

In 1889, the new bridge, a privately owned wooden structure was constructed, and once again St. Andrew's Parish was connected to the city of Charleston. A brochure published by the Charleston Bridge Company detailed the opportunities for planters and with the new bridge they could efficiently move produce to market. At the turn of the century, the War Department established the South Atlantic Naval Station on a site along the Cooper River. The economic stimulus provided by truck framing, dairy production, and availability of jobs at the new naval yard began to have a modest impact on St. Andrew's Parish. In 1921, the toll was lifted and, according to the St. Andrew's Parish Exchange Club brochure, "the Parish reached its turning point and proceeded into the present era."

By now, the living conditions on the peninsula had become congested and residents began to look to St. Andrew's Parish as a place to build homes. Wappoo Heights was one of the first residential developments established in 1924 by George A. Nash. With the construction of the bascule bridge in 1926, the development of Windermere and The Crescent quickly followed along land adjacent to the Ashley River Memorial Bridge. For the next decade, growth was rapid. Soon, the residents found themselves in need of infrastructure in the form of bus service, phone service, fire and police protection, and schools. It was also decided that a service club was needed and the Exchange Club of St. Andrew's Parish was formed in 1941. The United States's entry into World War II was looming and the leaders and residents felt preparation and organization was needed.

Two prisoner of war (POW) camps functioned in the Parish during World War II. One camp along the Ashley River housed German POWs and the other camp along Savannah Highway housed Italian POWs. Numerous stories circulate about the POWs and as best that can be discovered, they were mostly "hired-out" as day laborers to the local farms. Housing continued to be at a premium as more workers were recruited for jobs at the naval yard. Developers continued rapidly building neighborhoods. Avondale, Byrnes Downs, and St. Andrew's Homes are examples of this expansion. Businessmen set up shop and churches and schools were organized. In 1945, peace was declared and the ground of St. Andrew's Parish had been planted with the seeds for a different type of community. The agrarian lifestyle was giving way to a suburban lifestyle. Gathering places like Bootle's BBQ stand, Roy Hart's, Ashley Theater, Cavallero, and the numerous gas stations were becoming popular with the local people.

By the mid-1950s the discussion of incorporation was on the table. The pros and cons of incorporation were debated and published in the local newspaper the *News and Courier*. In the end, Mayor Palmer Gaillard proposed annexation into the city of Charleston and during the mid-1960s, most of St. Andrew's Parish voted to become part of Charleston. When Bernard Hester designed the emblem for the St. Andrew's Parish High School, he included the Latin phrase *Sapere Aude* which translates to "Dare to Be Wise"—perfect advice for a community growing into its own.

At the end of the section titled, "Its Historical Past—Its Progressive Present and Its Glorious Future" in the brochure, this sentiment is expressed, "Much more can be written of the loves and lives of St. Andrew's Parish and of its ascendency and decline as a political, economic and social factor in the Carolina Lowcountry, and of the effect its early culture had on many parts of America, but it is not possible in the scope of this modest brochure to do more. Predictions of the future of St. Andrew's Parish also are beyond the scope of this book, but it is obvious that, with the continued growth in population and the many progressive steps taken in recent years to give residents all facilities of urban life, it takes no eye of prophecy to foretell that the future of St. Andrew's Parish is to be a substantial one and that during the postwar period she will contribute to the welfare of her state and nation and will return again to the glories that were part of her past."

Libraries, local bookstores, and archives are replete with the history of Charleston, a town whose influence on the beginning of our country is placed alongside Boston and Philadelphia. The contribution of the life and times west of the Ashley River were a significant part of not only this early Colonial time but also the plantation era. With all due respect to our place in this history, I present this book as a preface to a more modern history—the 20th century history of St. Andrew's Parish, West Ashley, as it changed from an agrarian lifestyle to the community we love and live in today.

One

Postwar Recovery

Prior to the Civil War, St. Andrew's Parish was the home to some of the grandest plantations of the colonies. Parish residents were signers of some of our country's most hallowed documents and the institution of slavery provided the system where plantations could accumulate great wealth. Postwar recovery would take a completely different direction, as the financial backbone of the area had been broken. The discovery of plentiful phosphate resources, the beginning of a fertilizer manufacturing industry, and the ability to enrich the land for crop farming gave the area the means to find the road to recovery. Dr. St. Julien Ravenel was instrumental in refining the chemical process, transforming phosphate to fertilizer and for the physiological understanding of its application to crops. The port of Charleston began shipping both raw ore and processed fertilizer. By 1930, there were 16 fertilizer plants in the greater Charleston area, and it had become the world's largest producer. Pre–Civil War plantation life had attempted to replicate the elite British society; however, this was not the case for the plantation owners who participated in the mining industry. The social and political prominence of the Parish was now a page for the history book. Farming provided another mechanism for financial recovery. Joseph Harrison, Edmond Ravenel, Francis Hanckel, William Kennerty, Ernest King, and Charles Ravenel are a few of the men who either used the family land or purchased land in the early 20th century to set about making a living from cabbage, potatoes, or milk. With the abolition of slavery and the opportunity for jobs in the phosphate and farming industries, freed slaves also found a road to recovery. Mary Mathews Just purchased land from the Hillsborough Plantation using the wages she earned in the phosphate mines, and the African American town of Maryville grew out of this opportunity. The South Carolina Legislature revoked the town's charter in 1936 and Maryville was divided by the construction of St. Andrew's Boulevard (also known as Highway 61), however, the community survived. The neighborhood along the west bank of the Ashley River is known today as Ashleyville and the section across the boulevard retains the name of Maryville. St. Andrew's Parish, west of the Ashley River, was now in the 20th century.

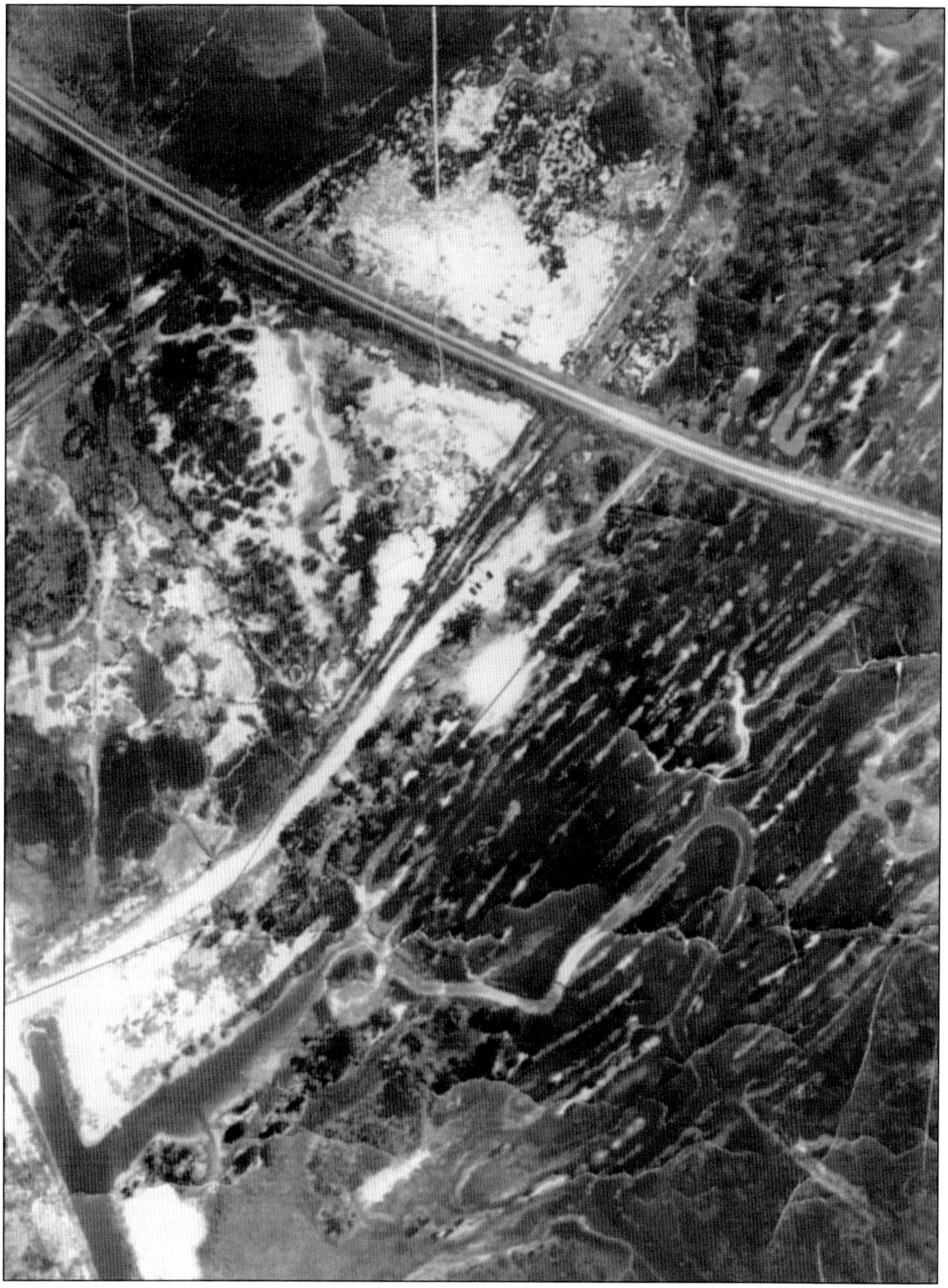

The marshes bordering the Sylan Shores subdivision show some of the scars left in the St. Andrew's Parish landscape by phosphate mining. Charleston was the top producer of phosphate in the nation and mining provided a windfall for an area in economic ruin after the Civil War. Both landowners and freed people shared in this windfall. (Courtesy of Jack Eades.)

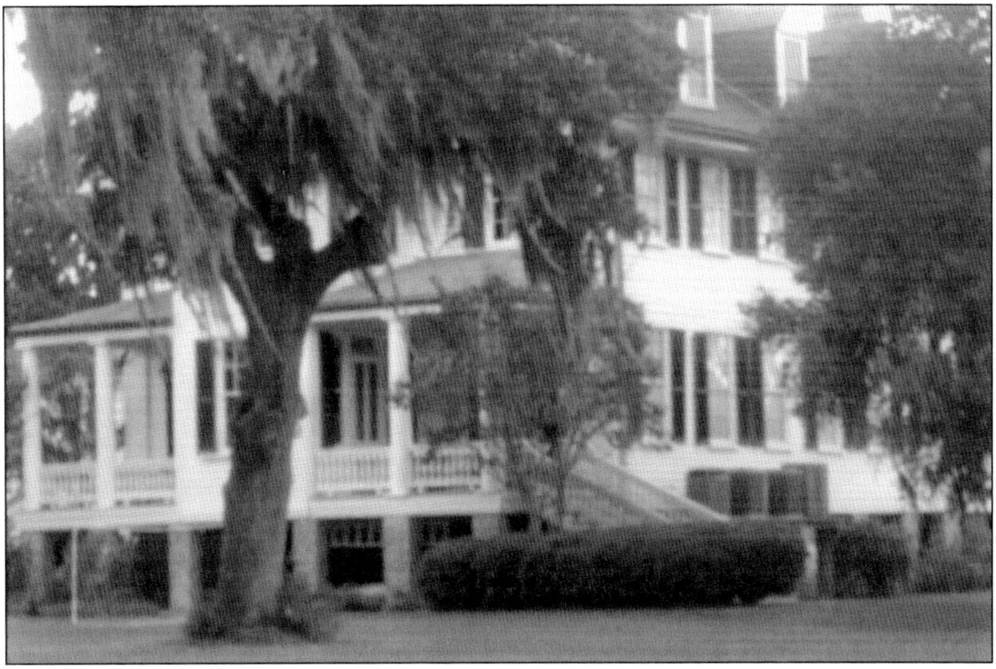

William Ravenel moved his family into this house at Farmfield in 1854. The story is told that a slave named William built the home for William Ravenel as a thank you for keeping his family together. William served as the executor to numerous estates and was known for keeping slave families together, often moving them to his farm. Rose Pringle Ravenel wrote the delightful *Piazza Tales* about her memories growing up on Farmfield, the Ravenel genealogy, and war times. (Courtesy of Arthur Ravenel Jr.)

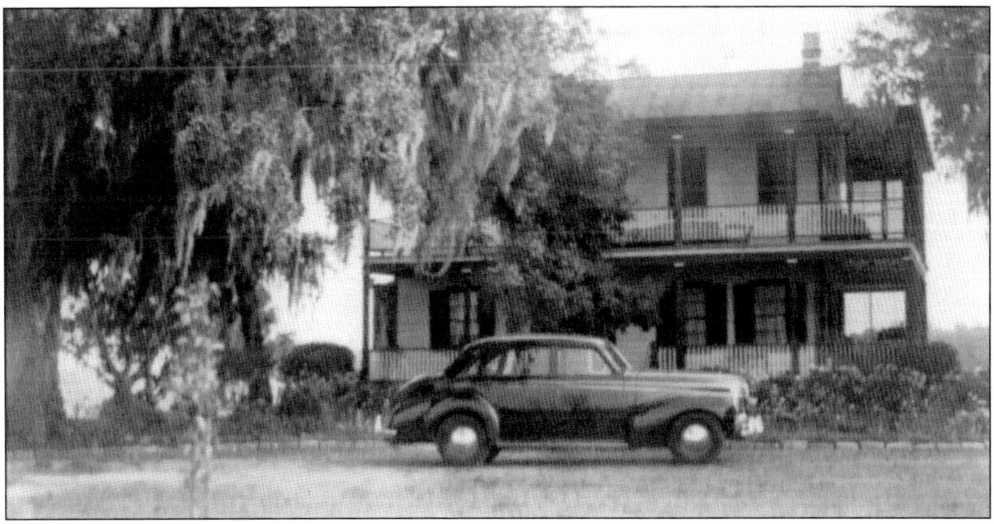

Located in Harrison Acres, 30 Betsy Road was the home of Gus Flood, the overseer of Joseph Harrison's farming endeavors on land known as the Voorhees Plantation. In an earlier time, the land was known as Bluff Plantation and owned by Col. George Lucas, the father of Eliza Lucas Pinckney. Eliza's experimental work cultivating indigo helped create another cash crop for the colony. In 1976, a plaque in her honor was dedicated at the site. (Courtesy of Barbara Burk DeWitt, Ruth Burk Gay.)

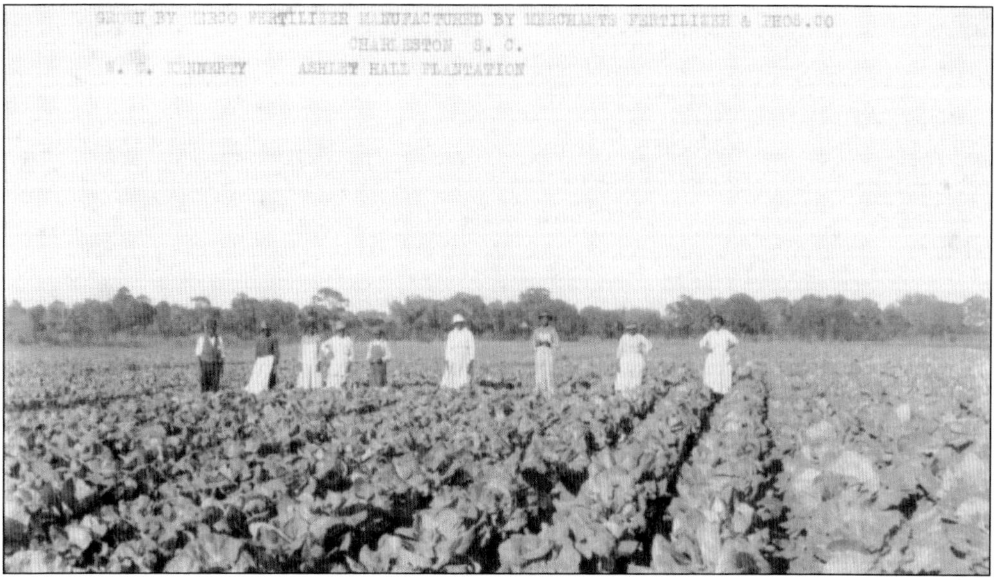

A vivid and acrid memory for the residents is the smell of cabbage when it was past its prime in the fields. Cabbage was one of the crops planted not only at Ashley Hall Plantation but also other farms in St. Andrew's Parish. When W.C. Kennerty purchased the property in 1919, he set about restoring the plantation grounds and turning Ashley Hall into a successful farm. Trains were important in moving produce to market. In this unique photograph, workers pose at one of the stations near Pierpont. There were two stops in this area: the Jahnz Station and the Radium Station. (Both, courtesy of William C., Joan Kennerty.)

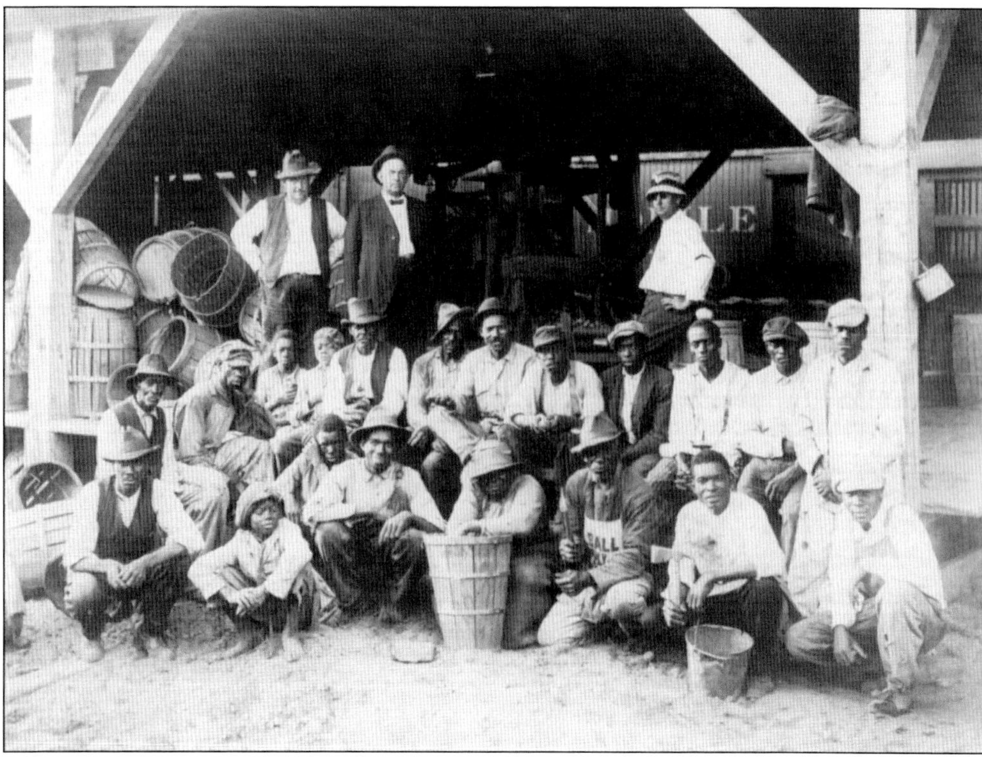

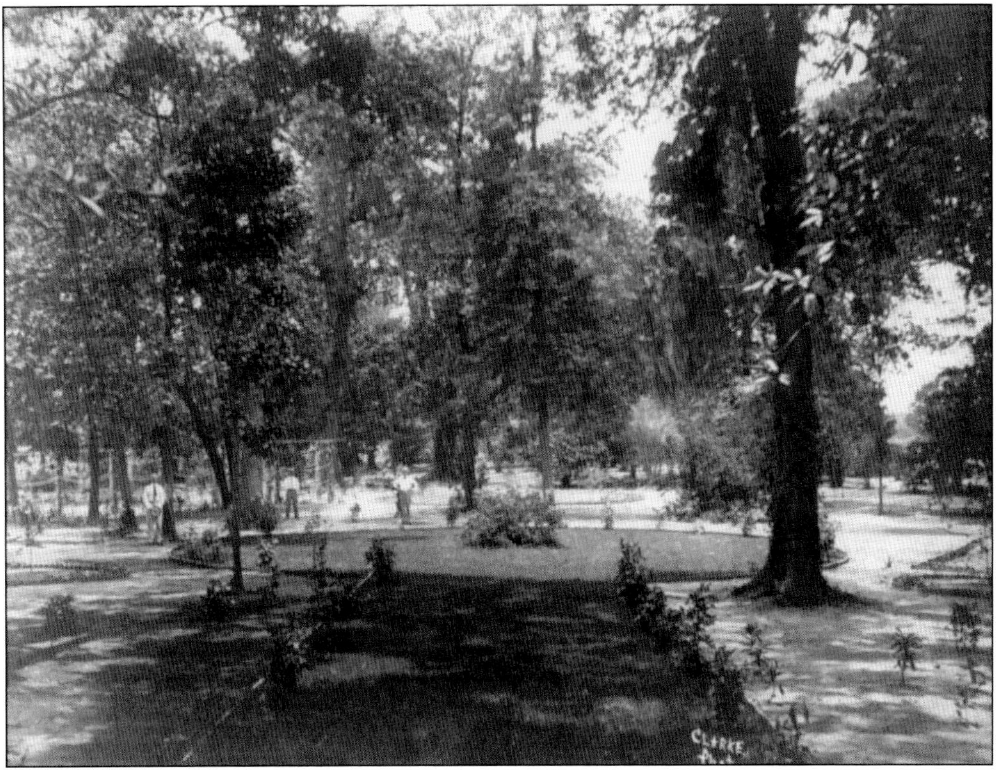

Gardens adorned the front of the family home at Ashley Hall Plantation. Stephen Bull, one of the first English colonists to set foot west of the Ashley River, was granted the land that would become Ashley Hall Plantation. There is a deep and rich history encompassing Ashley Hall and the surrounding plantations. In 1983, Rosina Sottile Kennerty published a synopsis of this history titled *Plantations on the South Side of Ashley River.* The Kennerty family became the current owner of the property in 1900. There was a brief period when it changed ownership, but W.C. Kennerty purchased the property back in 1919. William C. Kennerty Jr., born and raised on Ashley Hall Plantation, poses with a butter churn. The avenue of oaks along Ashley Hall Road remains as a canopied memory of the history of this land. (Both, courtesy of William C., Joan Kennerty.)

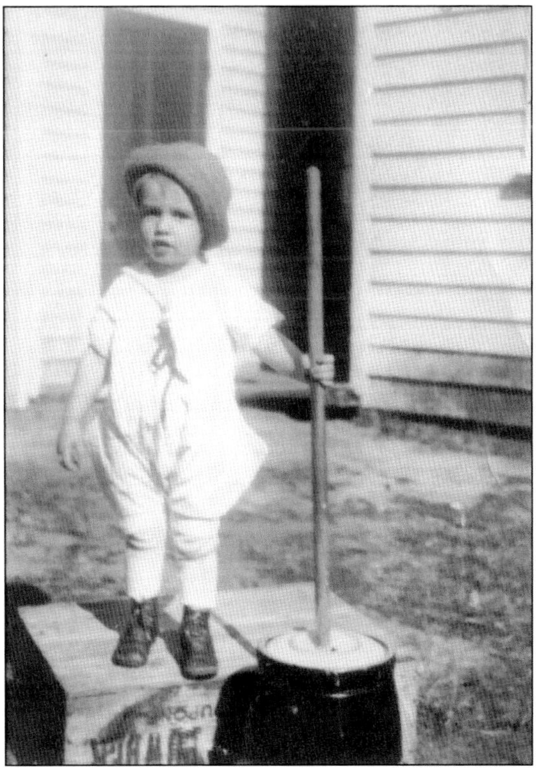

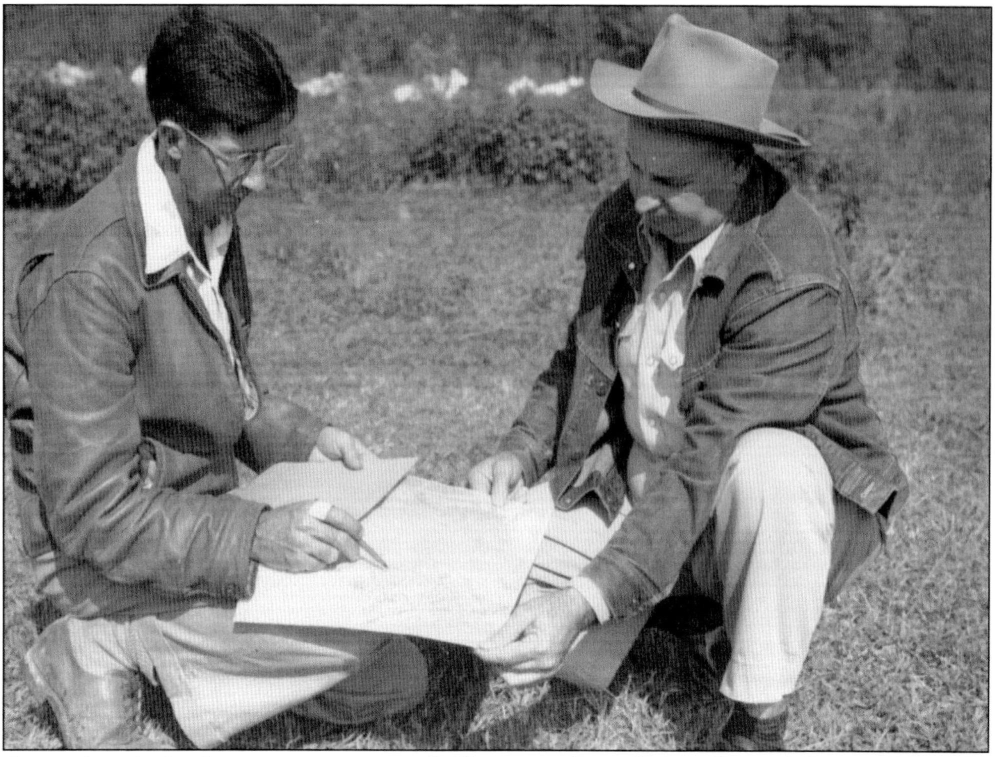

An unidentified soil conservation agent (left) reviews farm plans with G. Philip Higdon at Mr. Higdon's Springfield Farm. Mr. Higdon raised Brahma cattle on this farm. He founded both the South Carolina Brahma Breeders Association and the South Carolina Quarter Horse Association. The farm would later be developed into the Springfield Subdivision. In the below photograph, Mr. Higdon and G. Philip Higdon Jr. strike a proud pose with the Brahma bull named Geech. Geech's nature was unusual for a Brahma bull: he would allow riders. Mr. Higdon also owned other farms in St. Andrew's Parish. His son Philip recalls that Italian POWs worked on the other farms. The family grew close to a few of the men, maintaining connections long after the end of World War II. (Both, courtesy of Philip Higdon Jr.)

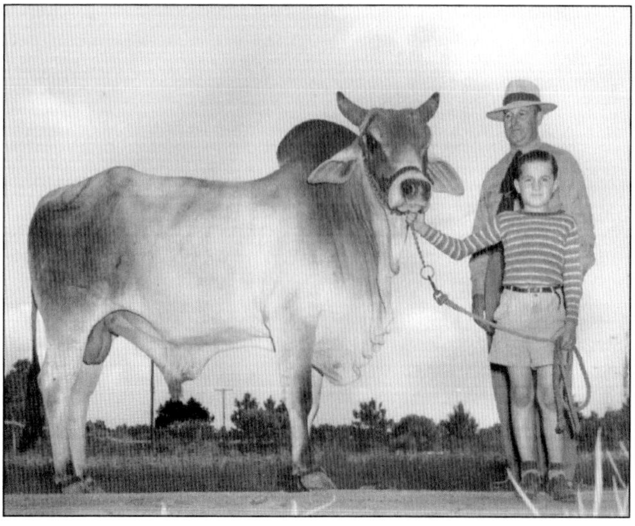

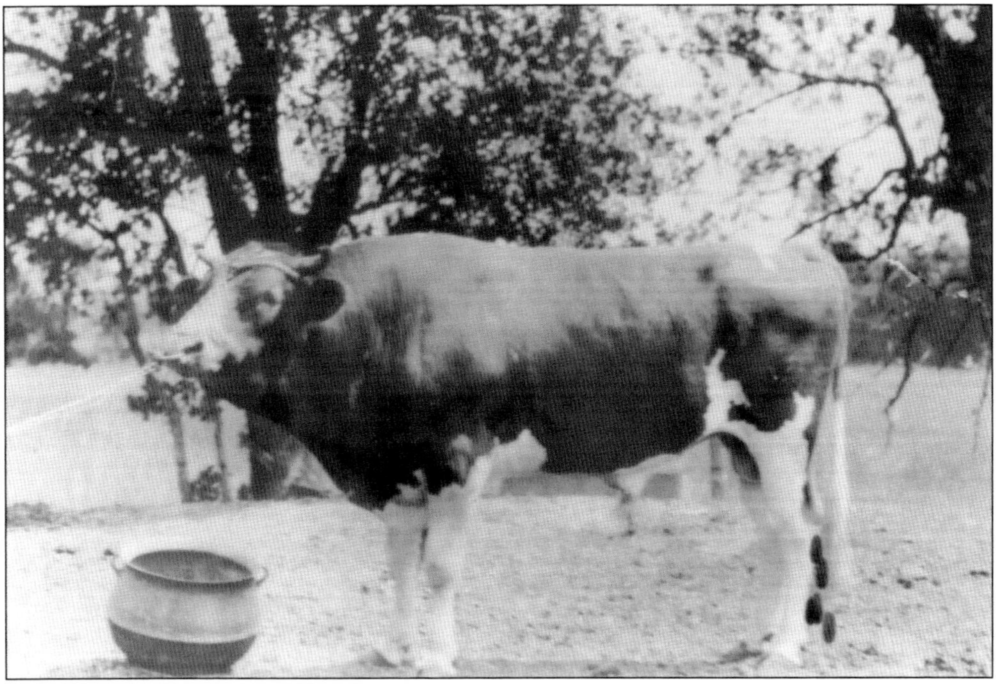

In 1921, Francis S. Hanckel Jr. and I.D. Auld established the dairy on Coburg and since that time, the dairy has played a strong role in St. Andrew's Parish. Charlotte Hanckel Hay remembers having to get up early for the school bus in time to make it down the dirt road, now known as Coburg Road, past the railroad track, now the West Ashley Greenway, to Savannah Highway before the cows blocked the road. (Courtesy of Frank Hanckel, Charlotte Hanckel Hay.)

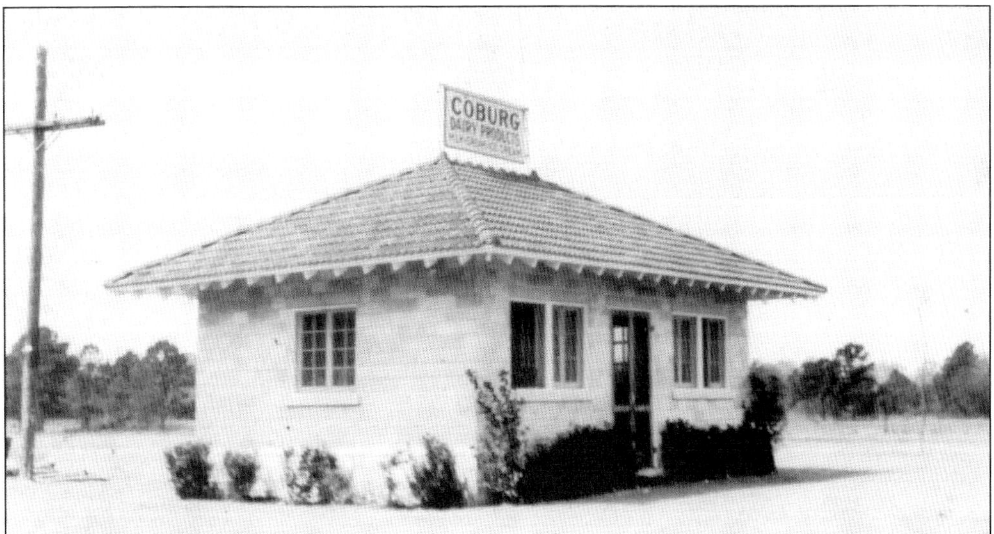

Coburg Dairy sold dairy products from this store on Savannah Highway. During World War II, the building was used as a Draft Board. In the late 1950s, St. Andrew's Center was constructed on this site. For many years, the Coburg cow and sign at the corner of Coburg Road and Savannah Highway have been the iconic reference point for St. Andrew's Parish. (Courtesy of Frank Hanckel, Charlotte Hanckel Hay.)

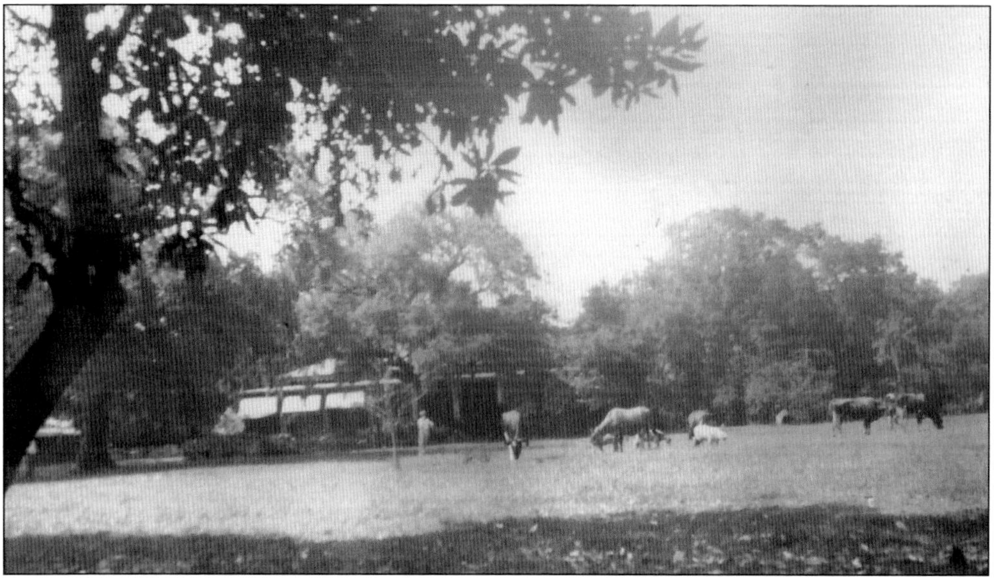

In 1916, Rene Ravenel surveyed a tract of land along the west bank of the Ashley River for Joseph M. Harrison. The story is told that the home on the site had been built in 1845 as a dance hall and Mr. Harrison converted it to his home. Mr. Harrison was an agricultural entrepreneur, according to Arthur Ravenel Jr. He grew cabbage and corn, kept chickens, goats and cows, and many memories are related about the narcissus that was grown on part of the farm that is now Moreland. Today, many yards in this neighborhood still bloom with narcissus in January and February. In the above photograph, Mr. Harrison is seen in the yard with his cattle, while the below photograph shows moss-draped trees shading the farm outbuildings. (Both, courtesy of Barbara Burk DeWitt, Ruth Burk Gay.)

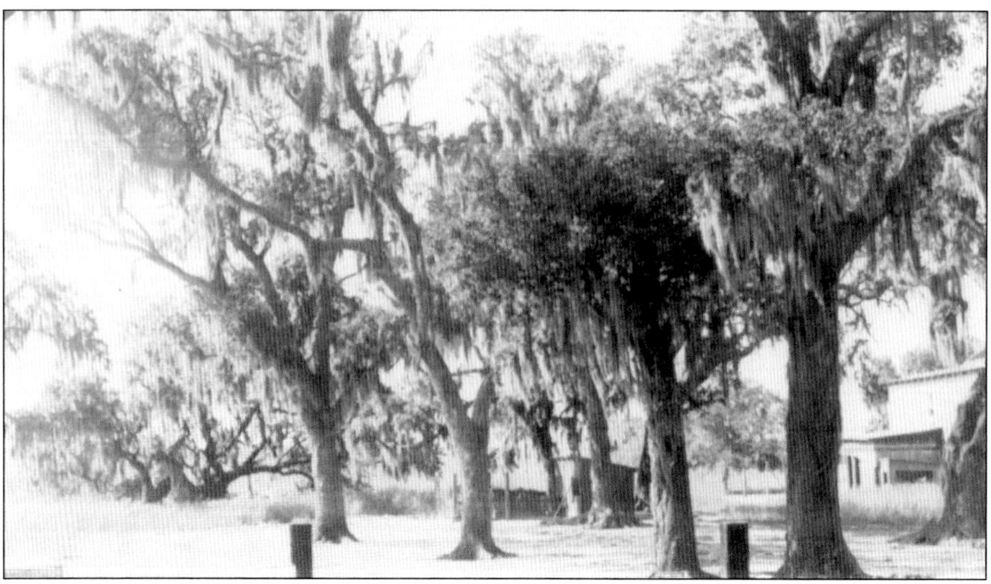

In addition to his farming endeavors, Joseph M. Harrison served as a commissioner on the Charleston County Police Commission organized under the 1937 Act of the South Carolina General Assembly. (Courtesy of Barbara Burk DeWitt, Ruth Burk Gay.)

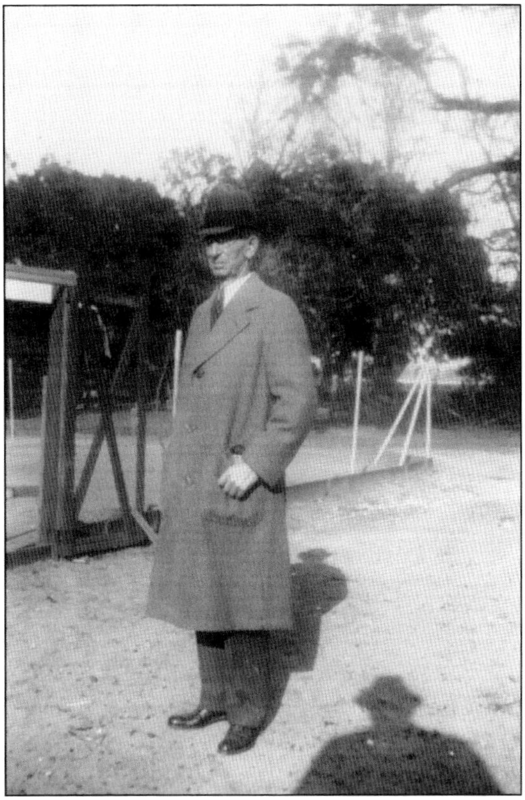

In this undated photograph, Savannah Highway is lined with cars for a farmer's convention. The wood structures behind the cars on the left were erected at the turn of the century on the Voorhees land as housing for farm laborers. Painted a dull red, the line of shanties was known as Red Row. Mamie Harrison, Joseph's second wife, did not drive. When it was time to collect the rent from the Red Row tenants, she would ask her niece Irene Burk to drive her. (Courtesy of Barbara Burk DeWitt, Ruth Burk Gay.)

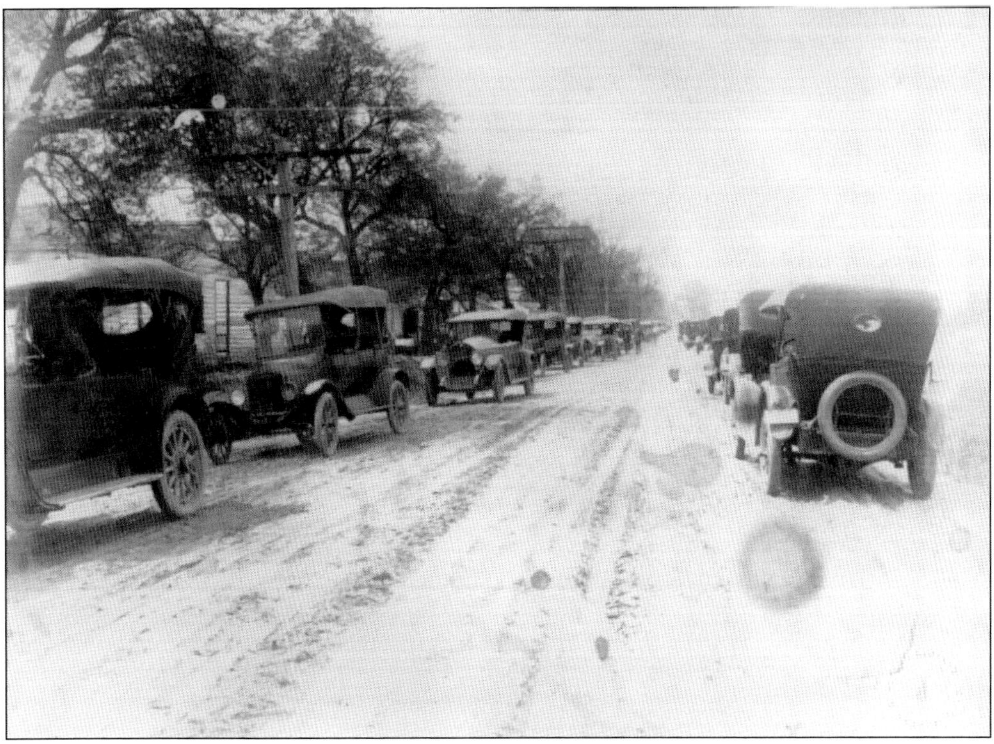

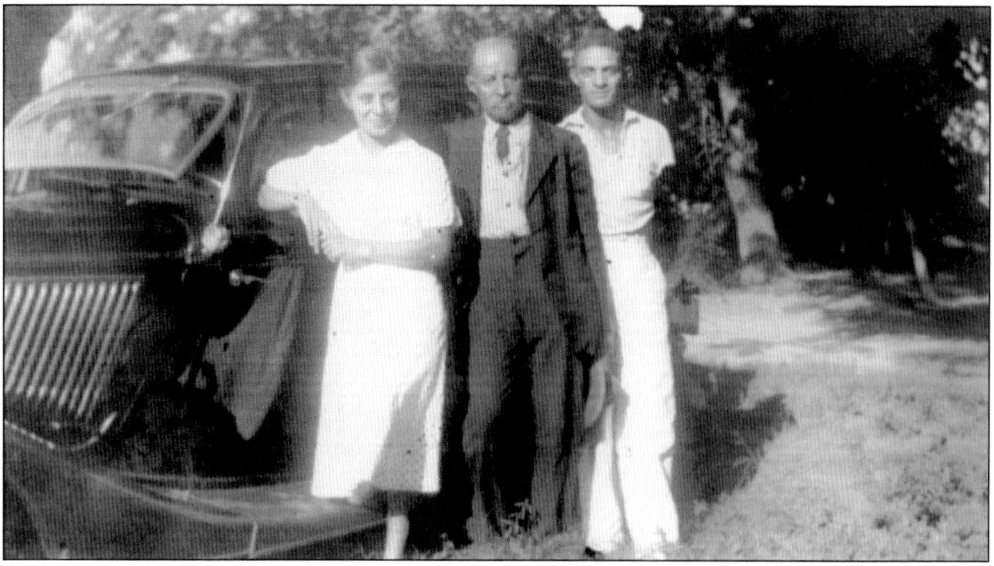

The handwriting on the photograph says "Sister, Dad, Me," which denotes Mary Ruth Carr, Thomas Tobias Carr Sr., and John Wesley Carr posing with their car at the family home on Main Street. Their home, shown in the below photograph, is located on the Ashley River side (Ashleyville) of Maryville. Thomas Carr was the last mayor of the town of Maryville. In 1936, the South Carolina Legislature revoked the town's charter. Many of the Carr family papers and photographs have been archived at the Avery Institute. (Both, courtesy of the Avery Institute.)

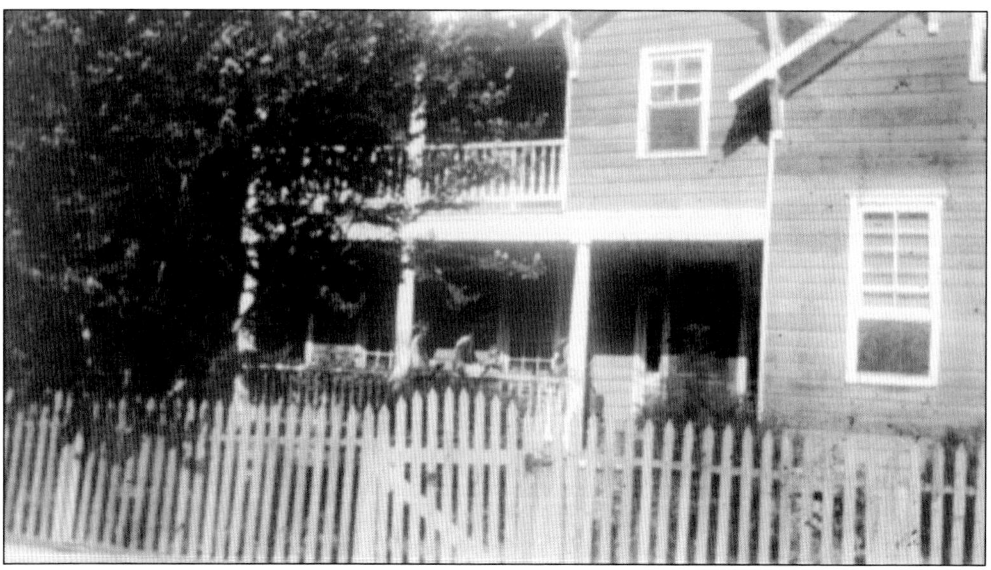

Two

St. Andrew's Parish's Turning Point

In the 1943 St. Andrew's Parish Exchange Club brochure, an unnamed author attributed the lifting of the toll on the new bridge in 1921 as the Parish's turning point. Access to the fertile land "West of the Ashley" was now easier for everyone. Farming continued to be an important and successful staple for the Parish. The opening of the Clemson College Truck Station and the US Department of Agriculture Vegetable Breeding Laboratory was indicative of a community with strong ties to an agrarian way of life. Soon, developers began to see the potential in land for suburban neighborhoods. Housing was at a premium due to the increase of workers at the Charleston naval yard. The naval yard employed 10,000 workers during World War I, according to Fritz Hamer in his book *Charleston Reborn: A Southern City, Its Navy Yard and World War II*. Advertisements announcing the attractiveness of living west of the Ashley River appeared and families were enticed to move across the river. Wappoo Heights, Windermere, The Crescent, Edgewater Park, St. Andrew's Heights, Stono Park, and Pinecrest Gardens were all established prior to 1930. Guest Homes were constructed along Highway 17 South and Folly Road for tourists who came to enjoy the magnificent gardens or to participate in the Azalea Festival. It was during 1925 that P.L. Bootle opened his famous barbecue stand near the foot of the Ashley River Bridge. Joseph Harrison donated land to Lewis Burk for the WCSC (Wonderful Charleston South Carolina) radio transmission tower in 1930. Arthur and Harold Ravenel developed Carolina Terrace in 1931. Soon, Monnie Carter established a gas station along Savannah Highway near Carolina Terrace where he became one of the first residents. Society was still suffering from the impact of the Civil War, World War I, and the Great Depression. Segregation, racial tensions, and economic uncertainty were still evident, but at this turning point, a community began to reemerge with a sense of pride. The landowners, businessmen, and homeowners of the Parish found themselves building a new suburban life, but with the threat of World War II ever present in their mind.

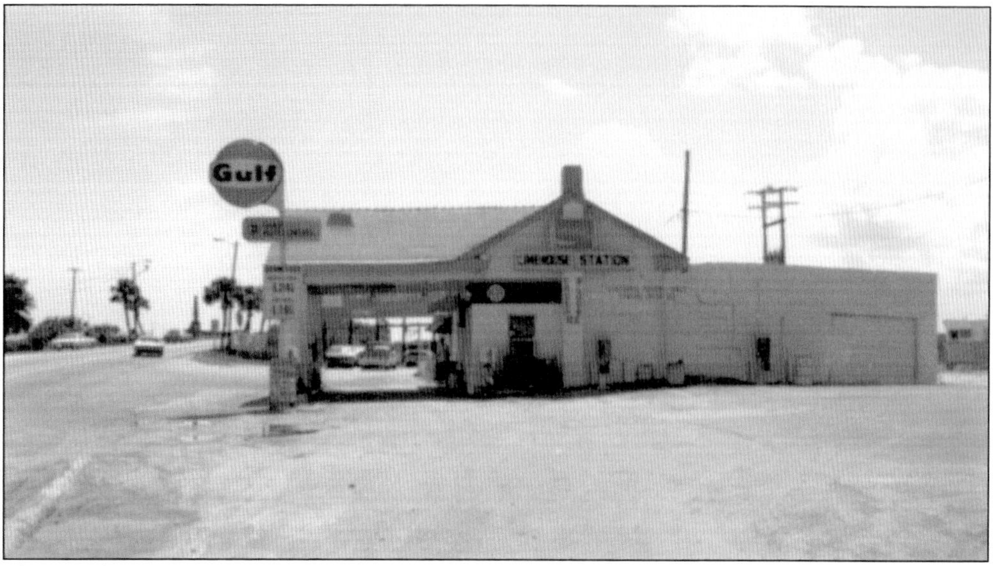

The Limehouse Service Station was a landmark that announced the start of the Ashley River Bridge on the east side of the river. J.S. Limehouse, the owner, advertised his station as "Open all Nite" in the 1940s. Cars were becoming more widely used and stations functioned both for service and as a gathering place. Today, the Bristol Marina entrance is located at the site where the station once stood. (Courtesy of Avram Kronsberg Jr.)

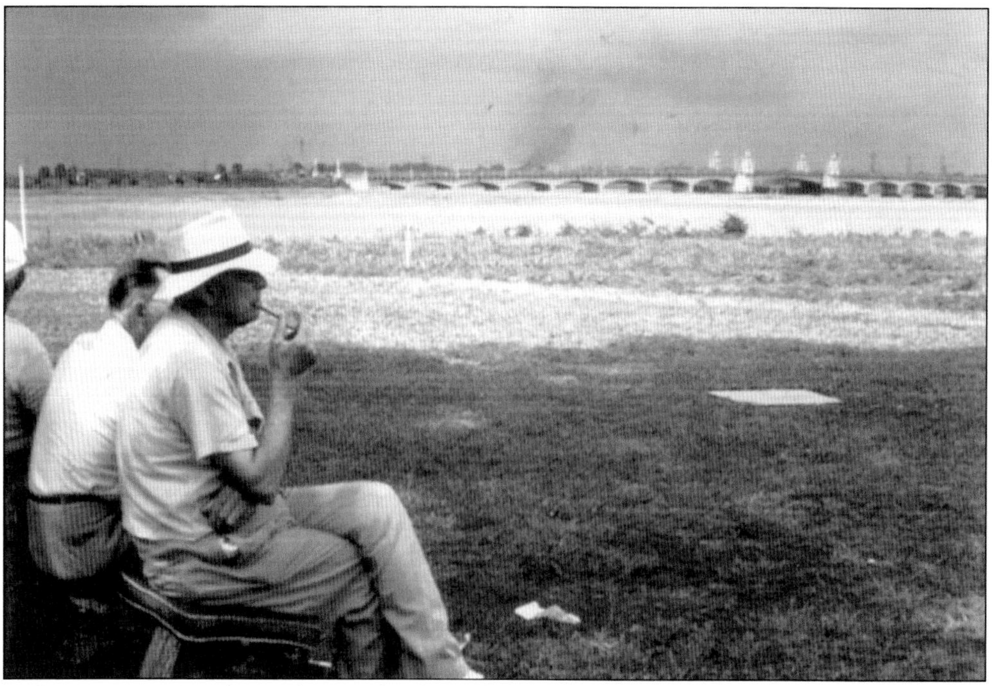

W.O. "Sammie" Bootle was known for three things: competitive skeet shooting, hunting, and barbecue. Along the high ground on the west bank of the Ashley River was the Charleston Skeet Club range. Sammy's father, Philip Lorraine Bootle, smokes a pipe as he watches the target practice. The Ashley River Bridge can be seen in the background. (Courtesy of P. Luther Bootle Jr., Ina Bootle.)

Monnie Lamar Carter Sr. and Monnie Lamar Carter Jr. are all dressed in the living room of their Carolina Terrace home. Monnie Sr. built a gas station, repair garage, and ice cream shop on lots three and four on Carolina Terrace in 1936 and 1937. Today, a bank occupies the station's site at the corner of Radio Road and Savannah Highway. Monnie Sr. was an active member of the community and initiated a petition "for the discontinuance of all illegal and undesirable businesses" at the Welcome Inn located near his home. His activism resulted in his assault by the inn's owner's son. News of the assault was published in the *Carolina Free Press* on February 9, 1940. (Courtesy of Monnie Lamar Carter Jr.)

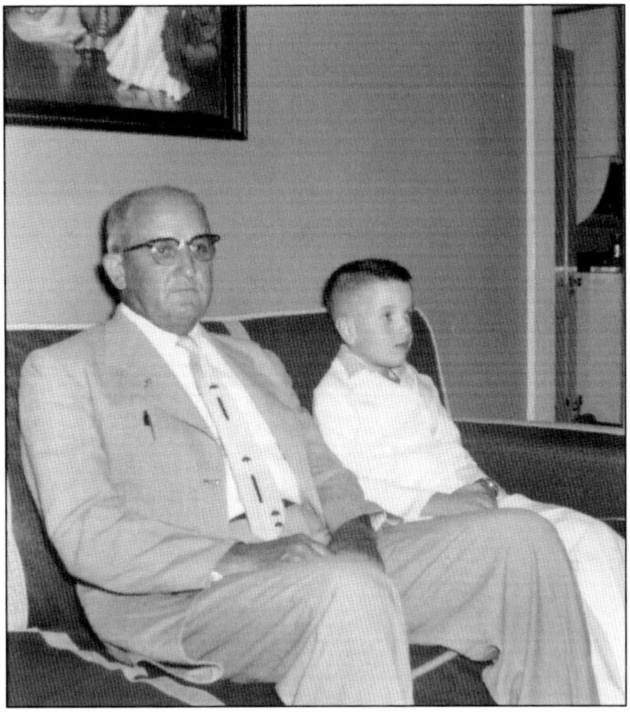

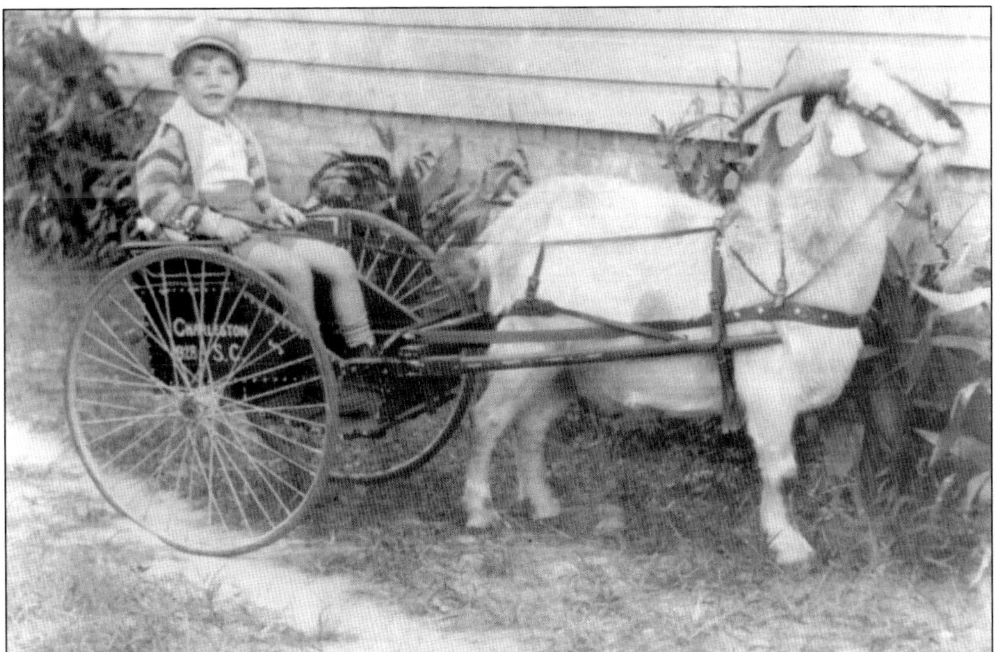

There was a time when it was popular for photographers to walk through neighborhoods with goat-drawn carts or saddled ponies to pose with local children for photographs. In this 1928 photograph, Robert F. McNab Jr. (Bob) smiles for the camera from a goat cart. Bob took up photography as a hobby and started building darkrooms in his childhood home in Windermere and in the home he built on Woodward Road in Moreland. (Courtesy of Robert F. McNab Jr.)

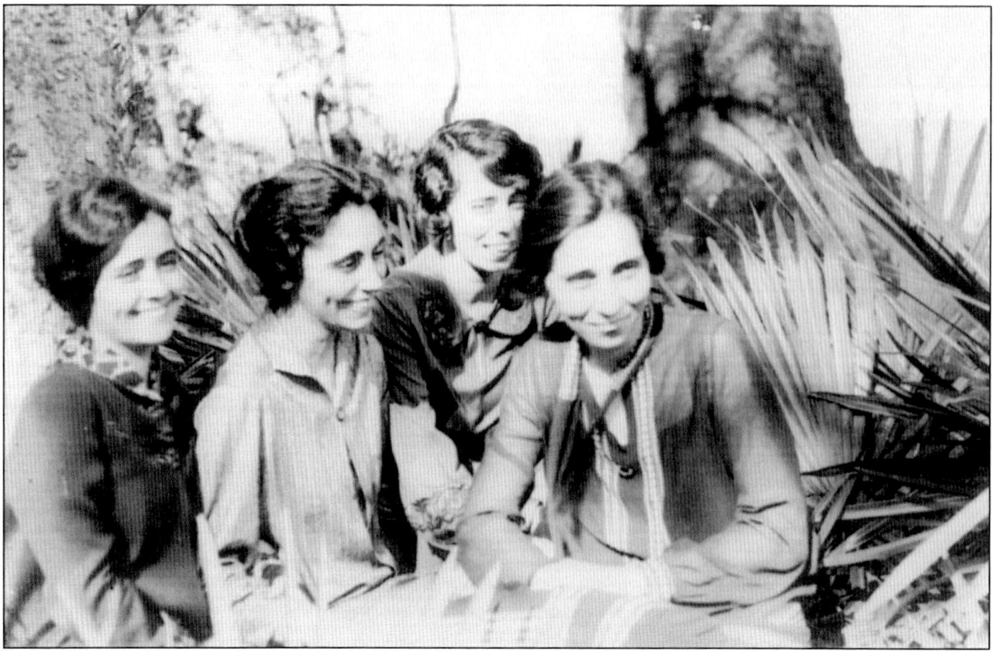

On the grounds of the Harrison farm, the four Santos sisters gather for a photograph. From left to right, Dolly Santos Reynolds, Mamie Santos Harrison, Inez Santos Grayson, and Irene Santos Burk are smiling, but not at the photographer. Dolly, Mamie, and Irene pursued careers as nurses at St. Francis Hospital. (Courtesy of Barbara Burk DeWitt, Ruth Burk Gay.)

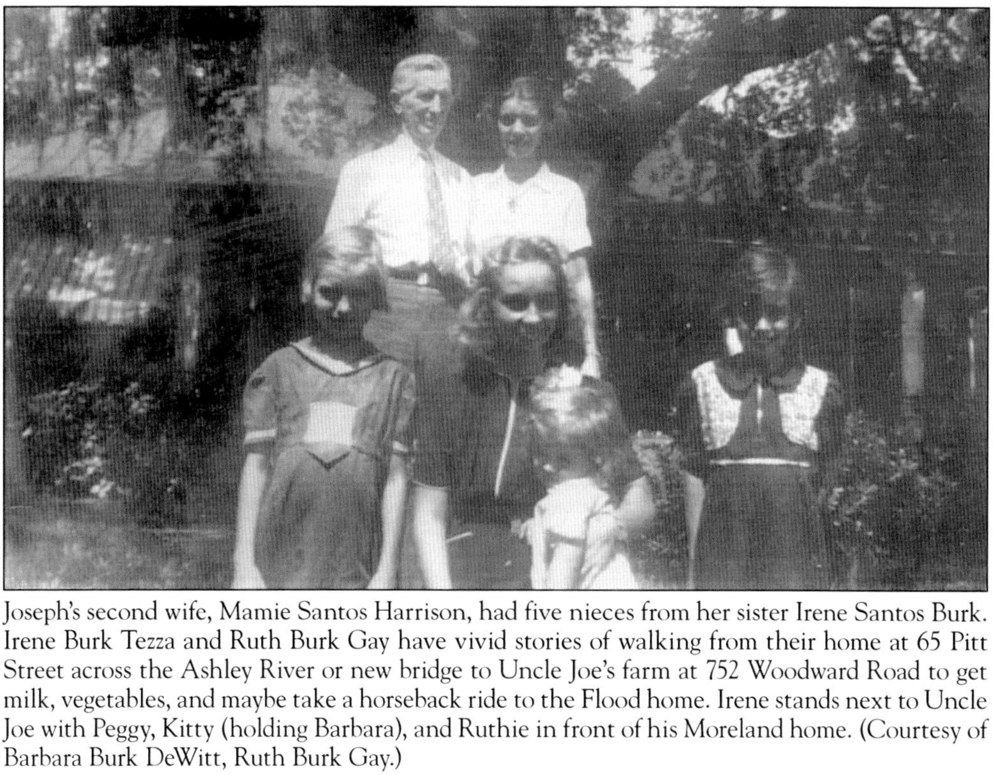

Joseph's second wife, Mamie Santos Harrison, had five nieces from her sister Irene Santos Burk. Irene Burk Tezza and Ruth Burk Gay have vivid stories of walking from their home at 65 Pitt Street across the Ashley River or new bridge to Uncle Joe's farm at 752 Woodward Road to get milk, vegetables, and maybe take a horseback ride to the Flood home. Irene stands next to Uncle Joe with Peggy, Kitty (holding Barbara), and Ruthie in front of his Moreland home. (Courtesy of Barbara Burk DeWitt, Ruth Burk Gay.)

Uncle Joe and Aunt Mamie pose with their niece Barbara Burk and "Uncle Bubsy" with a view of Charleston in the background. Uncle Bubsy was the brother of Joseph Harrison's first wife, Alma Geraty. Riding along Woodward Drive in Moreland today, the view from Joseph Harrison's farm across the Ashley River is still breathtaking. (Courtesy of Barbara Burk DeWitt, Ruth Burk Gay.)

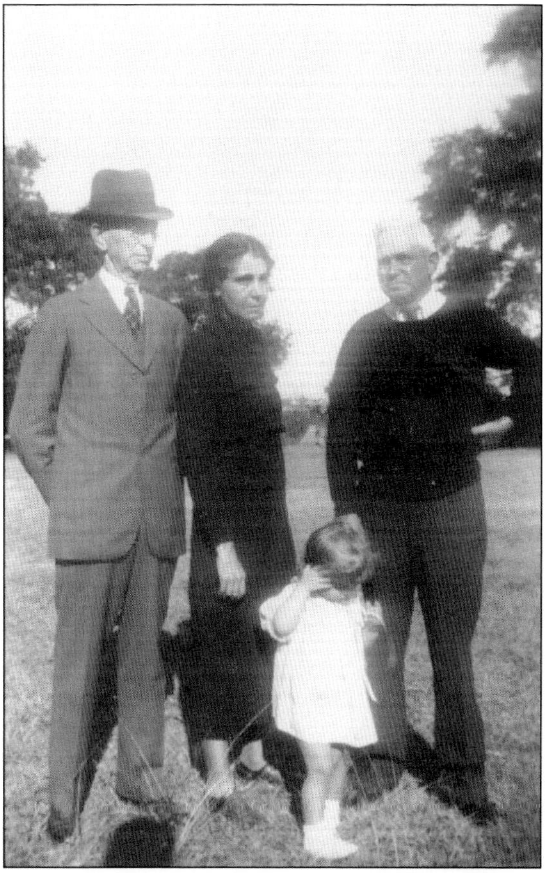

Pictured from left to right, Robert F. McNab Jr. (Bob), William I. Peek, and William C. Kennerty were roommates at Clemson during the 1941 and 1942 school year. The young men called St. Andrew's Parish home. Bob spent his youth exploring the banks of the Ashley River and developed affection for the land owned by Joseph Harrison. Bob's father, Robert F. McNab Sr., handled Joseph Harrison's stock investments. When it was time to subdivide and sell the Moreland property, Bob asked his father to place a down payment on the lot he had selected in his elementary school days and where he would later build his home. (Courtesy of Robert F. McNab Jr.)

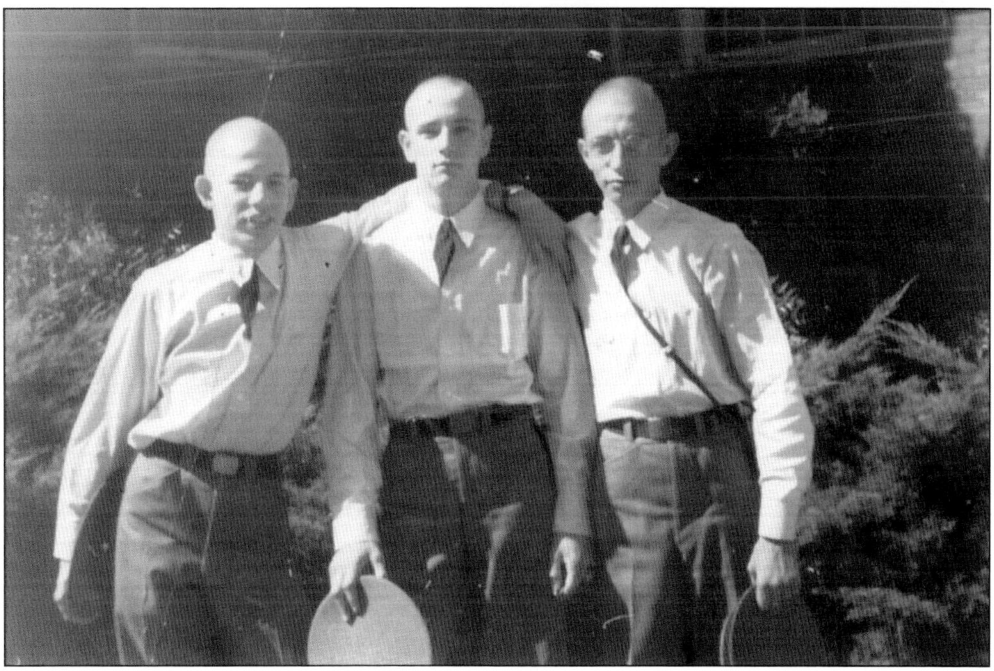

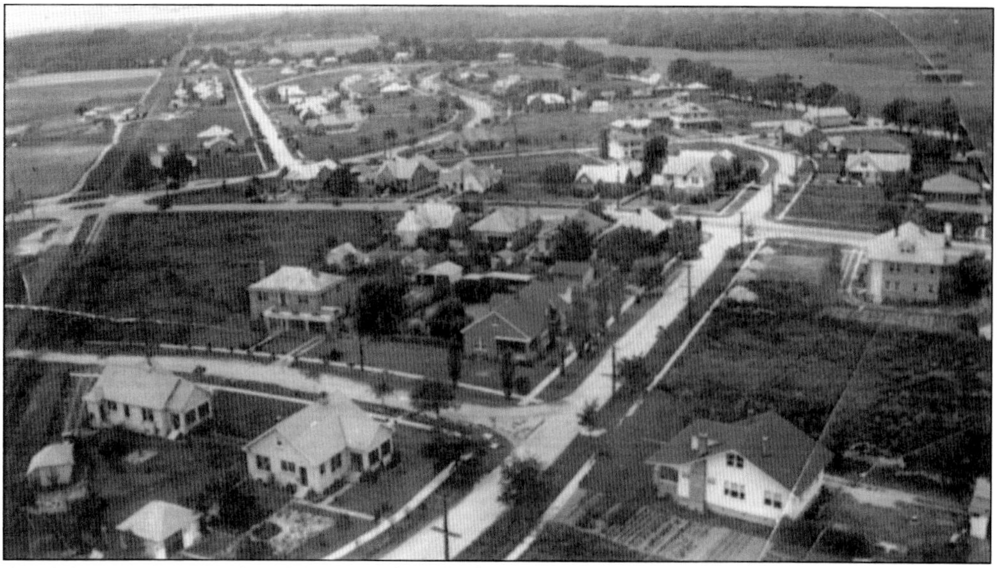

At 12:30 p.m. on May 5, 1935, an unidentified shutterbug climbed the water tower located near the Windermere neighborhood and took this photograph. This 70-plus-year-old perspective is amazing, for it only took 15 years for the area to develop into a thriving community. (Courtesy of Carolee Williams.)

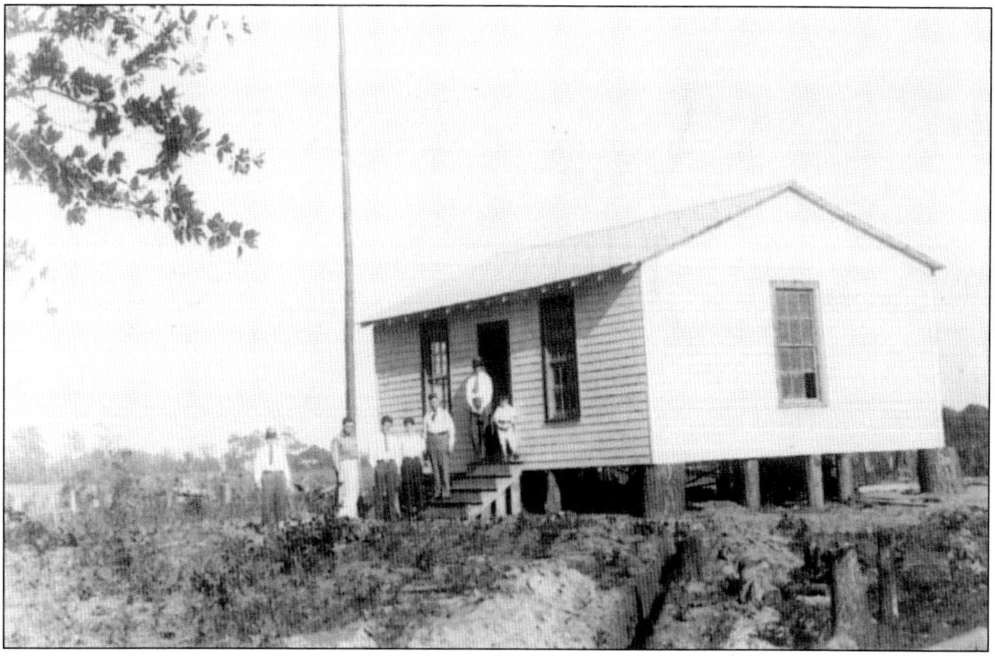

WCSC 1360 began broadcasting from the Francis Marion Hotel in May 1930. Lewis Burk and Fred Jordan were partners in this new technology. Lewis Burk was a harbor pilot with a passion for radio. Fred Jordan owned Jordan's Music House where Lewis would repair radios when not guiding ships into the Charleston Harbor. Joseph Harrison, related by marriage to Lewis, donated land near Harrison Acres to establish the first transmitter station. Photographed at the site are Joseph Harrison (far left), Lewis Burk (standing by tower), and Fred Jordan in the doorway. (Courtesy of Barbara Burk DeWitt, Ruth Burk Gay.)

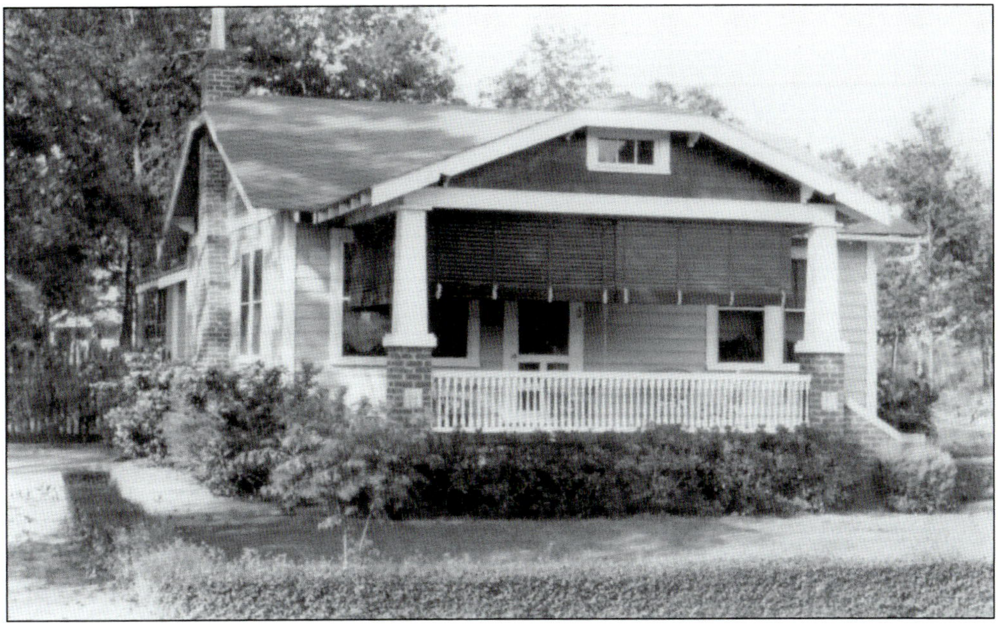

The home at 2 Tall Oak Drive was built in 1937 by Angelo and Amelia Marie Ferrillo. The family name was originally spelled "Fiorillo," and they emigrated from Goeta, Italy. When their grandson Bud Ferillo came to Charleston for a visit, he knocked on the door of the current owners, Chris Abbey and Angela Sanchez, and related this family history to them. (Courtesy of Bud Ferillo.)

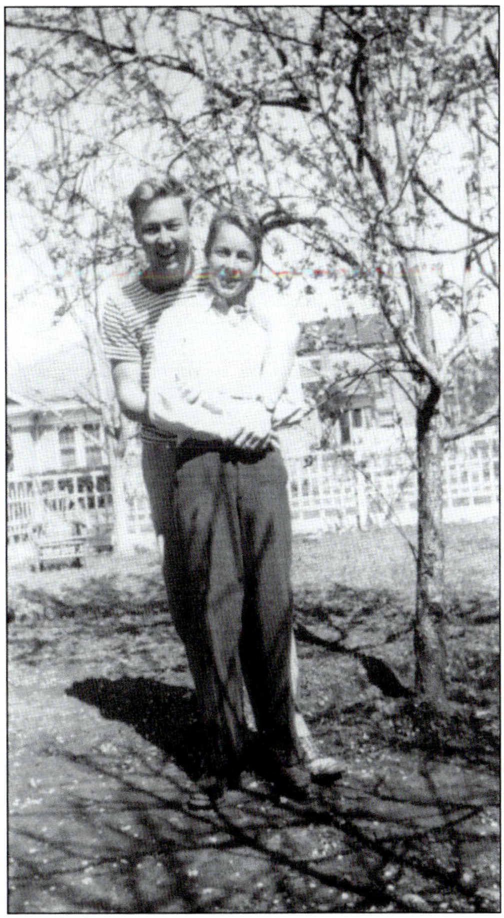

The Schaffer family moved into their home at 37 Fenwick Drive in August 1929. Mrs. Schaffer was fond of fruit trees and planted several in the yard. Her sons, Wally Schaffer (back) and Henry Schaffer, pose beside one of the fruit trees. Henry Otto Hasselmeyer, the father of Mrs. Schaffer, started the famous Henry's restaurant of Charleston. Mrs. Schaffer coached the girls' basketball team at St. Andrew's Parish High School. (Courtesy of Henry Schaffer.)

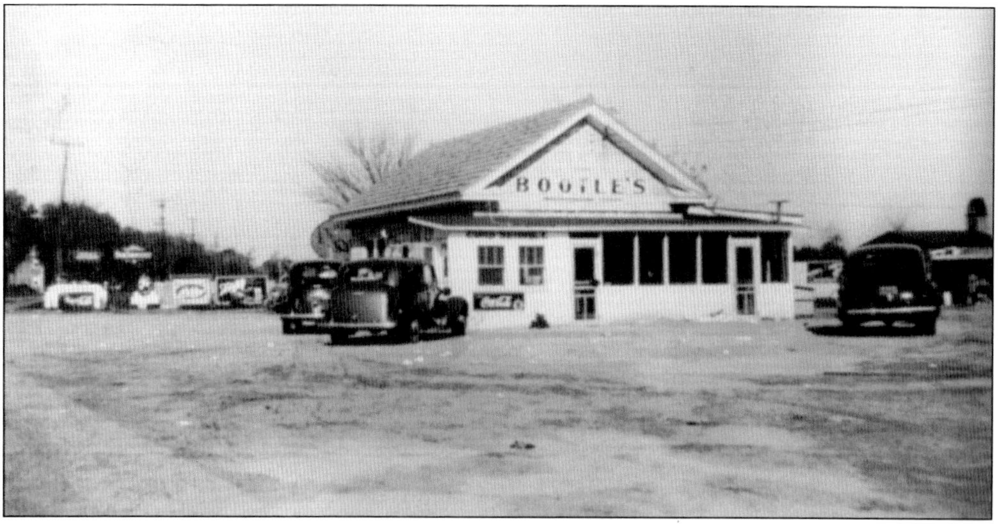

Southerners are passionate about their barbecue and Philip Lorraine Bootle was famous for his. Phillip learned the barbecue technique from a relative in Brunswick, Georgia, while working in the sawmill business. He returned to South Carolina in the early 1920s, purchased property across the river, and opened his first barbecue establishment called Sunshine Cabin. The building in the above photograph was constructed after the cabin burned and was known in the family as "the BBQ stand." The below photograph, taken in 1939 of the inside of Bootle's, evokes delicious memories. Sandwiches sold for 15¢. Locals claim that the neon sign pointing to the wooden pig at Bootle's was the first in the area. (Both, courtesy of Ina Bootle.)

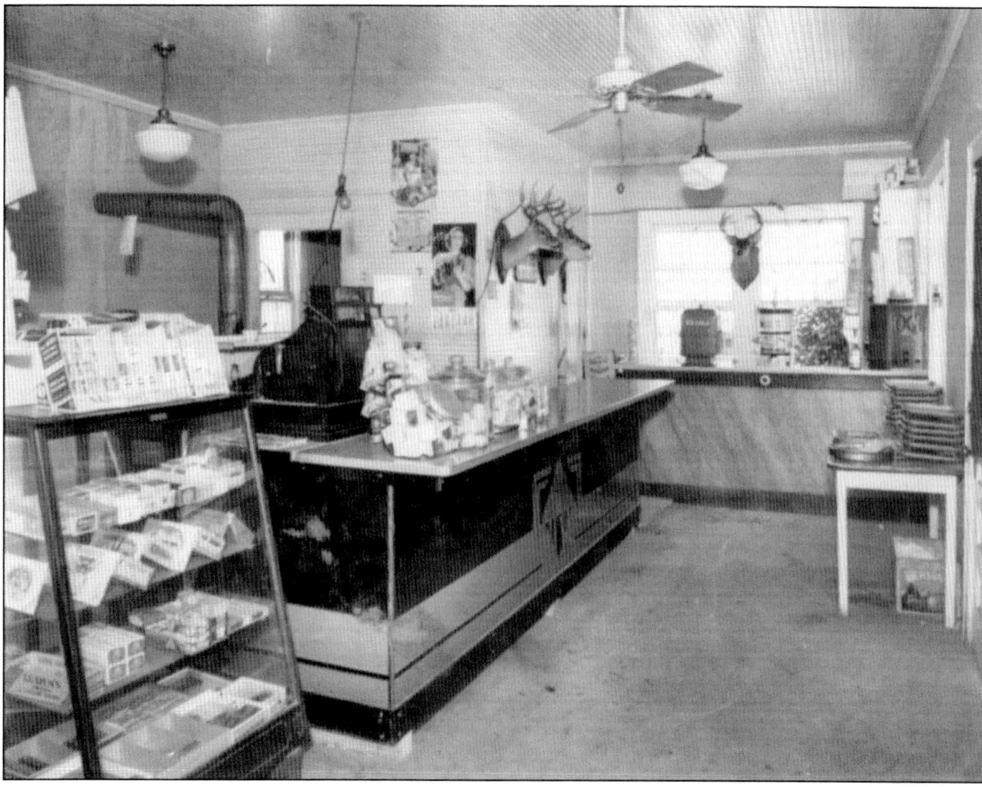

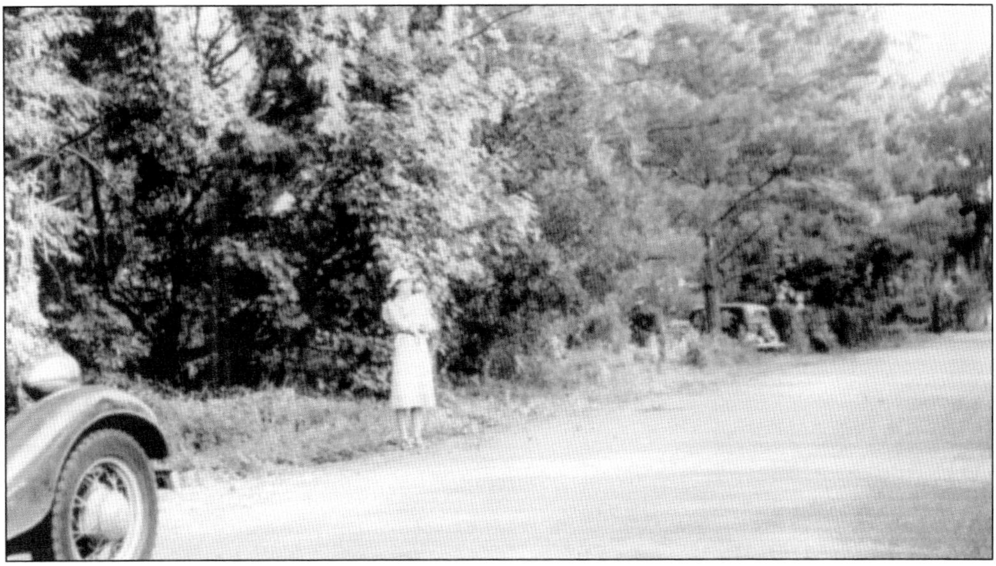

George Nash purchased 45 acres of high ground and 27 acres of marsh from the Wappoo Realty Co. in 1924 and named it Wappoo Heights. The land had been part of The Crescent Plantation and was owned by Joe Harrison prior to this purchase. Elsie Melchers Lunz, holding her daughter Elisabeth (Betsy), stands in front of the wooded lot at 7 Azalea Road in Wappoo Heights in 1939. The road name would later change to Formosa Drive. Her husband, Robert, cleared the land and built their home that same year. A few years later, Robert's parents, George Robert and Mary Whilden Lofton Lunz, built at 9 Azalea Road. Seated on the bench in front of 7 Azalea Road are Betsy and Elsie Lunz, Margaret Bonnoit (of 11 Azalea Road), and Mary Whilden (Minnie) Lunz. Today, Rev. Dr. Betsy Lunz is a Presbyterian minister in Georgia. (Both, courtesy of Betsy Lunz.)

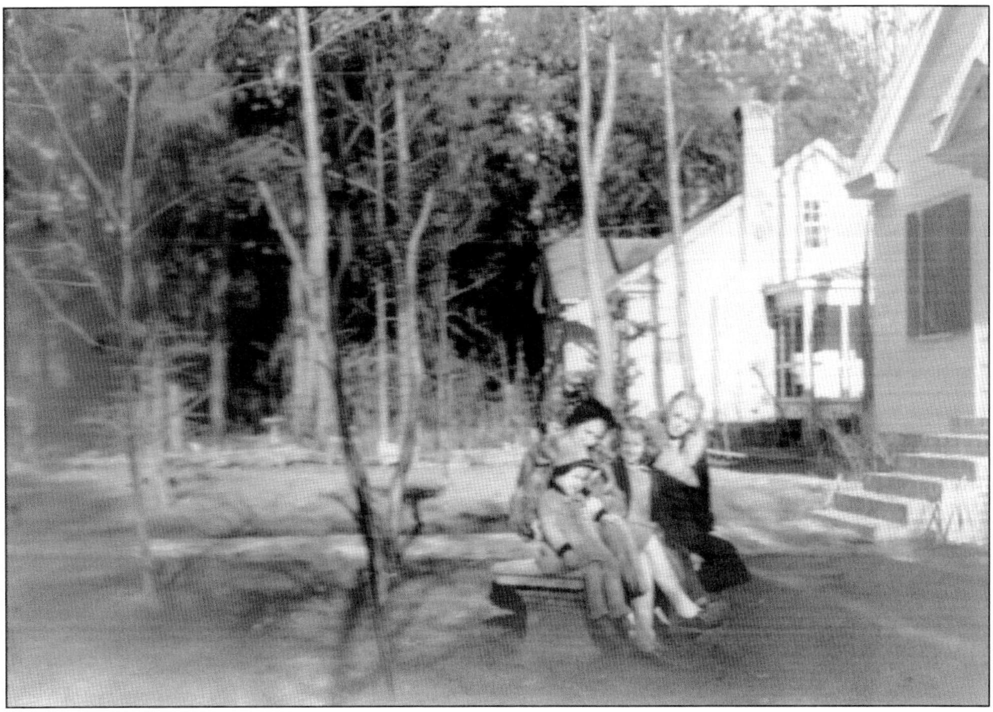

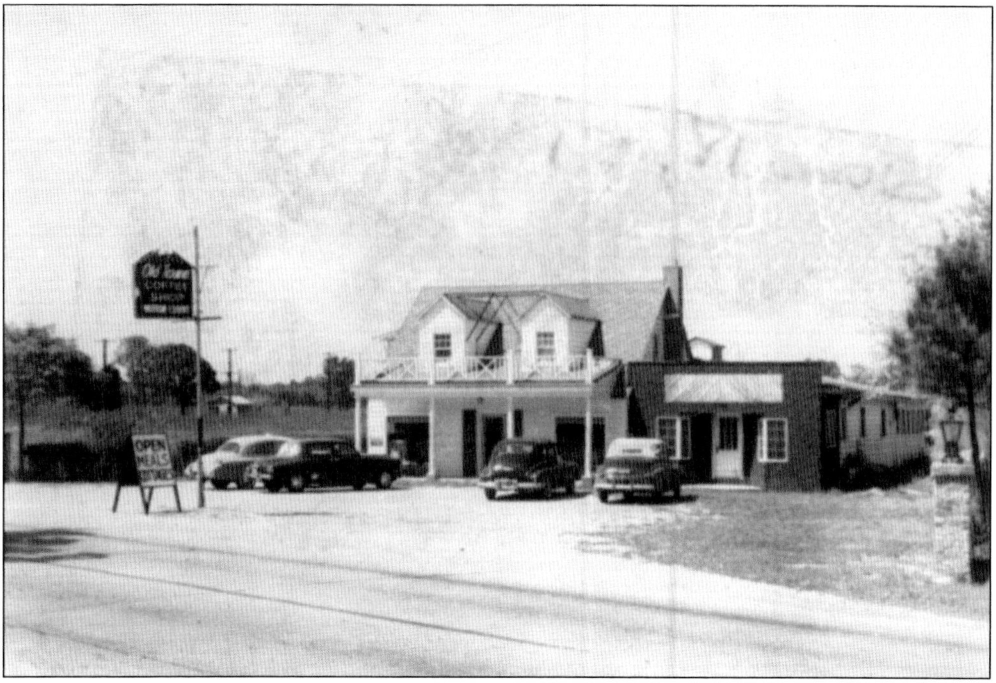

Dan H. and Carnice L. Groves purchased the Old Town Motor Court on Savannah Highway in the late 1940s. There were small cabins in the back of the main building shown in this photograph that were rented to travelers. The story goes that "Gorgeous George" of professional wrestler fame once stayed at the Motor Court, arriving in a pink Cadillac. Today, the Pep Boys and Best Western occupy the site. (Courtesy of Yvonne Groves Gilreath.)

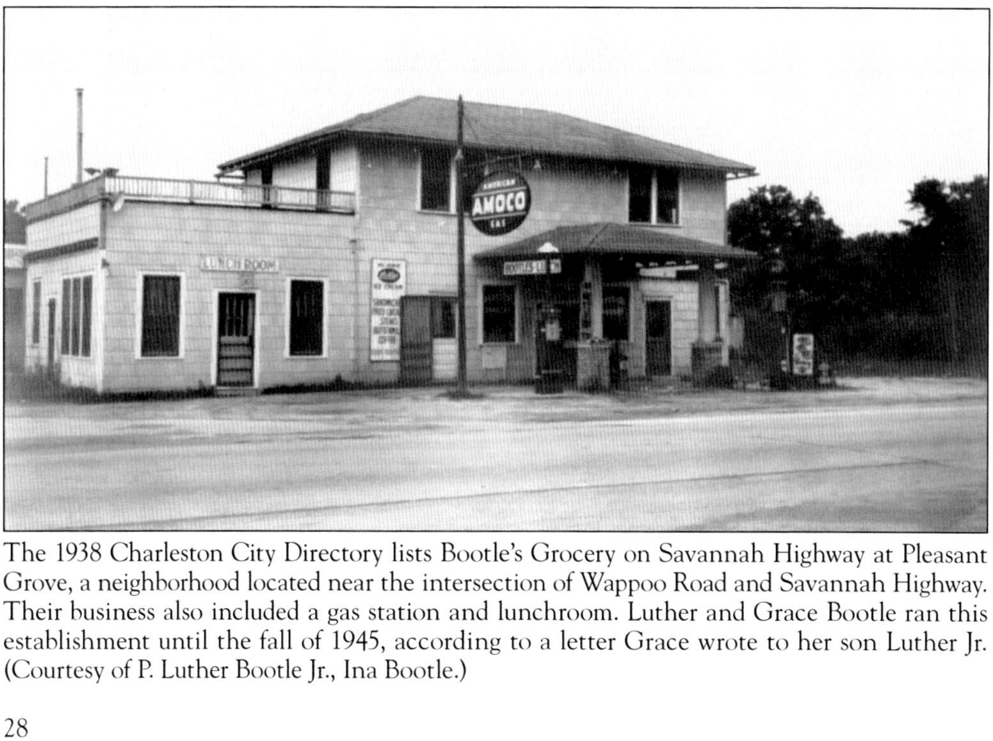

The 1938 Charleston City Directory lists Bootle's Grocery on Savannah Highway at Pleasant Grove, a neighborhood located near the intersection of Wappoo Road and Savannah Highway. Their business also included a gas station and lunchroom. Luther and Grace Bootle ran this establishment until the fall of 1945, according to a letter Grace wrote to her son Luther Jr. (Courtesy of P. Luther Bootle Jr., Ina Bootle.)

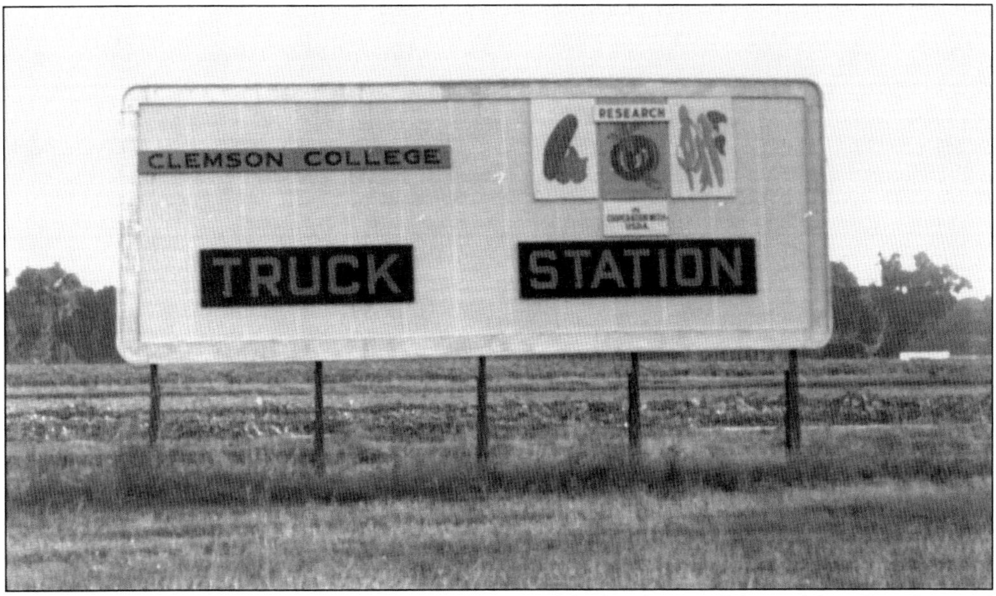

Truck or market farming became one profitable use of the land west of the Ashley after the Civil War. In 1931, the Agricultural Society of South Carolina purchased land on Highway 17 South to conduct vegetable crop research. Between 1939 and 1945, Clemson Agricultural College purchased this and other land to establish a truck experimental station to benefit local farmers. Clemson, now a university, continues this research in the areas of horticulture, entomology, and plant pathology. In 1936, the US Department of Agriculture established a vegetable breeding laboratory near the station. Since the 1940s, the Charleston County Market building on Wappoo Road has provided local farmers a site to sell their produce. (Above, courtesy of Yvonne Groves Gilreath; below, courtesy of P. Luther Bootle Jr., Ina Bootle.)

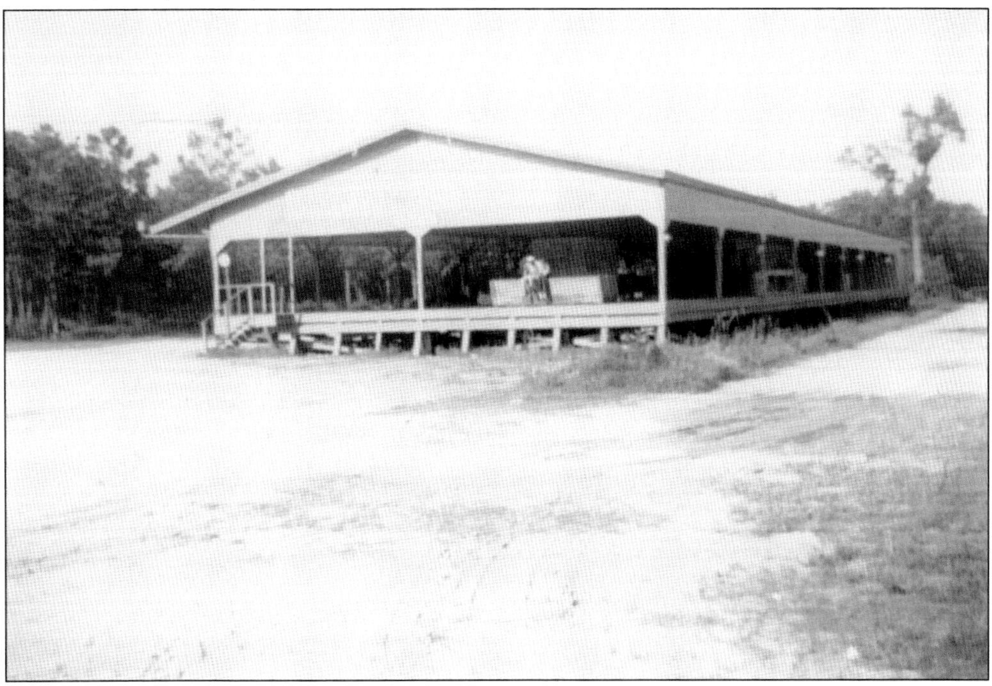

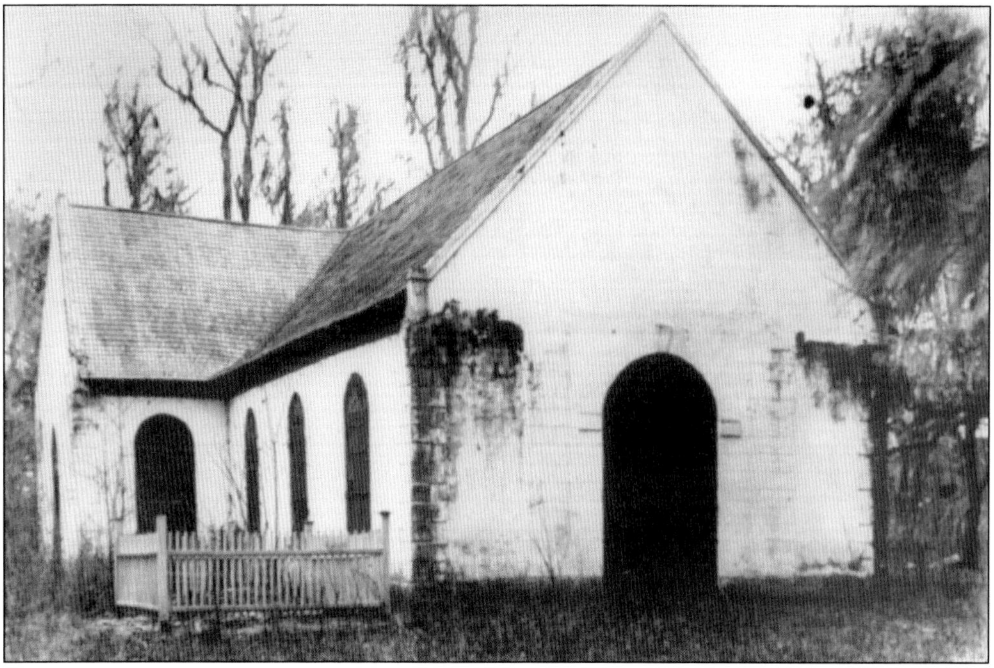

The St. Andrew's Parish Church, located on Ashley River Road, is the oldest surviving church building in regular use in the Carolinas and Georgia. Built in 1706, the church's history has seen periods of full congregations and of dormancy. This 1901 photograph shows the exterior of the church in a state of decay. An observer that year noted, "Presently it will crumble to dust and like the other holy and precious things, be no more seen . . ." This prophecy would not bear out. The Episcopal membership is active with regular services held every Sunday since 1948. (Courtesy of Old St. Andrew's Parish Church.)

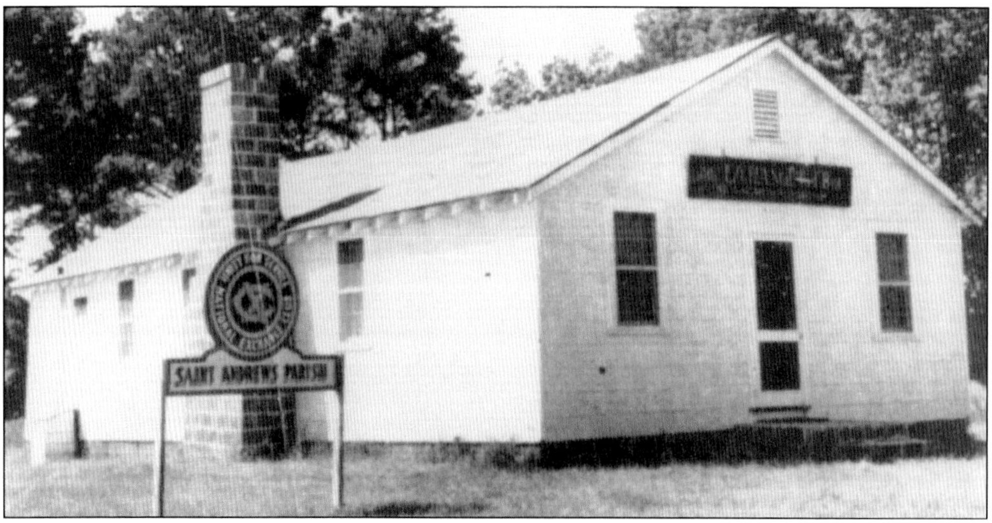

The St. Andrew's Parish Exchange Club held its permanent organizational meeting in February 1942. In June 1942, Francis S. Hanckel was elected president. He soon realized that a permanent meeting place was a necessity. This building was constructed on Savannah Highway near Coburg Road and was used by various organizations for meetings. On June 18, 1944, the John Wesley Church held its first meeting in the building. (Courtesy of John Wesley Church.)

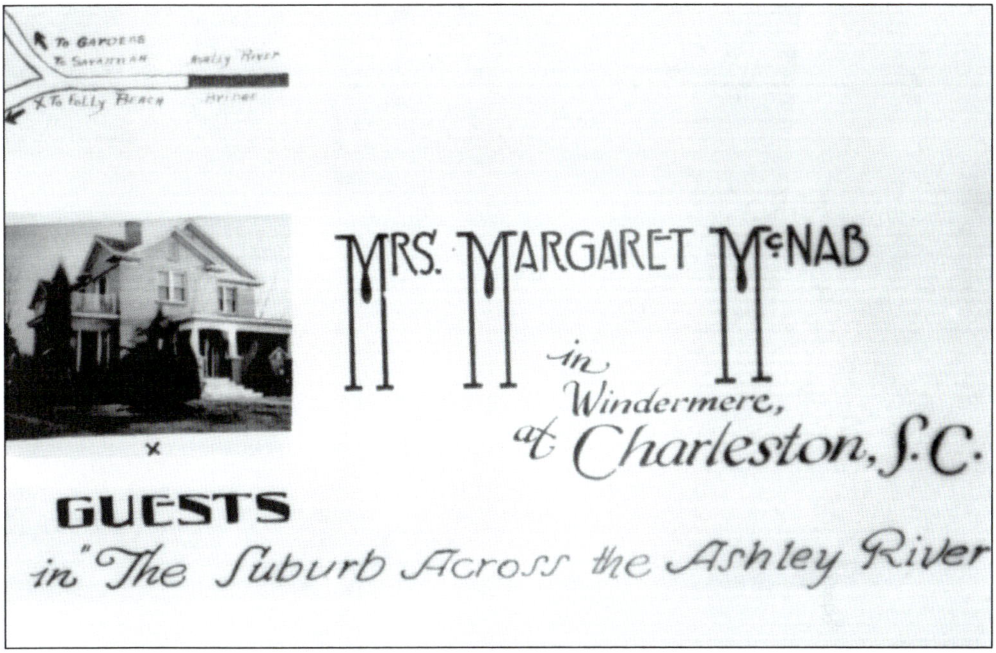

The Azalea Festival was founded in 1943, suspended from 1941 to 1947, and by 1948 there was reason to celebrate so the festival was held again. Tourists would come for the weeklong affair and it was common for families to rent out rooms in their homes. The McNab family lived on the first floor of 51 Folly Road and Robert McNab Jr. helped his father prepare this advertisement for their home. He also printed these cards in his photography dark room. (Courtesy of Robert F. McNab Jr.)

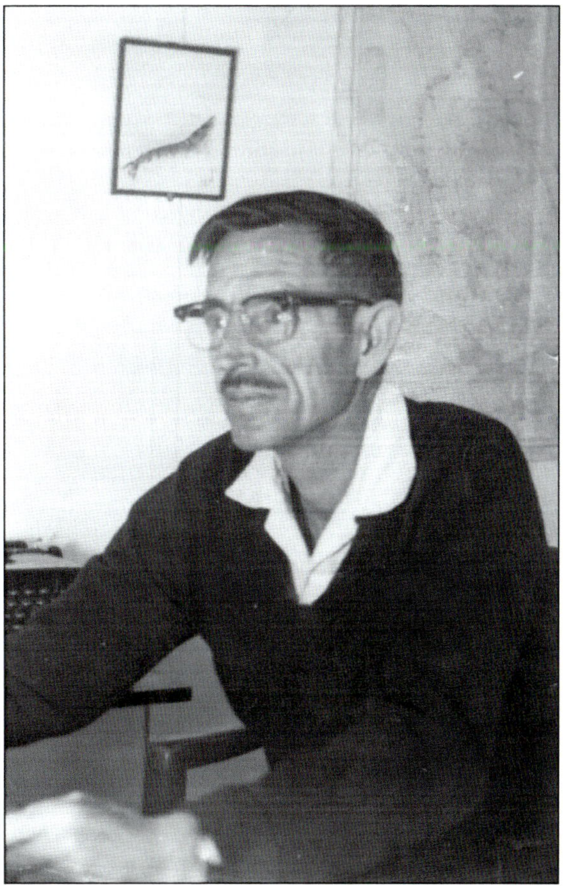

The graphic of a shrimp on the wall behind Dr. G. Robert Lunz Jr., an early resident of Wappoo Heights, is a simple reminder of Dr. Lunz's marine biology legacy. Dr. Lunz, known as Bob or Doc, began his career at the Charleston Museum where he became director of Crustacea Science. He was an early champion of shrimp farming, oyster cultivation, and marine conservation, conducting experiments at Bear's Bluff Laboratory where he served as the director from 1946 until his death in 1969. (Courtesy of Betsy Lunz.)

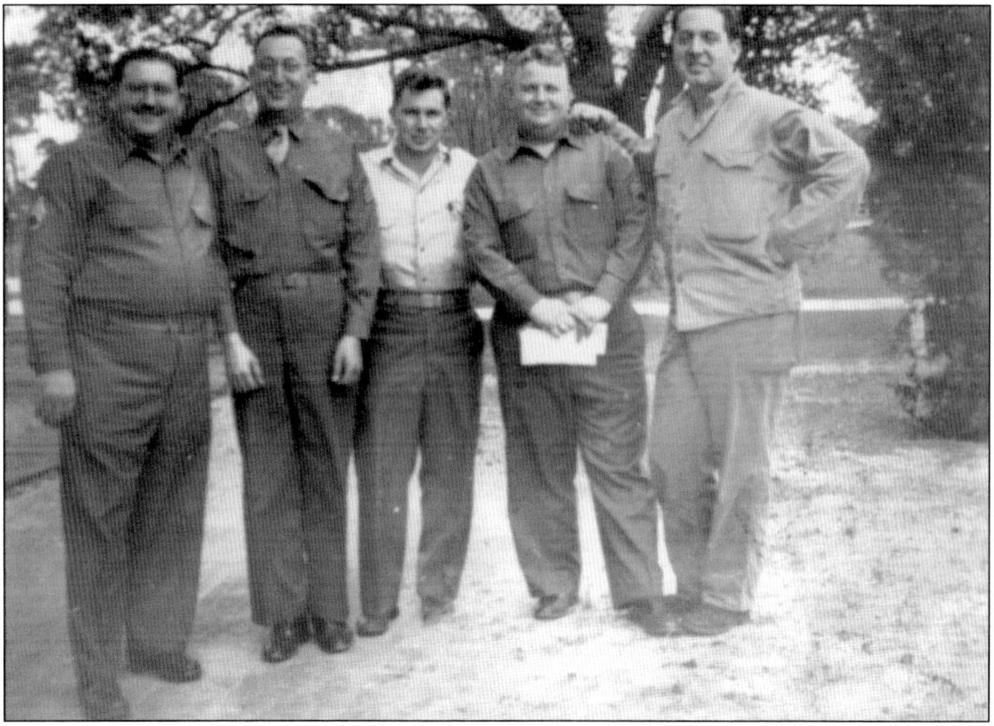

Very little has been discovered factually about the German and Italian Prisoner of War Camps located in St. Andrew's Parish during World War II. Anecdotal memories, however, could fill volumes. These unique photographs are now in the Special Collections at the College of Charleston. Milton Kronsberg, second from the left in the above photograph, was responsible for prison contract labor at the camp. The description given with the below photograph is "POW Street." The camp was located on the Ashley River side of St. Andrew's Boulevard along what is now Colony Drive. Remnants of the camp still exist in the area, particularly a chimney with an inscription "German Prisoners of War 19.1.1945." (Both, courtesy of Special Collections, College of Charleston; gift of Mickey K. Rosenblum.)

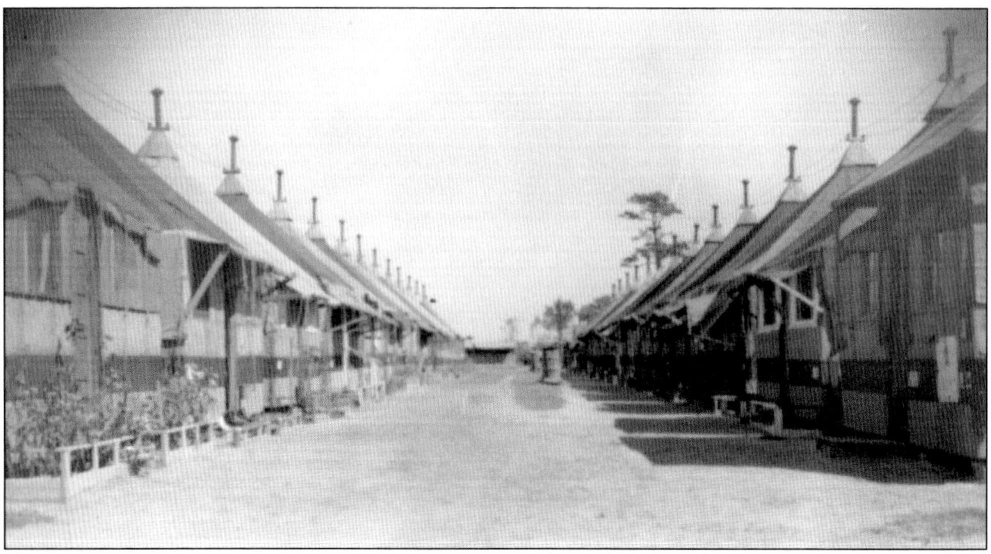

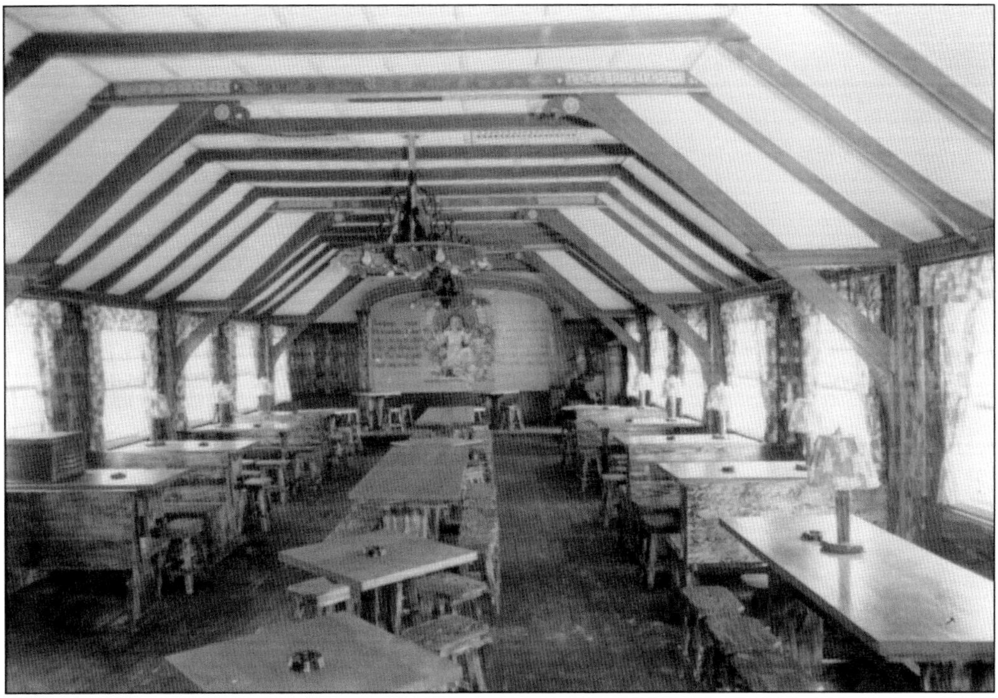

The POW barracks dining room (above) and POW camp mess hall from around 1943 (below), give us rare views into a beautifully appointed dining area in the camp. After the war, supper clubs were popular and some had their initial gatherings in this hall. One of the supper clubs is rumored to still have some of the furnishings. I.D. Peeks gave a game table from the camp to the Kennerty family. (Both, courtesy of Special Collections, College of Charleston; gift of Mickey K. Rosenblum.)

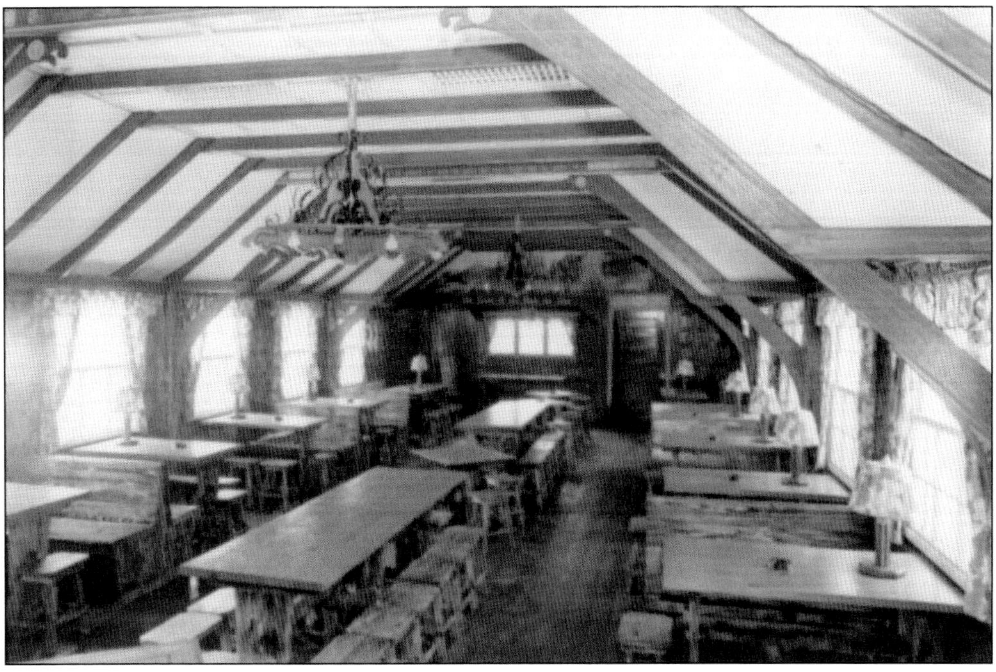

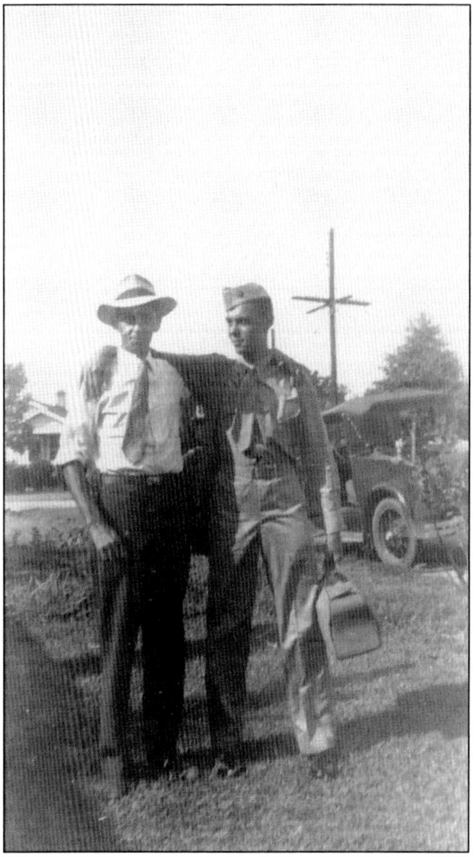

Like many of the young men of St. Andrew's Parish in 1944, Arthur Ravenel Jr. had enlisted. Arthur, dressed in his Marine uniform, holds his father, Arthur Ravenel, in front of the family home in Carolina Terrace. Arthur had returned from training at Parris Island and was on his way to Combat Infantry School at Camp Lejeune, North Carolina. The family's Model A is seen in the background. (Courtesy of Arthur Ravenel Jr.)

Arthur Ravenel Jr. General Contractor would do the framing and masonry work for Dan Groves's Howard Johnson on Savannah Highway. Arthur Ravenel Jr. attended the College of Charleston on the GI Bill earning a history degree. He landed his first job at the West Virginia Paper Mill and later branched out into commercial construction. Arthur went on to a career in politics, serving in the US Congress, the South Carolina State House of Representatives, and the South Carolina State Senate. (Courtesy of Yvonne Groves Gilreath.)

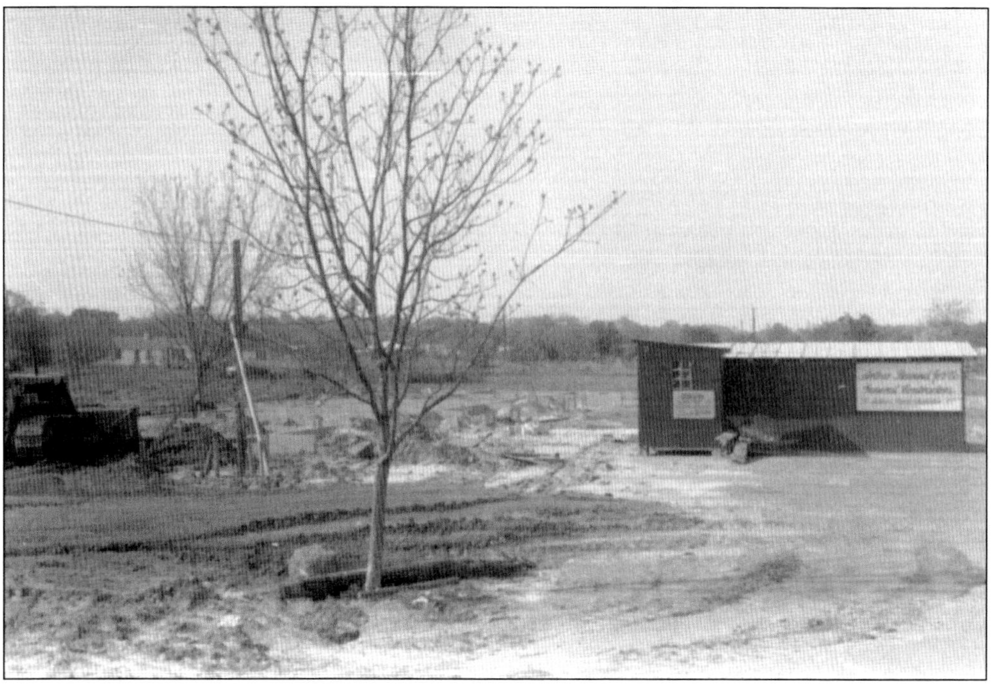

Three

St. Andrew's Parish's Suburban Life

World War II presented a dichotomy for the area. On one hand, the nation's sons were fighting a war, commodities were in short supply, and rationing existed, but the expansion at the naval yard gave the area an economic boost with a corresponding ripple effect. The continued influx of workers at the naval yard meant that developers were continuing to build houses. The neighborhoods of Avondale, Byrnes Downs, and Carolina Terrace that were once farmlands were now listed as FHA housing by private contractors. In 1943, St. Andrew's Homes was built as public housing on Arthur Ravenel's "Little Farm." The war ended in 1945, and by 1947, the population of St. Andrew's Parish exceeded 10,000 people. "Come visit me in the country" or "I'm moving to the country" was a sentiment that was often recounted as families moved from downtown Charleston to the new neighborhoods sprouting up in St. Andrew's Parish. Advertisements from businesses located downtown that had once congratulated St. Andrew's Parish accomplishments now advertised their West Ashley locations. Gas stations, grocery stores, guest homes, hotels, 5¢-and-10¢ stores, pharmacies, shopping centers, a car wash, a bank, and a post office opened to serve the community. The original church in the Parish, St. Andrew's Church was dormant, but soon Episcopalians living West Ashley breathed life back into it. The congregations of the Graham AME and the Emmanuel AME had gathered for worship in the Parish since the late 1800s. John Wesley Methodist, Blessed Sacrament, Ashley River Baptist, Lutheran Church of the Redeemer, and Holy Trinity Episcopal are just a few of the churches that were organized in the 1940s and 1950s. The General Assembly created the St. Andrew's Public Service District in 1949 to provide infrastructure—fire protection, garbage collection, street lighting, and a parish commission. A suburb is defined as a part of a city or residential area on the outskirts of a city or a smaller community adjacent to a city. St. Andrew's Parish was becoming a successful suburb, and soon incorporation would be a topic of discussion. With the explosion in growth came an equal explosion in stories about building this community, living in this community, and knowing your neighbors. Rich and fascinating, they would fill several volumes. St. Andrew's Parish had now become a place to live, a place to work, and a place to worship.

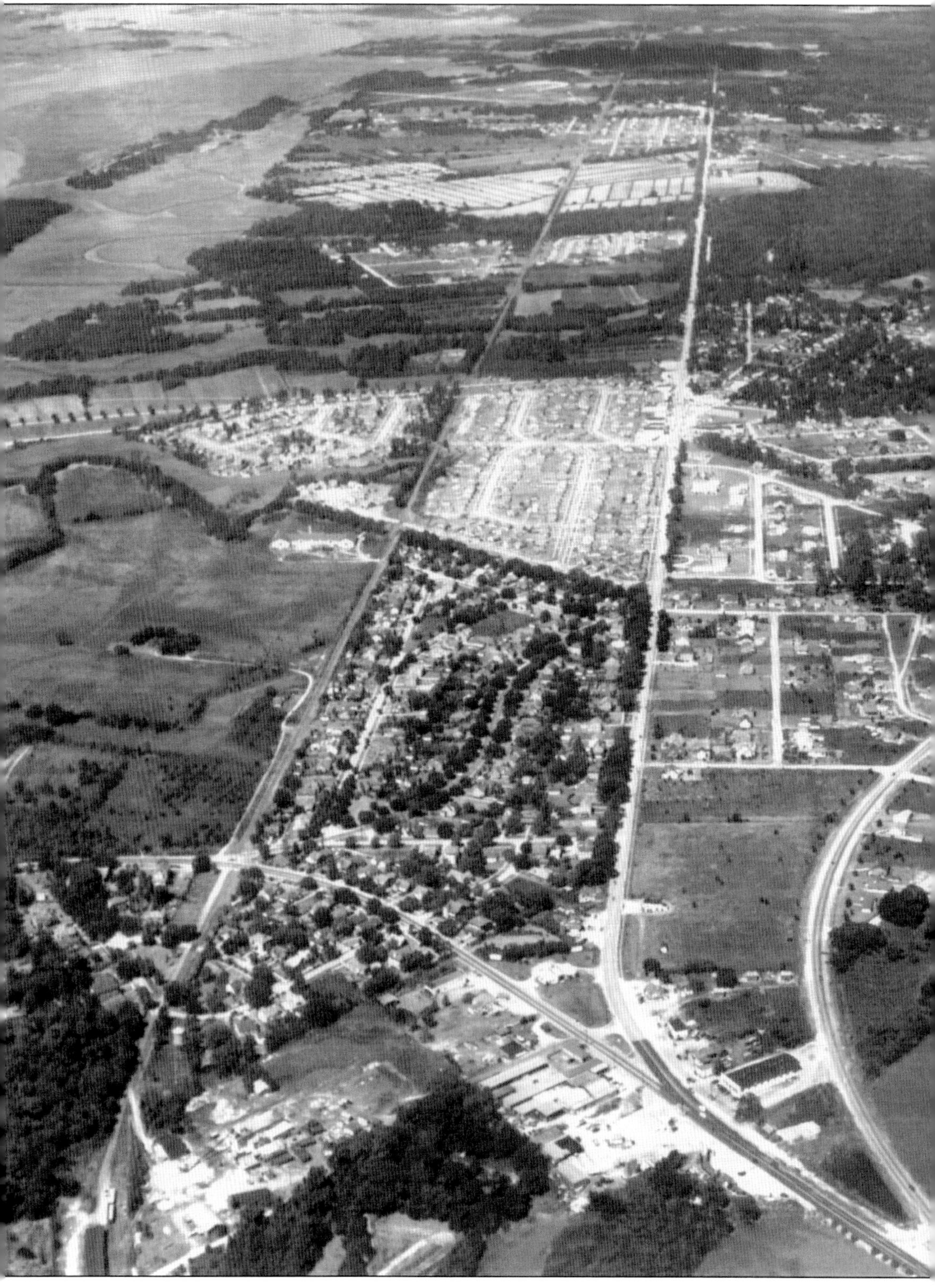

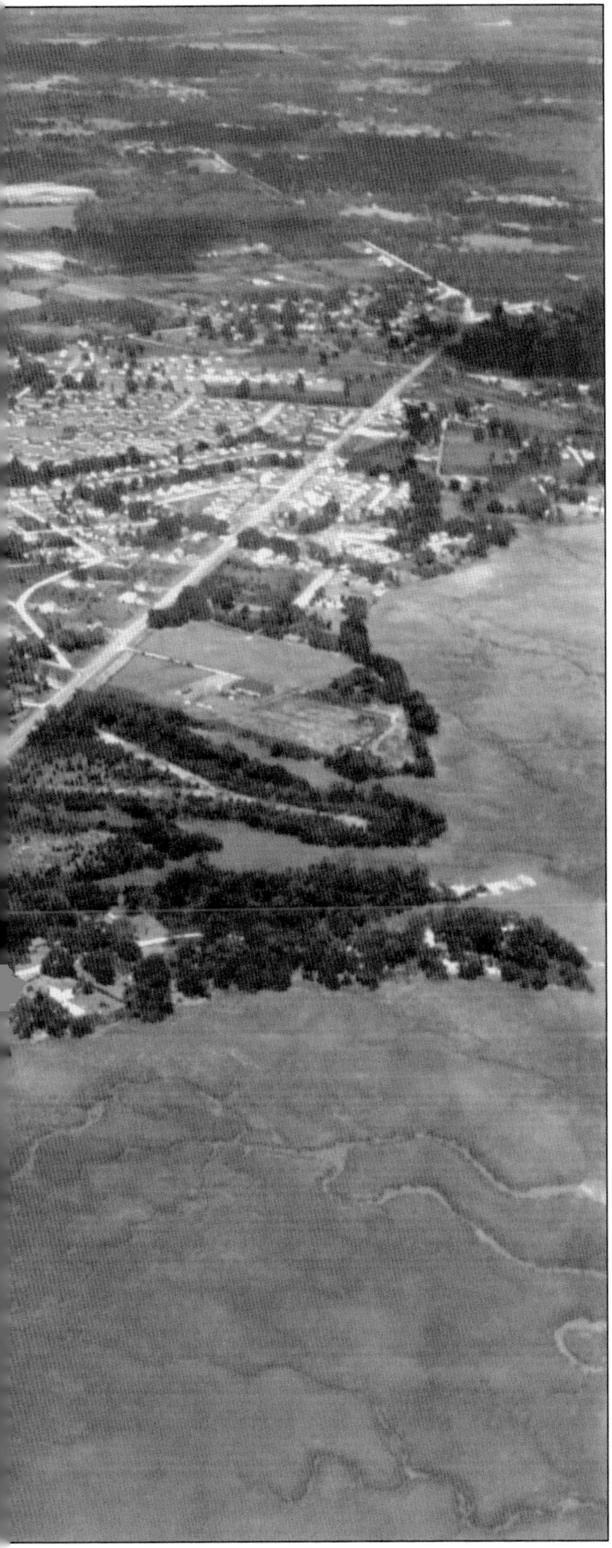

J.C. Hare hated to fly, but his good friend Roland Wooten, the postmaster for Charleston, had a passion for flight. This spectacular aerial was found among the papers of J.C. Hare. The speculation is that Roland took this photograph one day while flying and shared it with J.C., because J.C. and his wife wanted to move from their home on Tradd Street to the country. The presence and absence of certain landmarks date this photograph from late 1950 to early 1951. Some landmarks are St. Andrew's Elementary School with its original white facade, the tree-lined road to Coburg Dairy Farms, Windermere, Byrnes Downs, Avondale, the undeveloped land of the future Westwood, the Wessel home on the property that will soon become South Windermere, homes in Moreland, John Wesley Methodist Church, Blessed Sacrament Church, the Magnolia Theater, and the farmland that would become Harrison Acres. (Courtesy of Cantey Hare.)

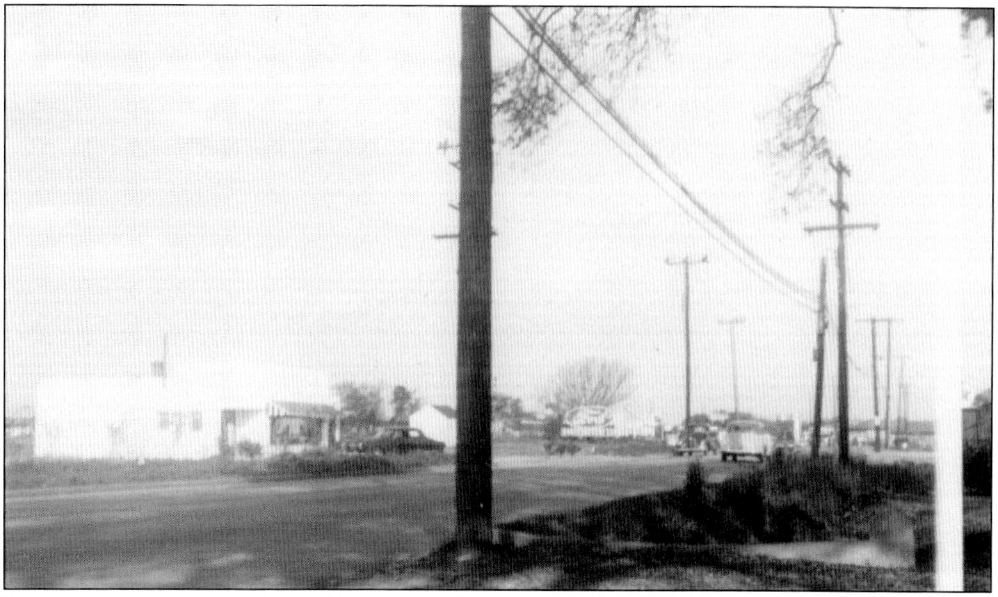

Does anyone remember the Golden Acorn? It was a gift shop located on Savannah Highway in a lone building with a striped awning in the space approximately in front of where the Sherwin Williams paint store is today. Savannah Highway is two lanes and the speed limit is 25 miles per hour. (Courtesy of P. Luther Bootle Jr., Ina Bootle.)

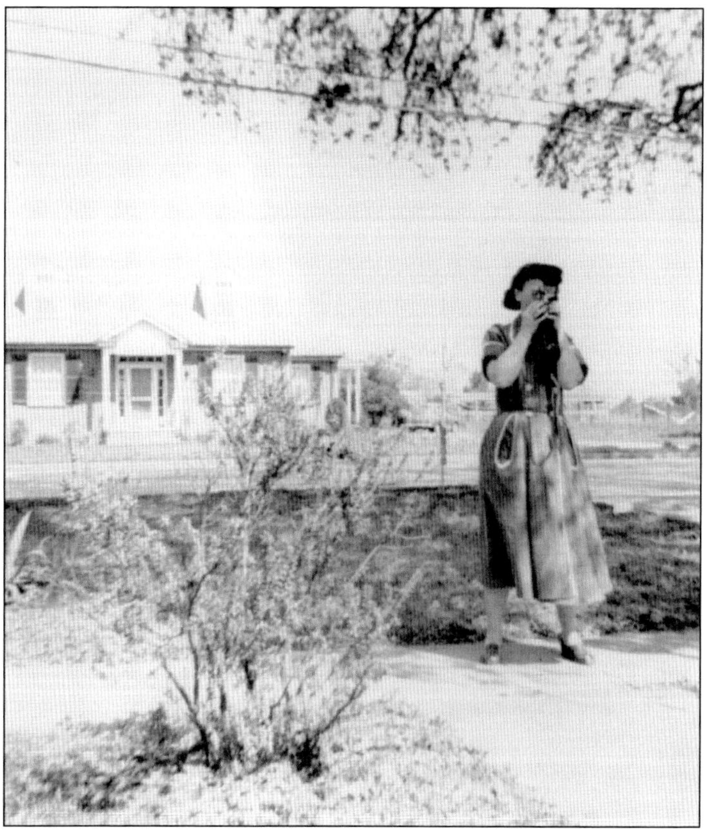

Another camera buff caught in action. The photographer is believed to be Jo Fogle, standing on Savannah Highway. Behind her is the home that now houses the dental office of Dr. Howard V. Peskin. Notice the field to the right. It is the property of Joe Harrison. Is this a packing shed in the background? Wesley Drive, known during this time as Wappoo Road, has not been extended from Savannah Highway to St. Andrew's Boulevard. The field would later sprout gas stations, a shopping center, the In and Out Car Wash, and Bill's Holly House. (Courtesy of Scott McClain.)

Arthur Ravenel Jr. identified the young man in this photograph as his good friend Edmund Fishburne Bellinger. Unfortunately we cannot see his feet, but the odds are that he is barefoot. Hugh Wayne and Edmund Bellinger were best friends. Hugh loved to go barefoot and Edmund challenged him to go barefoot to school. The "Boys without Shoes" spent most of their elementary school terms shoeless. (Courtesy of P. Luther Bootle Jr., Ina Bootle.)

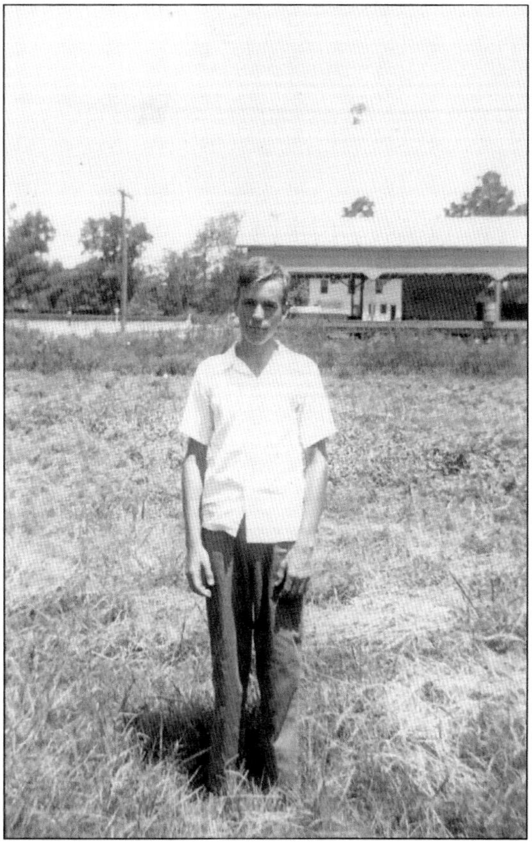

Philip Lorraine Bootle and Laura Lilla Benton Bootle sit in the glider behind Bootle's guest home on Savannah Highway. Standing behind them, from left to right and coincidently youngest to oldest, are their children: William Oliver (Sammie), Benjamin Thomas (Tommie), Leila Inez (Ina), William Augustus (Gus), Philip Luther (Luther), and Laura Lota (Lota). Philip and Lilla purchased the land from James Simmons in 1940 to build the guest home. Business cards advertised oil furnace heat, private baths, and showers. (Courtesy of P. Luther Bootle Jr., Ina Bootle.)

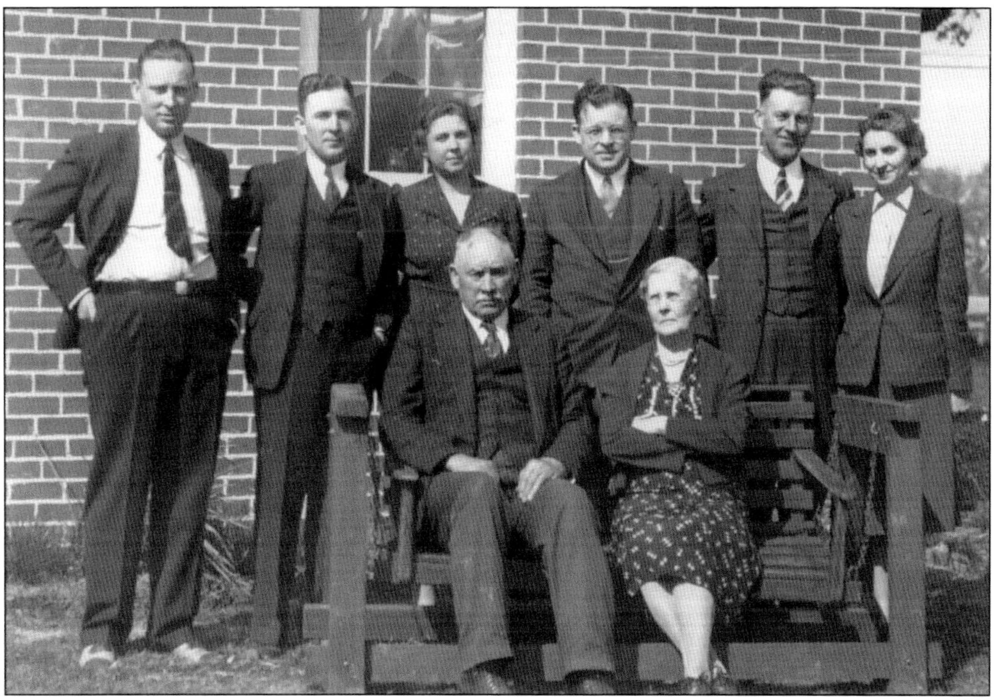

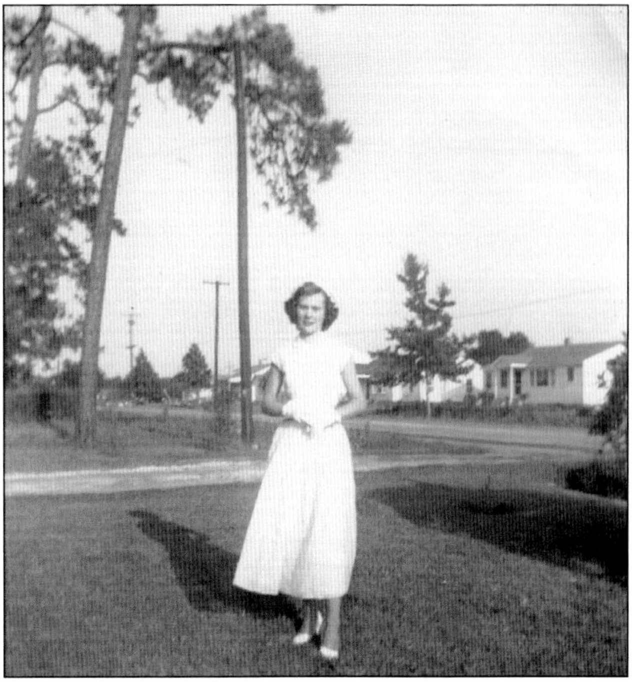

Stella Milton poses in the front yard of her home in Pinecrest Garden on Highway 61 near Wappoo Road. The neighborhood derived its name because of the tall pines that grew in the area. The family moved to the home in 1944 and Stella would ride her bicycle to St. Andrew's Parish High School on Wappoo Road. (Courtesy of Stella Milton Kearse.)

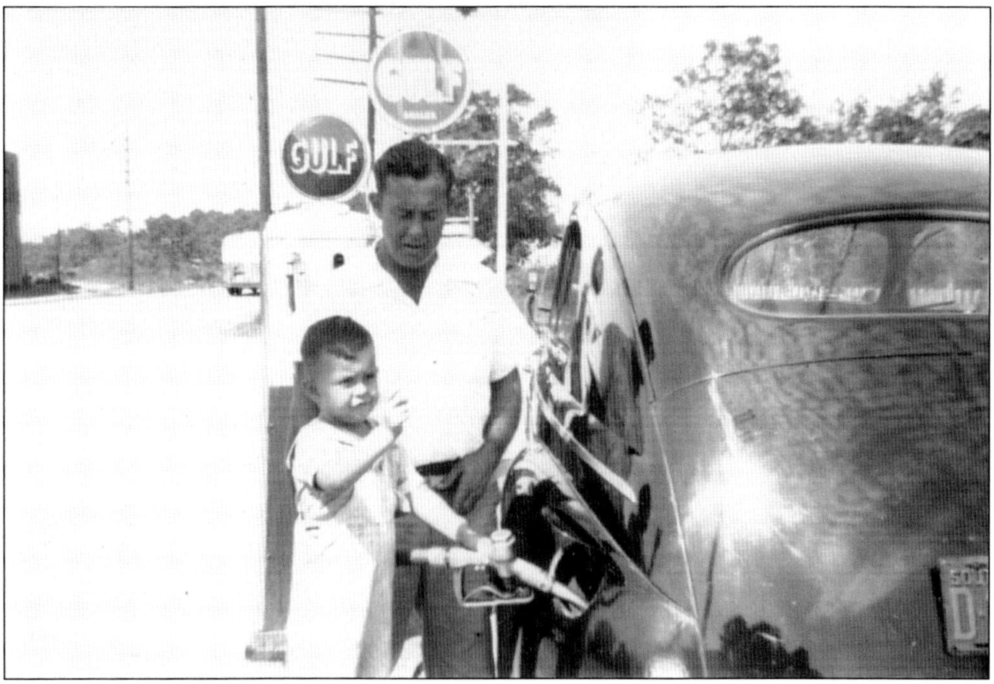

Albert Whaley teaches his son Albert Whaley Jr. the business of pumping gas at his Gulf Station. This station was located on the northwest corner of Wappoo Road and Savannah Highway. In 1946, Grace Bootle Long wrote to her son Luther relating that Albert was building a new gas station. This station would be located directly across Savannah Highway from the station in the photograph. Albert Whaley and Sammie Bootle were friends and Albert called Sammie every Christmas morning after he retired to Florida. (Courtesy of P. Luther Bootle Jr., Ina Bootle.)

Claire Krawcheck and Maurice Nussbaum were sweethearts when Maurice attended The Citadel in Charleston. They met at Jack Krawcheck's Men's Wear, one of Claire's father's retail stores, where Maurice worked part-time. They married in 1950 and in 1957 purchased their home in South Windermere. Maurice recalls that Ray and Nat Frisch built many of the houses in South Windermere, but not the one that became his family's home. (Courtesy of Maurice and Claire Nussbaum.)

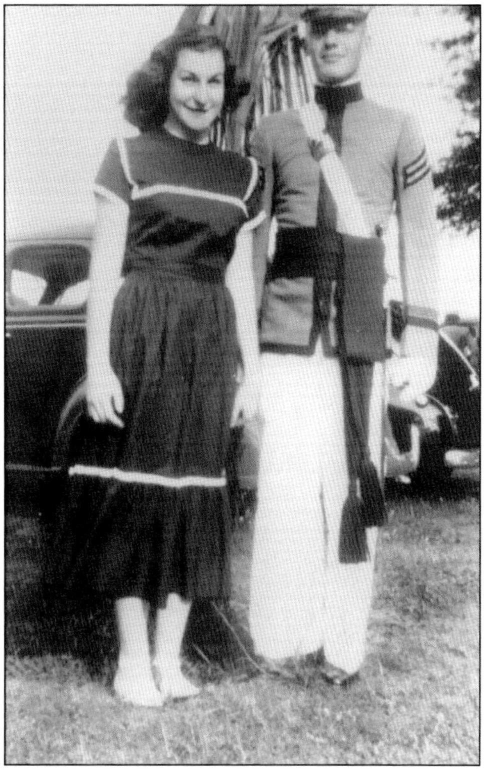

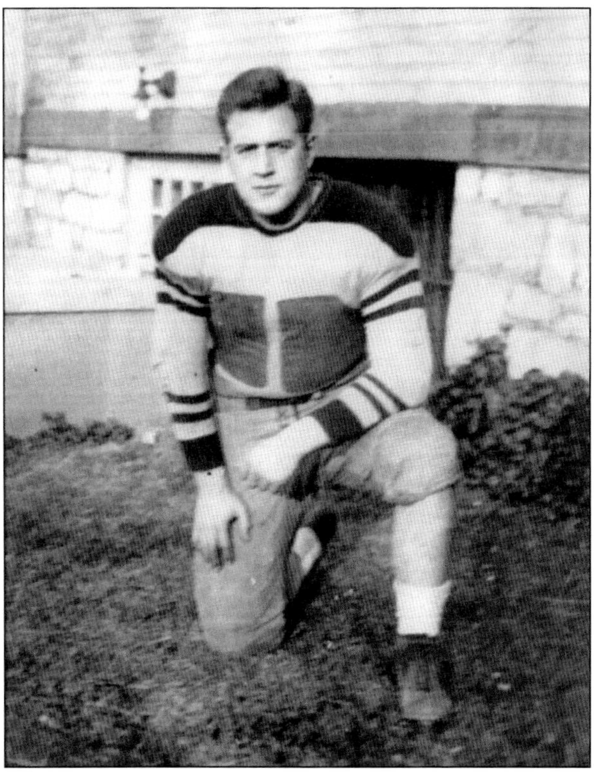

William Ackerman attended Dickinson College on a football scholarship graduating with a law degree. He entered the service during World War II and was stationed at Fort Jackson in Columbia, South Carolina. There he met his future wife, Jennie Shimel of Charleston. William was very active in the Charleston community. One of his many accomplishments was the West Ashley development of the South Windermere Shopping Center and South Windermere in the early 1950s. (Courtesy of the Jewish Community Center.)

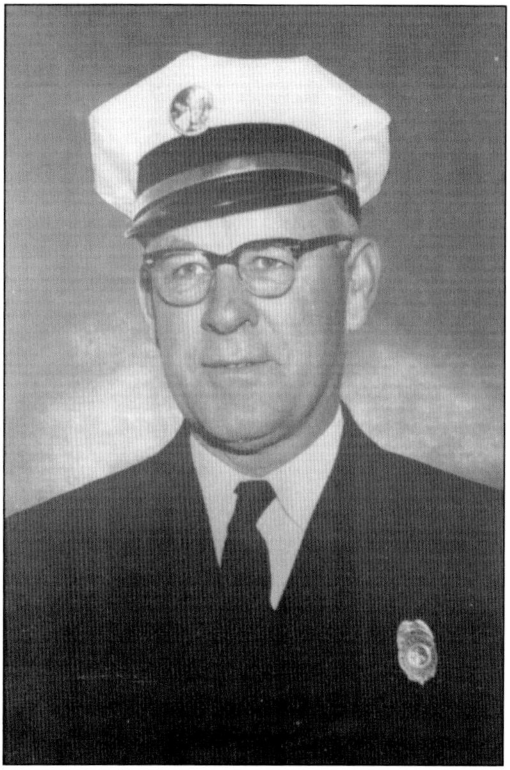

The 1947 St. Andrew's Parish Exchange Club brochure describes a "modern and fully equipped Fire Department." The personnel listed for the department where Chief R.F. Platt, P.L. Bootle, and R.B. Ramsey. Philip Luther Bootle was the chief of the St. Andrew's Fire Department from 1954 to 1956. (Courtesy of Ina Bootle.)

The occasion of this gathering of firemen and their equipment is unknown. The first fire station in St. Andrew's Parish was located at the junction of Folly Beach Highway and Savannah Highway near Windermere. To get oriented, visualize the Highway 17 overpass going north bisecting the photograph. Bootle's Barbecue Stand is the building on the left and Eden's Grocery Store is on the far right. (Courtesy of Ina Bootle.)

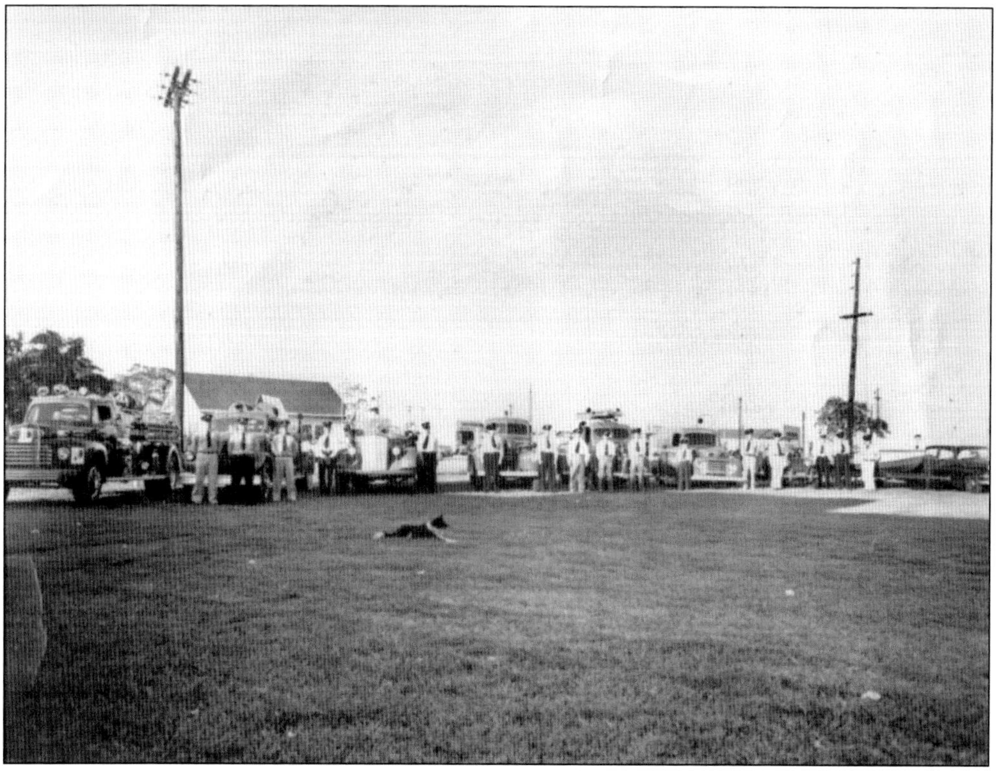

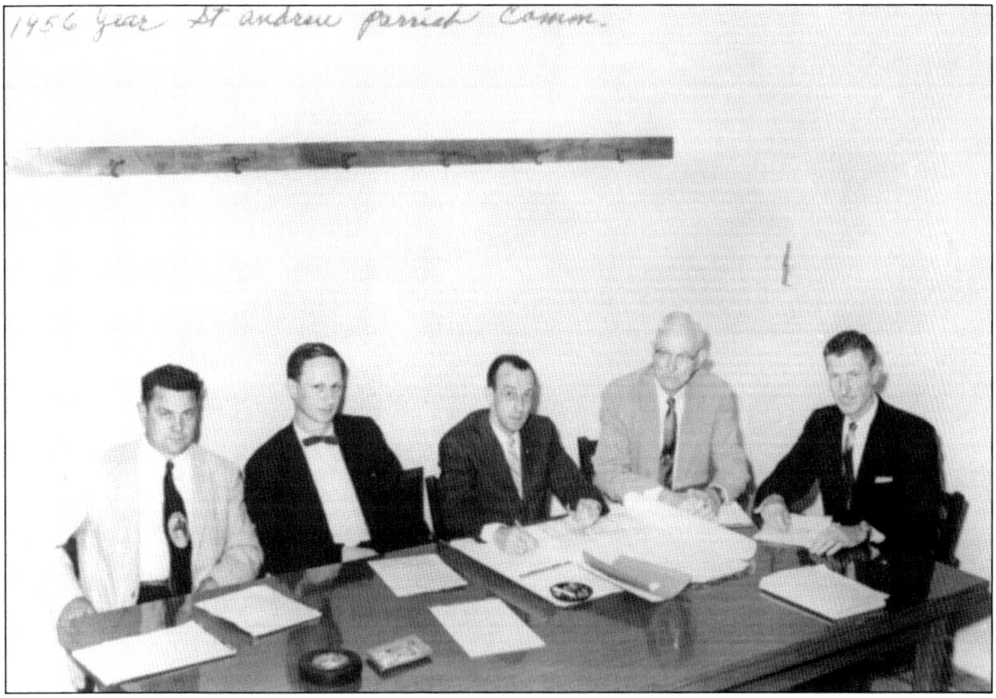

In 1956, the St. Andrew's Parish Commissioners were, from left to right, Richard M. Bunch, Clarence T. Hamrick Jr., Carl W. Welch Jr., and James H. Maquire. The man seated between Carl Welch and James Maquire is unidentified, possibly E.T. Friedell. The plaque that hangs in the Public Service District office lists the terms of the four identified men: Richard Bunch from 1956 to 1961, Carl Welch from 1955 to 1965, James Maquire from 1949 to 1961, and Clarence Hamrick Jr. from 1957 to 1978. E.T. Friedell is listed as a commissioner on the plaque at St. Andrew's Fire Station No. 2. (Courtesy of Richard E. Bunch.)

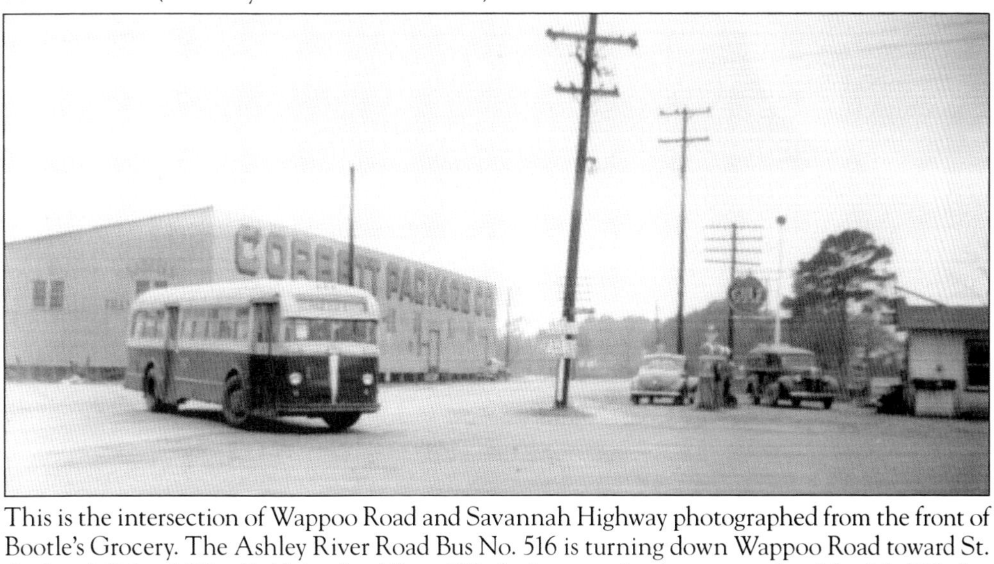

This is the intersection of Wappoo Road and Savannah Highway photographed from the front of Bootle's Grocery. The Ashley River Road Bus No. 516 is turning down Wappoo Road toward St. Andrew's School. The Gulf sign for Albert Whaley's gas station is seen on the right. Mr. Whaley would later build a new service station on the south side of Savannah Highway. (Courtesy of P. Luther Bootle Jr., Ina Bootle.)

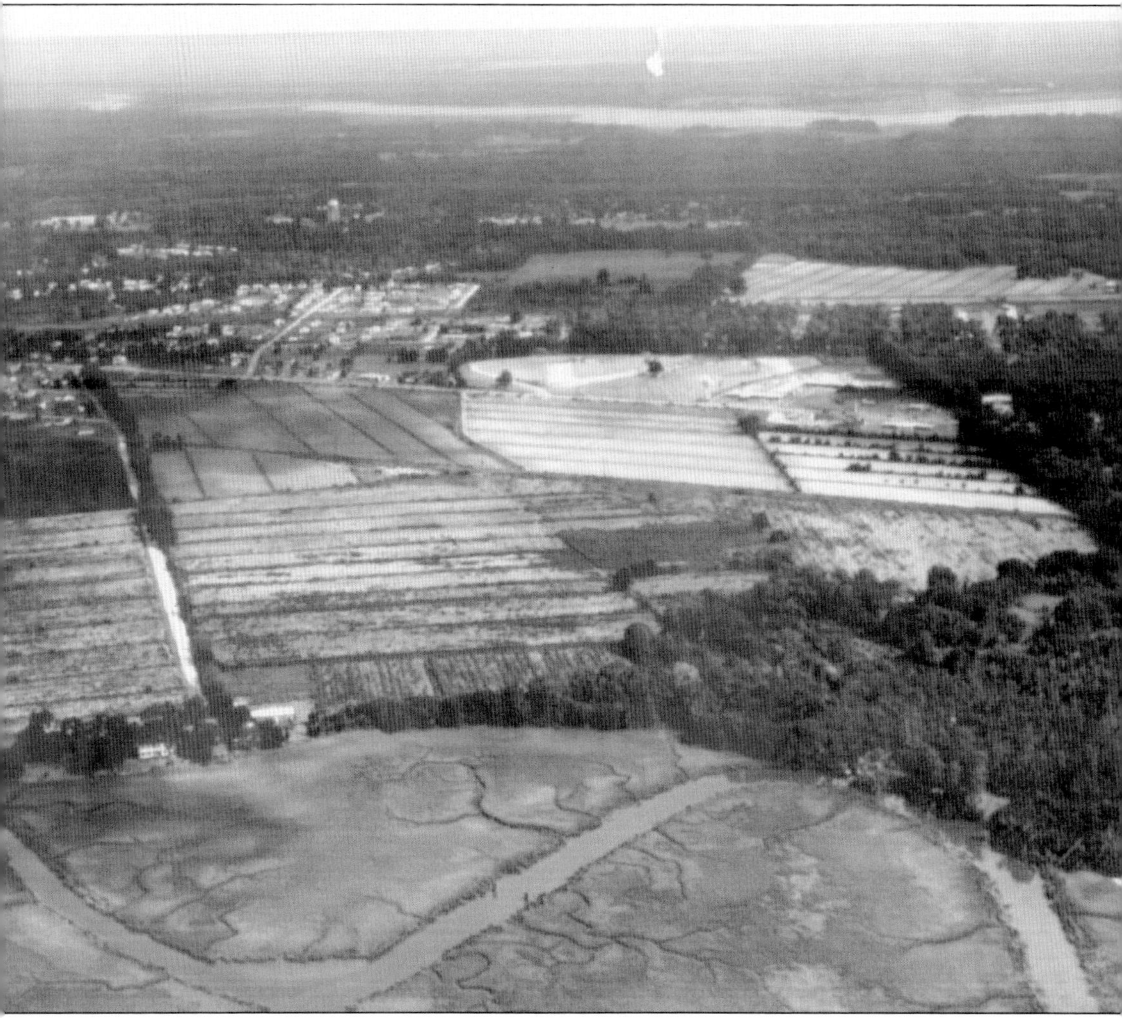

Two aerials, with slightly different perspectives of the Voorhees Plantation, capture the transition from farming to suburban life. William Voorhees, Martha W. Voorhees, and Lillian Voorhees Acken conveyed 470 acres of the Voorhees Tract and of Geddes Hall to Joseph Harrison in 1917. Mr. Harrison farmed the land until it was sold for development. (Courtesy of Irene Burk Tezza, Barbara Burk DeWitt, and Ruth Burk Gay.)

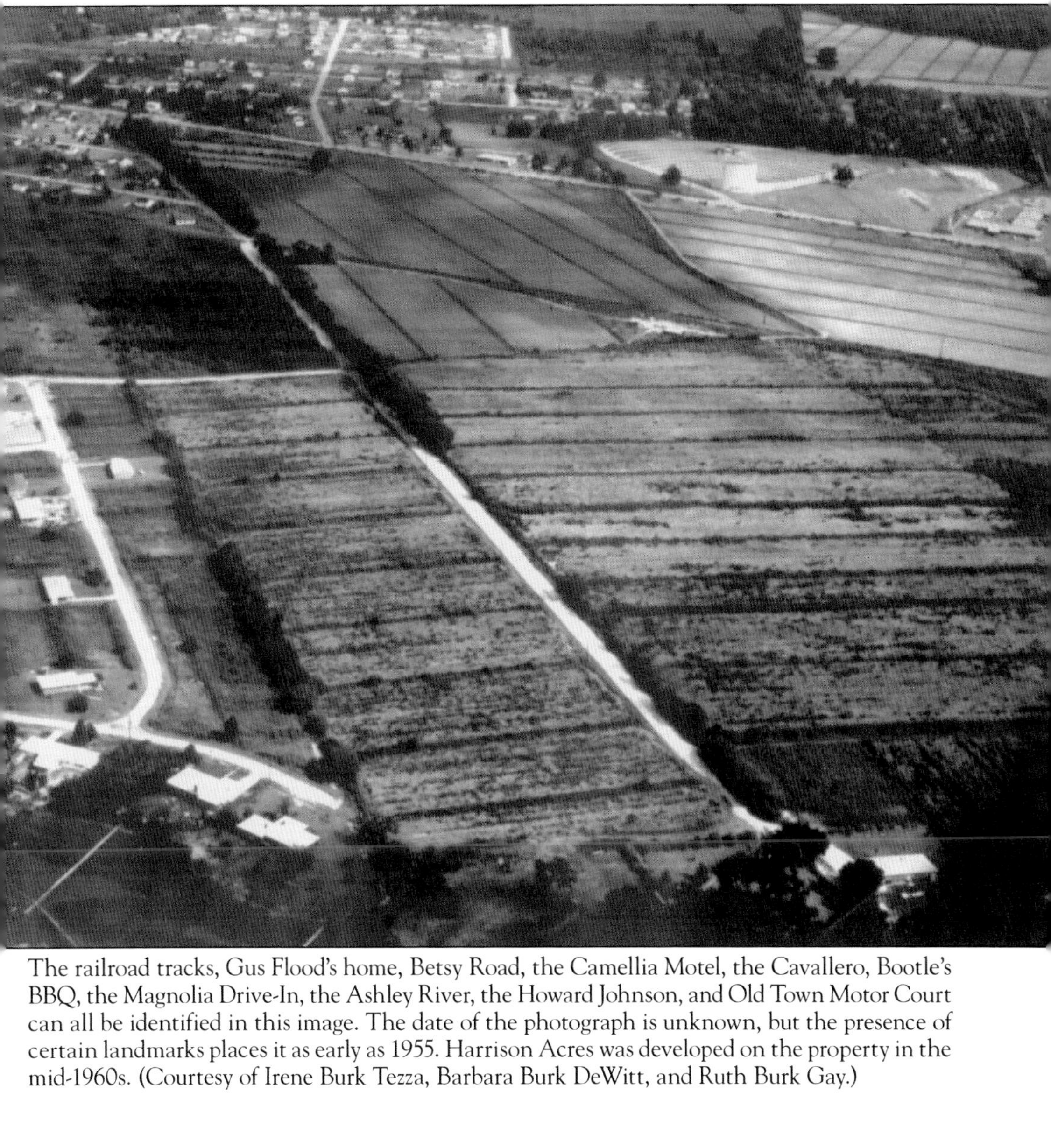

The railroad tracks, Gus Flood's home, Betsy Road, the Camellia Motel, the Cavallero, Bootle's BBQ, the Magnolia Drive-In, the Ashley River, the Howard Johnson, and Old Town Motor Court can all be identified in this image. The date of the photograph is unknown, but the presence of certain landmarks places it as early as 1955. Harrison Acres was developed on the property in the mid-1960s. (Courtesy of Irene Burk Tezza, Barbara Burk DeWitt, and Ruth Burk Gay.)

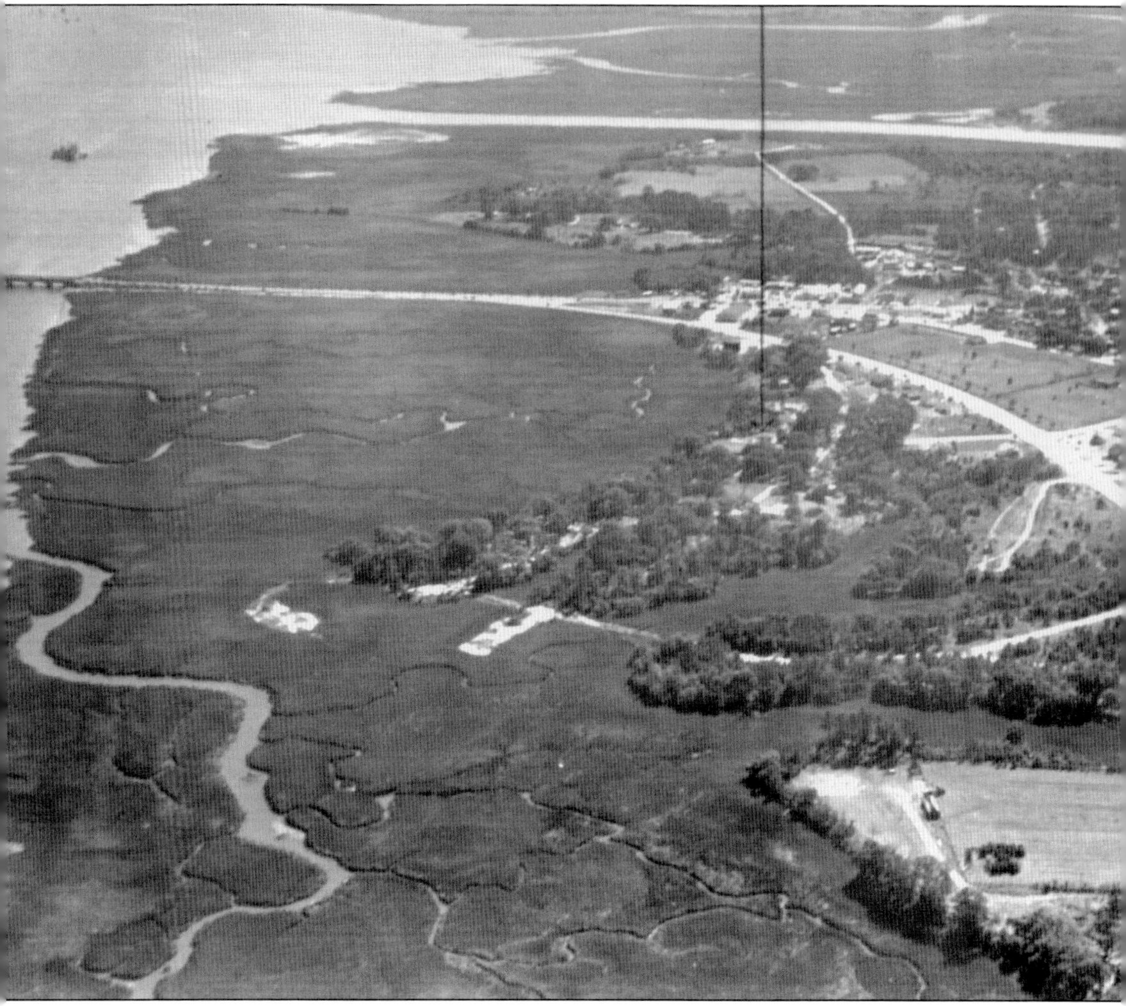

Albemarle Point is located on a piece of land along Wappoo Creek accessed by a causeway, graced by 10 homes, and embraced by the marsh along the west bank of the Ashley River. It can be seen in the upper center of this aerial. The residents recount with delight their childhood memories of riding horses, swinging in tire swings, walking along the railroad tracks to South Windermere Shopping Center, swimming in the man-made tidal canal, playing in the pea field that one day would become a tennis court and swimming pool, and exploring the surrounding farmland. West Ashley has boomed in the last 50 years, but the residents of Albemarle Point still feel the embrace of the marsh and the quiet solitude of the Point. (Courtesy of Cantey Hare.)

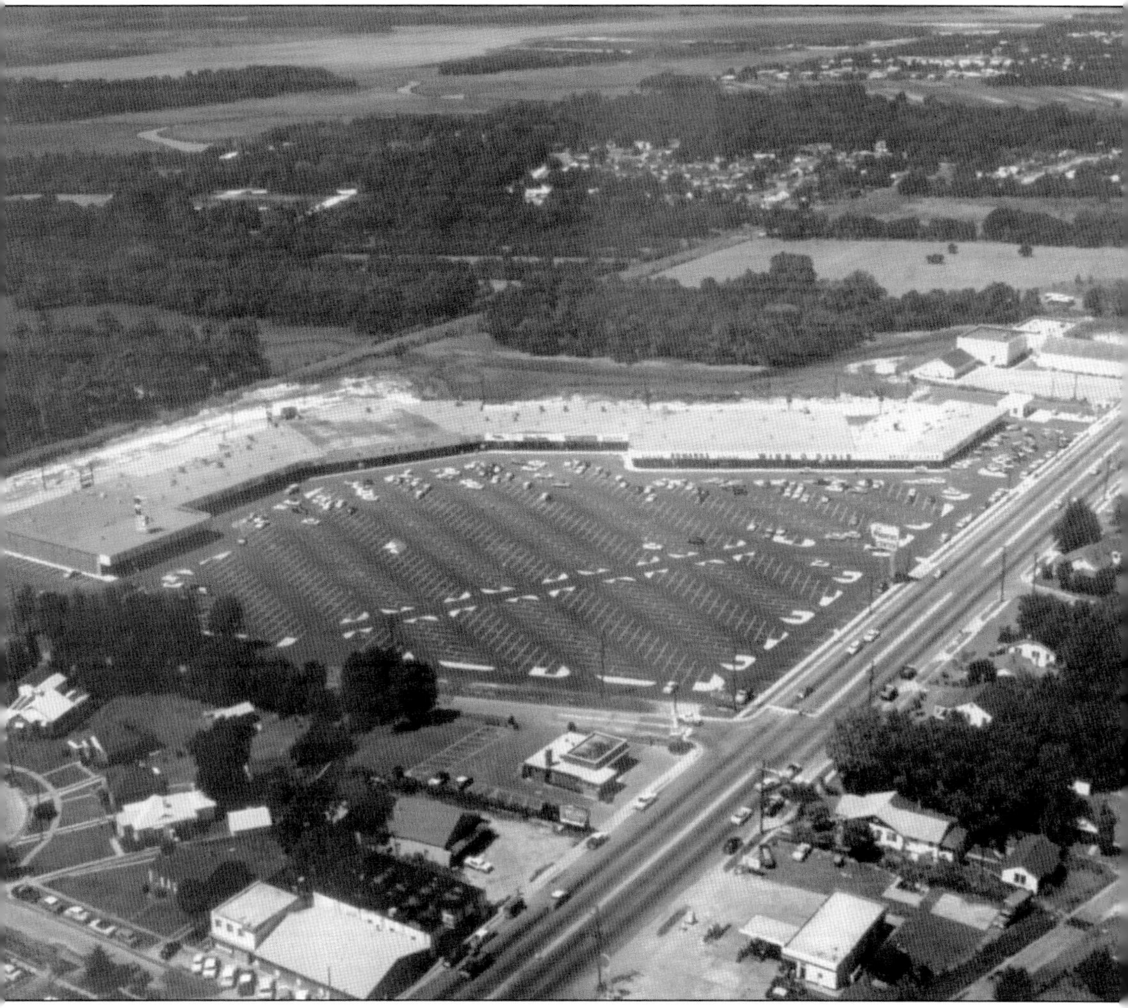

Francis Hanckel and Parish Realty Co. developed St. Andrew's Center that opened in 1959. Grant's, Winn-Dixie, Colonial, Kerrison's Department Store, Lorraine's Children Shop, and Hook Line and Sinker were a few of the 29 establishments originally located in the Center. The Center also had spaces available for the community, offering meeting rooms and sponsoring Easter Sunrise Services. Recently, Kimco Corporation, the current owner, gave it a face-lift and brought in new stores, including Harris Teeter. Some of the store fronts on Daniel Street and a few of the Byrnes Downs homes along Timmerman Drive can be seen in the lower left corner of the photograph. The Coburg Dairy sign marks the corner of the Center at Coburg Road and Savannah Highway. This favorite landmark is often used to orient newcomers to the area. (Courtesy of Frank Hanckel, Charlotte Hanckel Hay.)

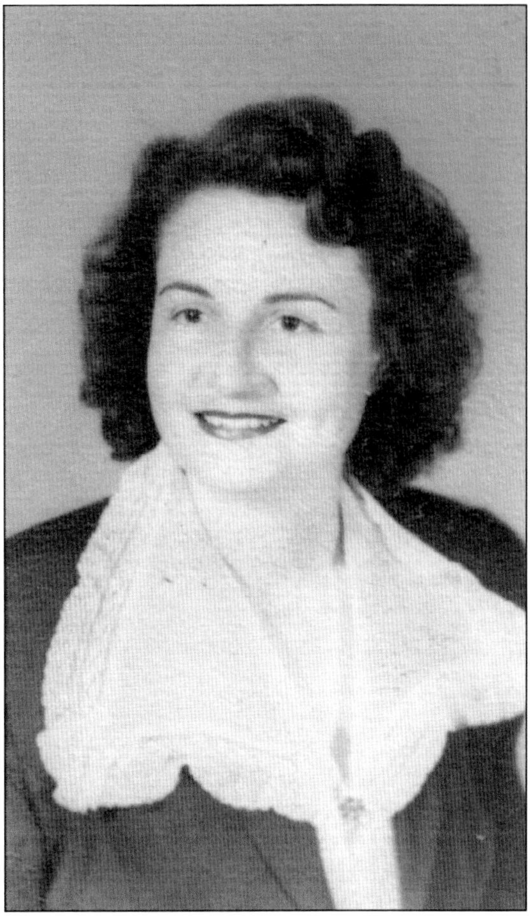

Margaret Flood Higdon, the daughter of Gus Flood, who worked for Joe Harrison, was a renowned horticulturist, developing the Old Fort Gardens and Nursery on land in Pierpont. She was often invited to judge both local and national flower shows and speak at local and national garden club meetings. G. Philip Higdon Sr. was responsible for the submission of the camellia variety that was designated the Margaret Higdon camellia. The Higdon camellia produces a pink blossom with white-tipped petals. (Courtesy of Philip Higdon.)

G. Philip Higdon Jr. stands on the entrance gates to Old Fort Gardens and Nursery. Beyond the gates is the structure that initially housed the nursery and later become the family home located near the 120-degree, arced fortification. The family also owned additional land in Pierpont where they lived and farmed. When they sold the farmland and renovated the nursery to the new home, Margaret Higdon built Higdon's Garden Center on Ashley River Road. Old Fort Gardens and Nursery had the contract for landscaping Byrnes Downs. (Courtesy of Philip Higdon.)

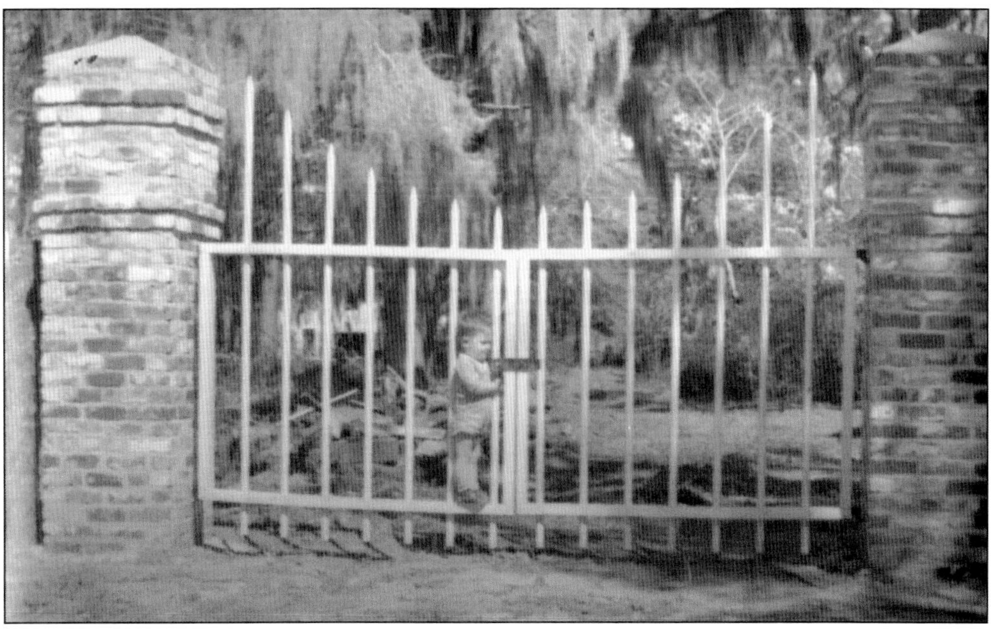

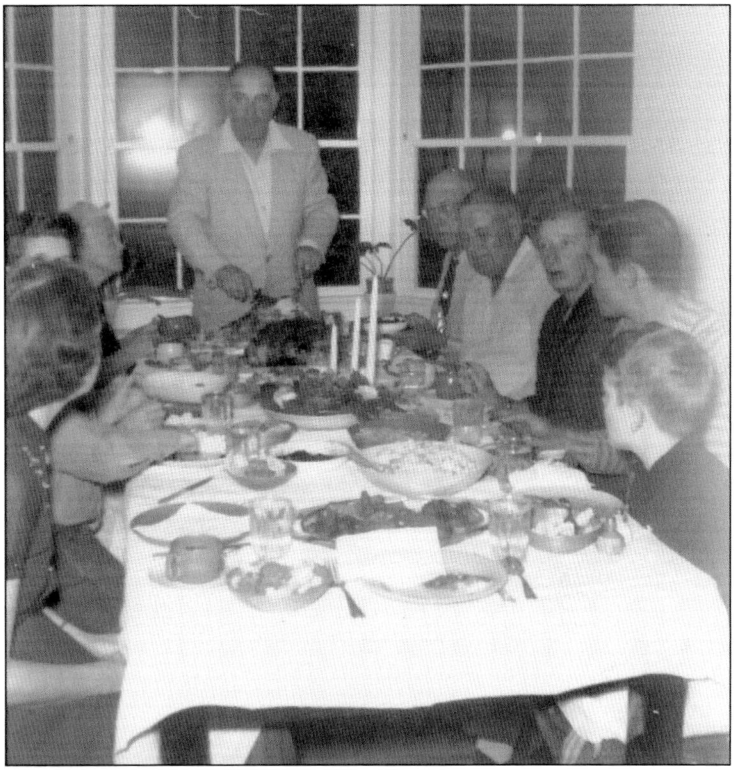

G. Philip Higdon Sr. carves the turkey for the holiday meal at their home in Pierpont. Gathered at the table are, clockwise, Margaret Higdon, John Philip Barker, Jack Barker, Trudy Higdon Barker, Grace Ellen McNally, Mr. Higdon, William Stacy, James Harvin, Molly Harvin, G. Philip Higdon Jr., and Jack Barker. By looking out the window, one could catch a glimpse of a 120-degree, arced fortification that was located near the house. (Courtesy of Philip Higdon.)

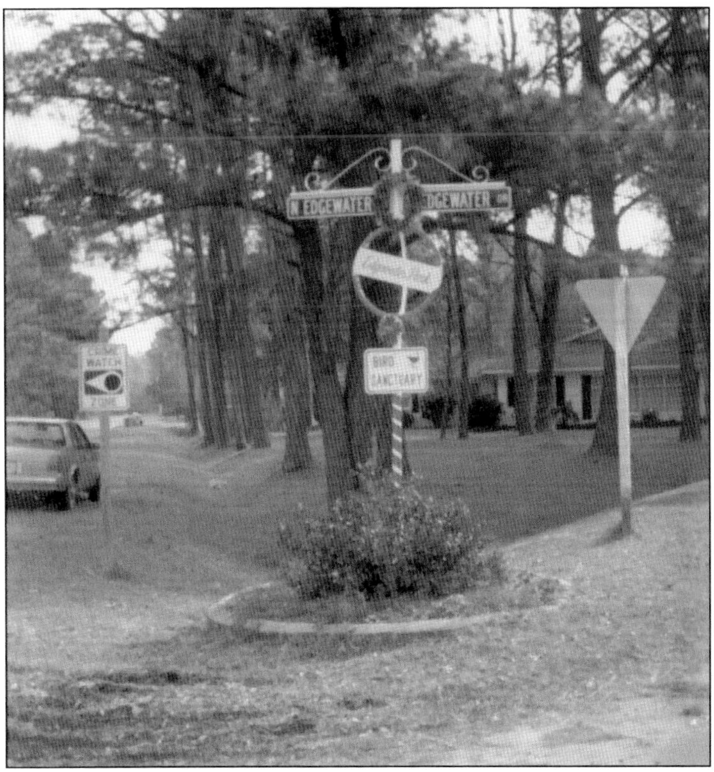

Edgewater Park is situated on land at the end of Wappoo Road accessed by a small bridge over Wappoo Creek with dramatic views of the Stono River and Elliot Cut. The Edgewater Park Garden Club, organized in 1955 with a mission to beautify the community, promote gardening, and protect wildflowers and birds, produces a yearly book of membership, club activities, and gardening tips. The sign at the old entrance to the neighborhood identifies it as a bird sanctuary. (Courtesy of Amy Elsey, past president of the Edgewater Park Garden Club.)

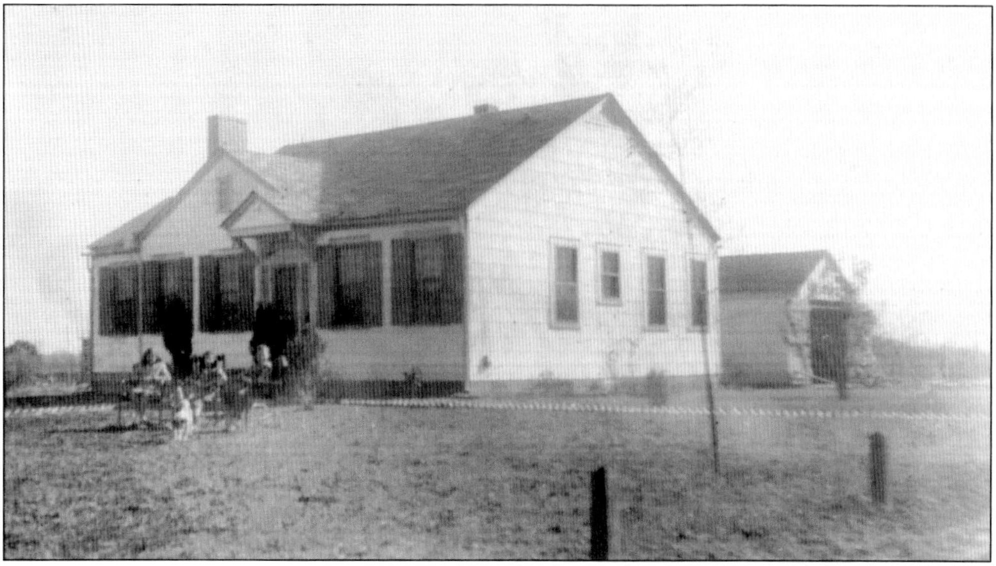

Martin and Gladys Holling built their home during the mid-1940s on Pinckney Park Drive in Stono Park, a neighborhood established in 1928. The neighborhood school, Stono Park Elementary School, would open with 11 classrooms on Garden Street in 1952. The school layout was similar to St. Andrew's Elementary built on Chadwick Drive in Windermere. (Courtesy of Carole Clark Earhart.)

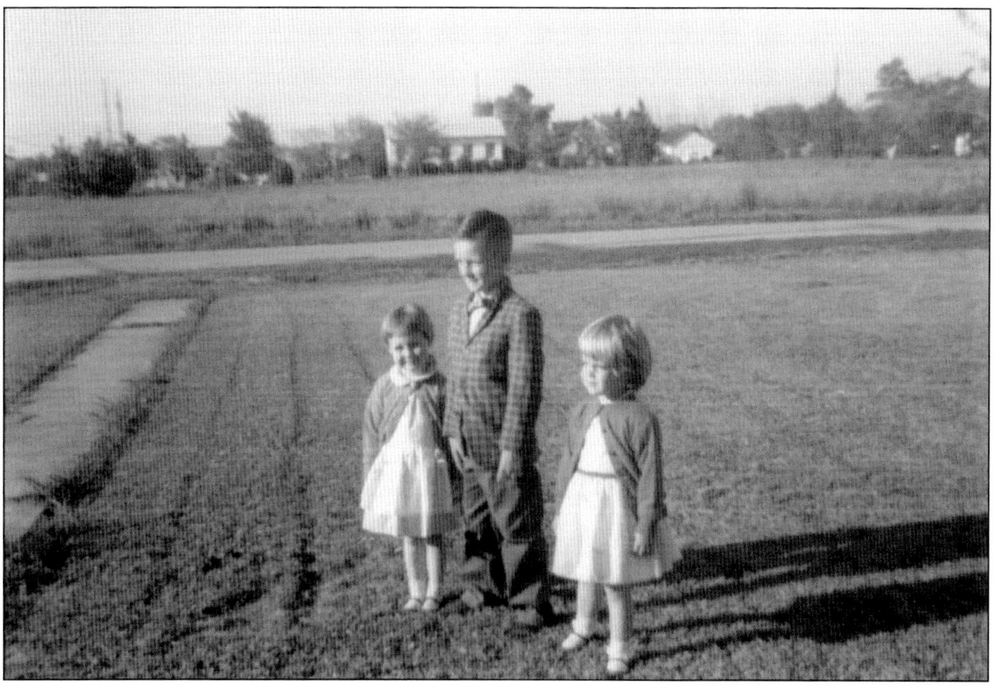

Carole Clark, her brother Marty Clark, and her cousin Sherri Clark are dressed for Easter. Maybe the Easter Bunny left treats in the front yard of their grandparent Holling's home in Stono Park. The building in the center background is the Stono Park Civic Club building. Randolph Park in Stono Park is named for Randolph Harrison, Joseph Harrison's brother, who owned the land before it was developed into Stono Park. (Courtesy of Carole Clark Earhart.)

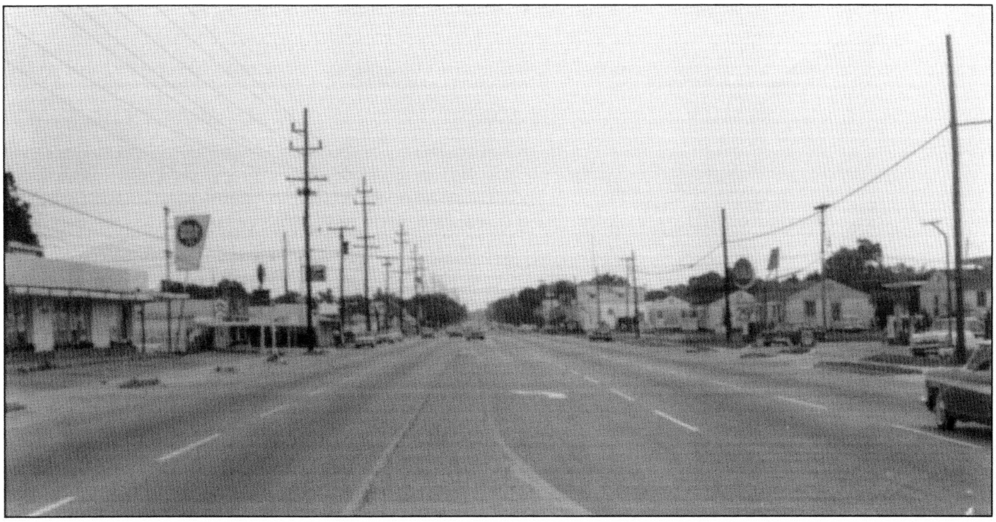

The photographer stands in the middle of St. Andrew's Boulevard, also known as Highway 61 and gives us a snapshot looking north. The small homes on the right of the road are the St. Andrew's Homes, built in 1943 as public housing. Today, the view has different landmarks with the Food Lion Shopping Center occupying the site that was once St. Andrew's Homes. (Courtesy of Yvonne Groves Gilreath.)

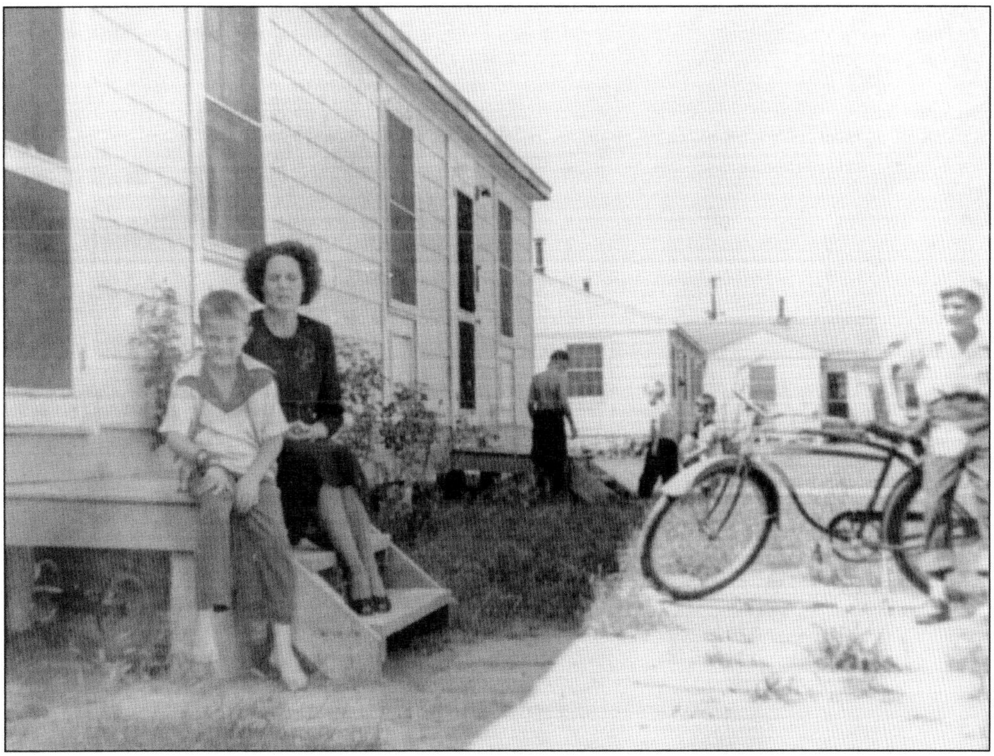

It is 1948, and Randy Mills sits on the steps of 112A Bibb Street at St. Andrew's Homes with his mother, Ethel Mills. Benson Faircloth leans on his bicycle and smiles for the photographer. Buddy and Charles Coleman hang out at the front door of the adjoining unit. (Courtesy of Randy Mills.)

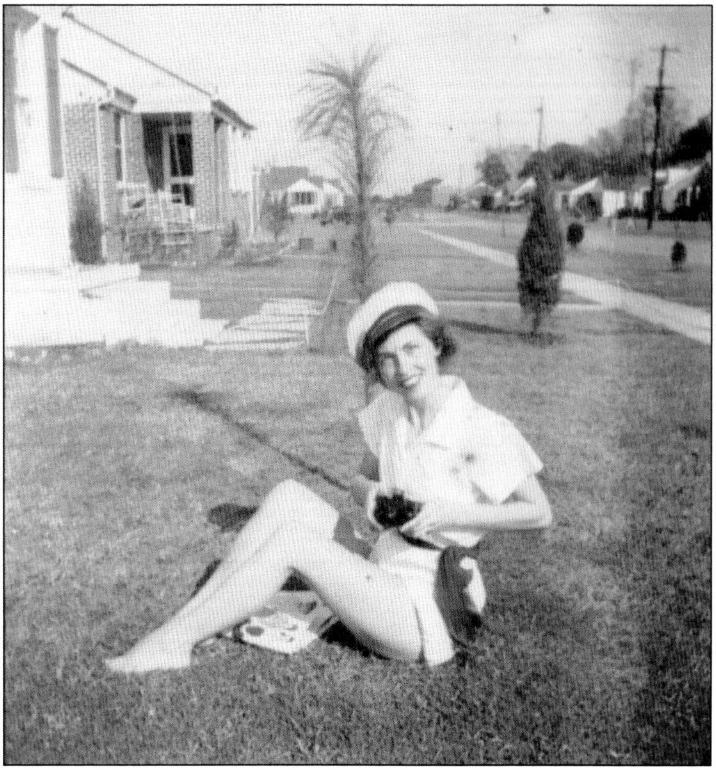

Janet Pearson sits on the front lawn of her home at 25 Campbell Drive in Byrnes Downs. She is smiling for the camera and holding a camera! "The Visitor," a column in the *Charleston Evening Post,* detailed the Pearson family and their artistic talents. Dimpy, Janet's husband, was a clarinetist, Janet was a painter, and their daughter Delores was an accomplished dancer. When it came time to decorate the front door for Christmas, sheet music for a Christmas carol seemed like the obvious choice. (Both, courtesy of Delores Pearson Rogers.)

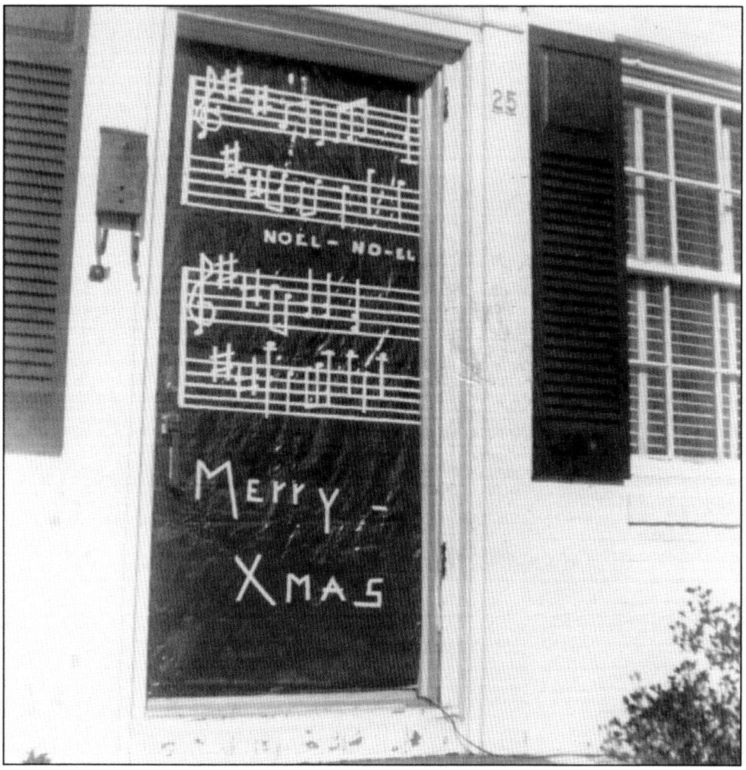

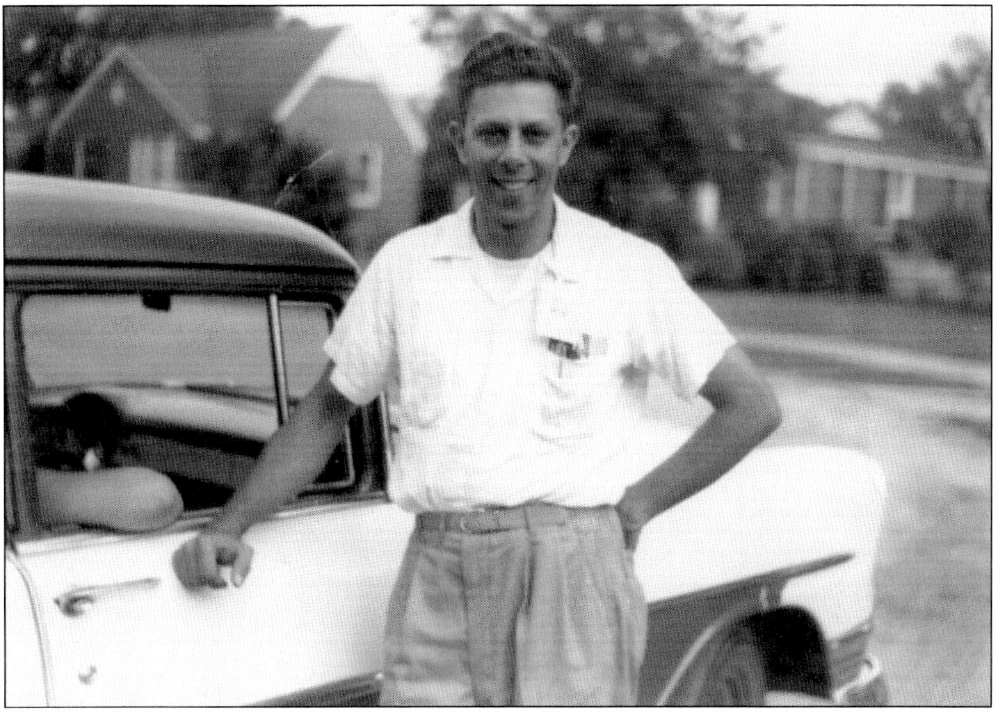

Herbert (Herb) S. Goldberg smiles for the camera while standing on the sidewalk near his first home on Yeamans (now known as Yeadon) Avenue in Byrnes Downs. Herb and his wife, Helen, lived in Byrnes Downs for more than 10 years before moving to Charlestowne Estates III. (Courtesy of Herb and Helen Goldberg.)

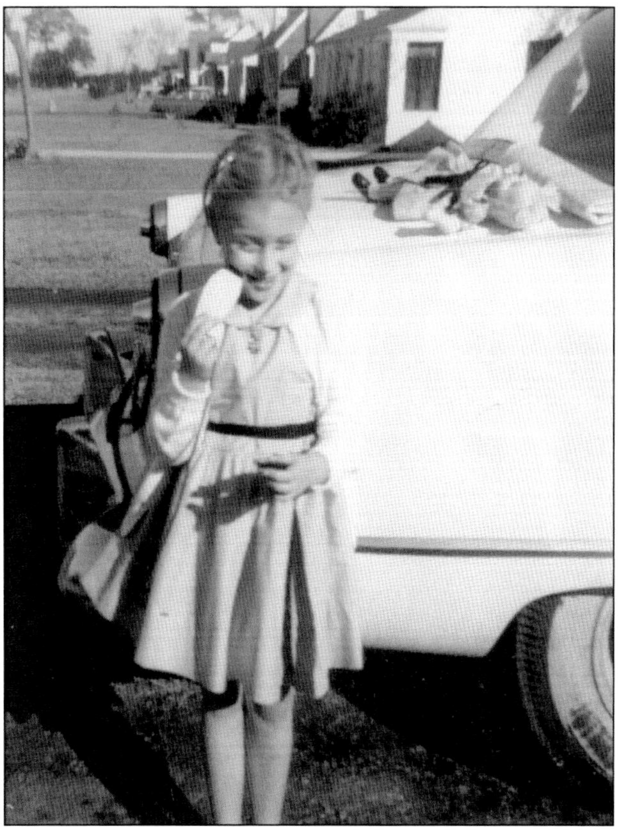

I.D. Peeks and C.P. Means developed the Avondale neighborhood in 1942. When Cecil Kearse was moved to the new West Ashley branch of Citizens & Southern National Bank, he wanted to move his family to the area and he settled on a home in Avondale. Cele, his daughter, stands by the family car with her doll on the hood of the trunk. Cele remembers attending Miss Till's kindergarten in Avondale. (Courtesy of Cecil B. Kearse.)

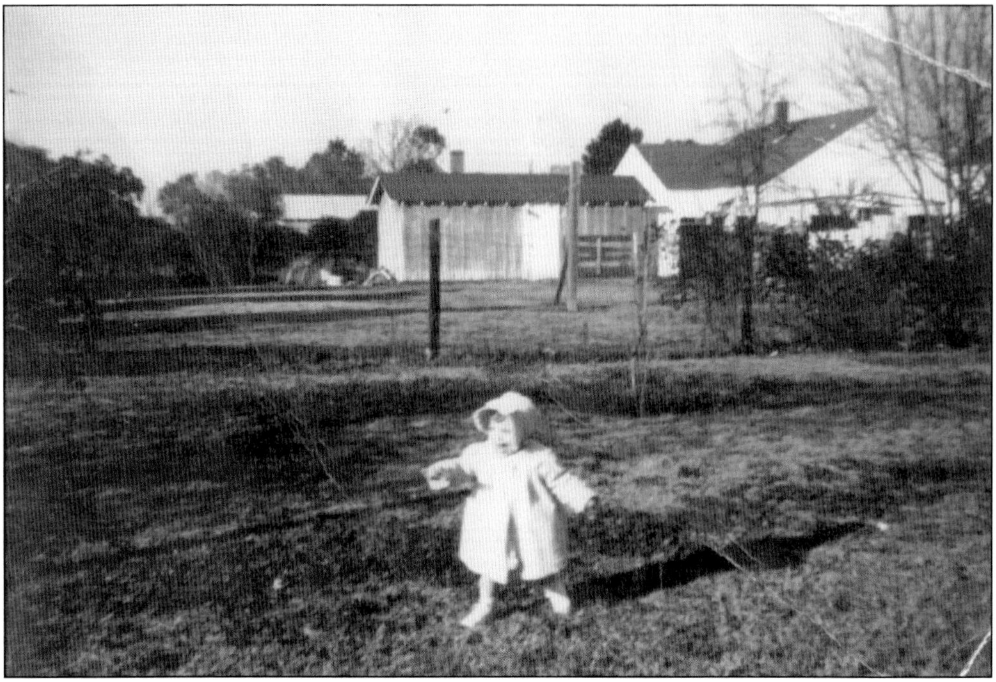

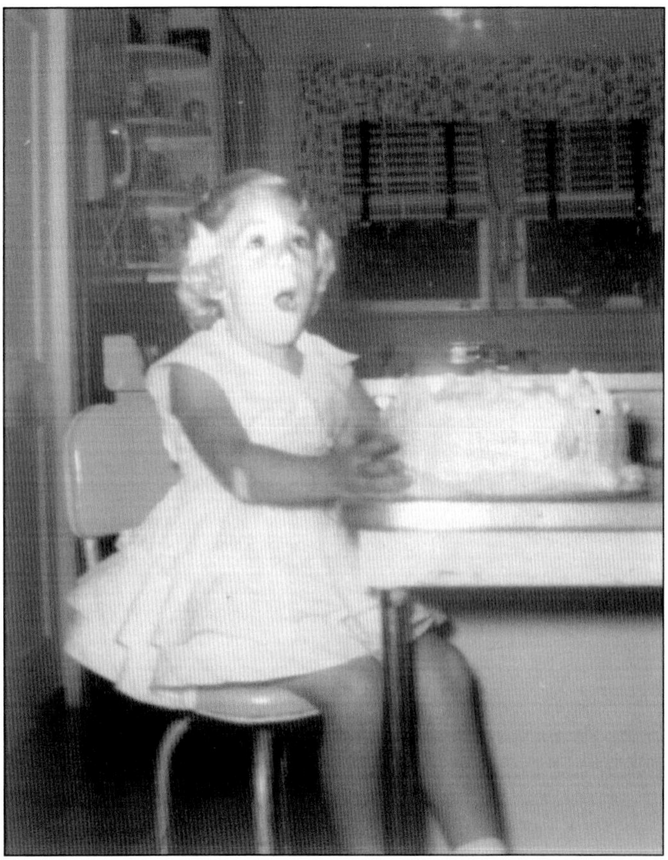

Debbie Reeves took her first steps in the backyard of her childhood home in Avondale. Bozman and Mozelle Reeves built one of the first homes in Avondale at 17 Lindendale in 1947. Mrs. Reeves designed the interior of the home. The elegant lovebird and floral wallpaper she used to decorate the dining room remains today. The owners were allowed to have large animals in the neighborhood. When Bozman (Bo) Reeves Jr. received bunnies for Easter, he housed them in the yard. Later, Mr. Reeves built a small barn in the backyard that housed Debbie's horse Layla. In the left photograph, Debbie celebrates her birthday with a cake at the kitchen table. (Both, courtesy of Debbie Reeves.)

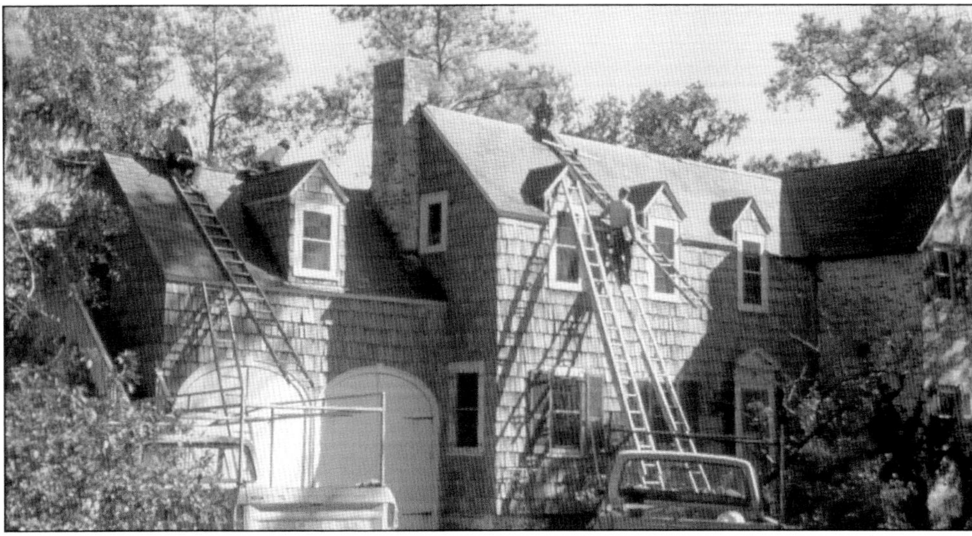

Two New Town Lane, known as Siskaya, is located in The Crescent. Siskaya is an alteration of the Cherokee term meaning "Place of Birds" and a fitting name for the home of Alexander Sprunt Jr., the noted South Carolina ornithologist. He purchased lot 7 block I constituting 0.97 acres in The Crescent on May 18, 1931. During the construction of his home, Alexander extensively documented the land, construction, workers, visitors, plants, birds, and other wildlife. This exquisite scrapbook conveys with the home to each new owner. (Courtesy of Jan McDougal.)

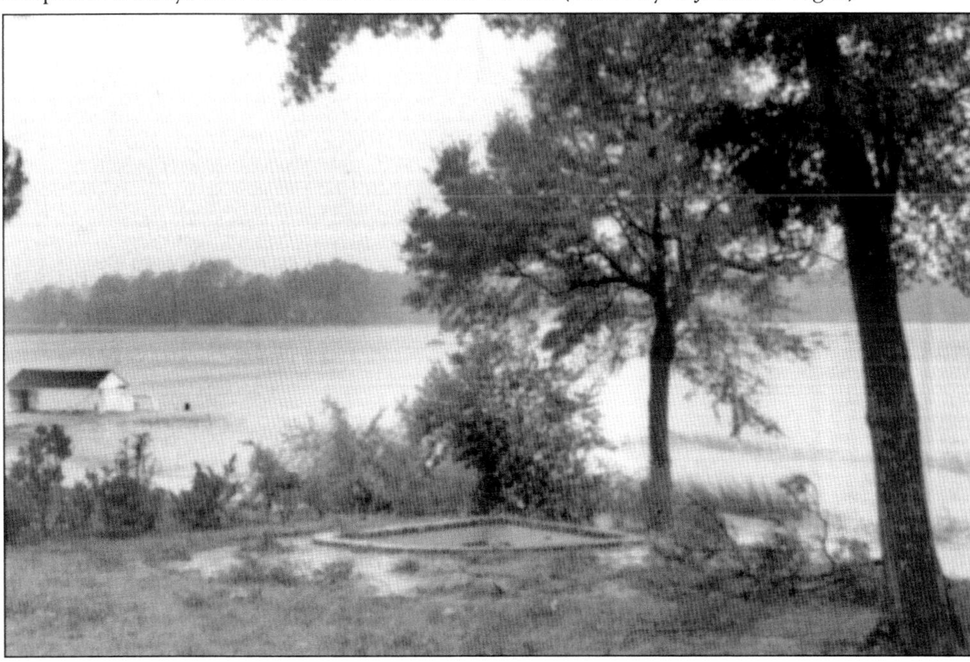

This view of Wappoo Cut from the country club looking toward The Crescent was taken from the home of "Lit" and Betty Wilson during Hurricane Gracie in September 1959. Four years earlier in 1955, a ferry service was located near their home at the base of the Wappoo Bridge. The tanker *Fort Fetterman* misjudged the approach to the Ashley River Bridge and destroyed it. Ferries, private boats, and the railroad became the only way into downtown Charleston. (Courtesy of Betty Smith Wilson.)

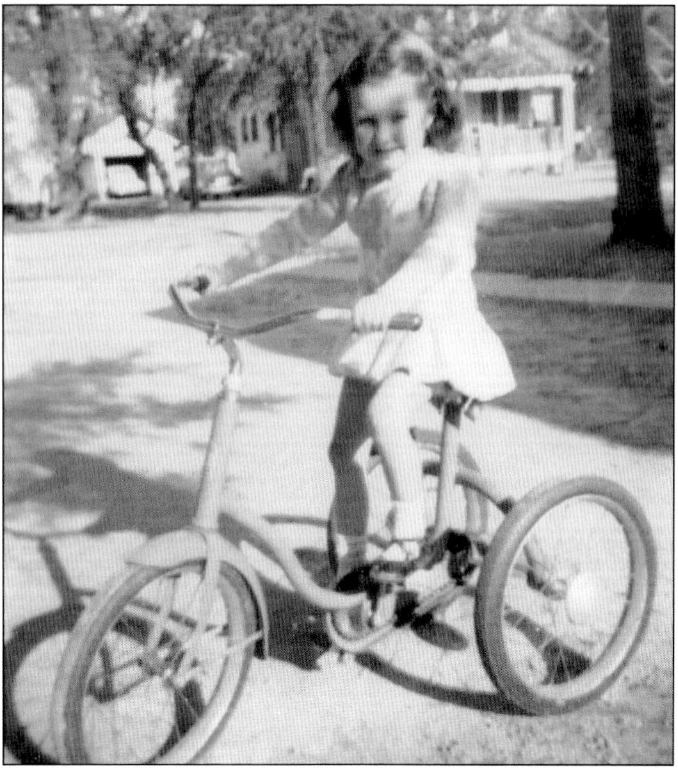

Every kid can't wait to ride on a tricycle and Catherine Louise Deets is no exception. The Deets family lived on Hickory Street in Ashley Forest, a neighborhood developed by J.C. Long in 1931. Louise's mother, Catherine Nolen Deets, and Martha Peeples' mother, Rita Nolen Peeples, were sisters and enjoyed raising their families close to each other. Their mother, Sophie, had raised them and their six other siblings by herself during the Depression. Sophie was blessed with 67 grandchildren. (Courtesy of Martha Peeples Attisano.)

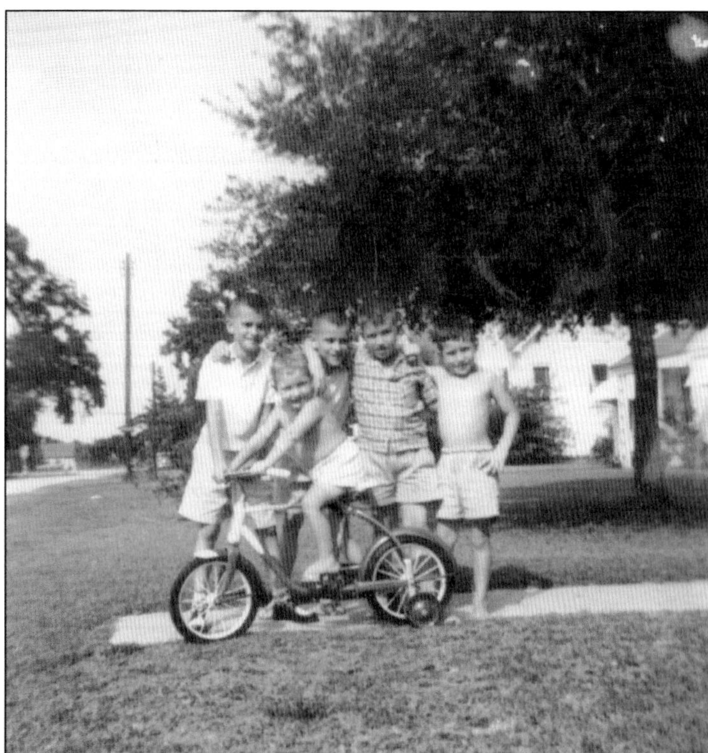

Cousins Roy Heissenbuttle, Steve Peeples (on bike), Ray Heissenbuttle, Ralph Peeples Jr., and Mike Peeples were inseparable and engaged in many adventures during their youth in Avondale. Roy and Ray's mother, Margaret Nolen Heissenbuttle, was one of Rita Nolen Peeples's sisters. The boys are locked arm in arm on the front yard of 7 Riverdale looking toward the Ashley River. The mischievous smiles suggest there might be an adventure afoot. (Courtesy of Martha Peeples Attisano.)

Everyone is dressed up and smiling for Sally Robinson's seventh birthday party at her home on Parish Road in Moreland. Pictured here are, from left to right, (first row) Paula Robinson, Meg Montgomery, Mary Ellen Eiserhardt, Caroline McManus, CeCe Montgomery, Cindy Robinson, Sandra Duncan, and Sandy Claire; (second row) unidentified, Susie Nepveaux, Sally Robinson, Betty Montgomery, Tommy Moss, David Runey, and Skip Condon. The Moreland Guest Home accents the background of the photograph. (Courtesy of Sally Robinson Whitlock.)

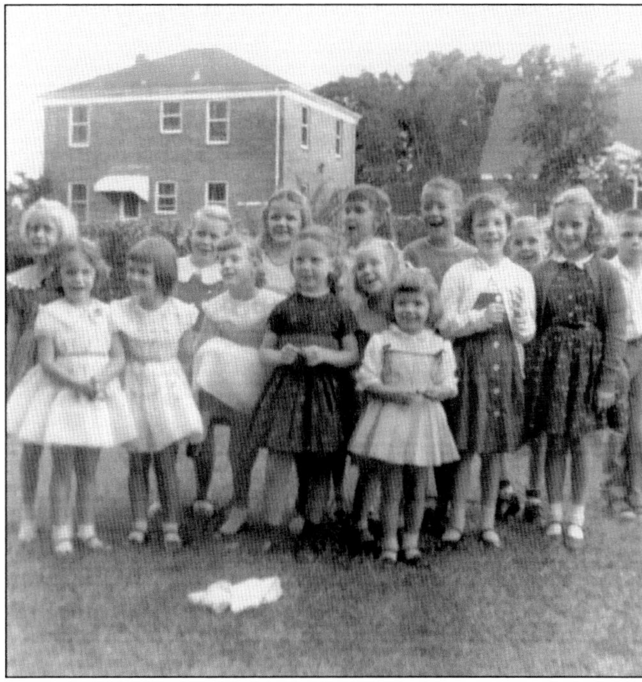

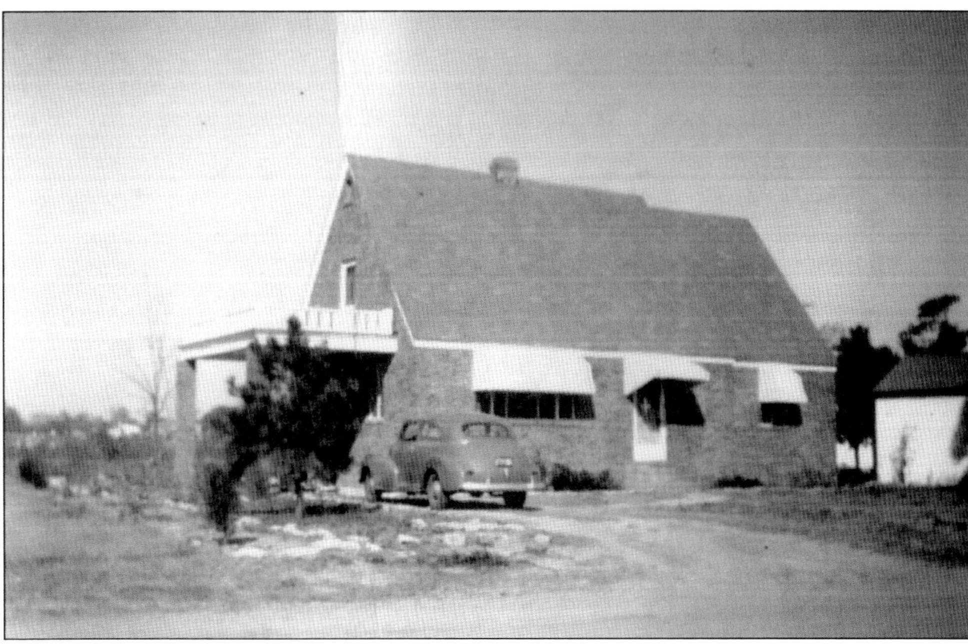

Sally Robinson Whitlock describes her childhood home on Parish Road in Moreland with "cabbage fields in back." Memories of farming and farmland are popular for the early suburban residents of St. Andrew's Parish. A more modern photograph of this neighborhood road would be graced with moss-draped oaks instead. William S. Means established Moreland in 1942. (Courtesy of Sally Robinson Whitlock.)

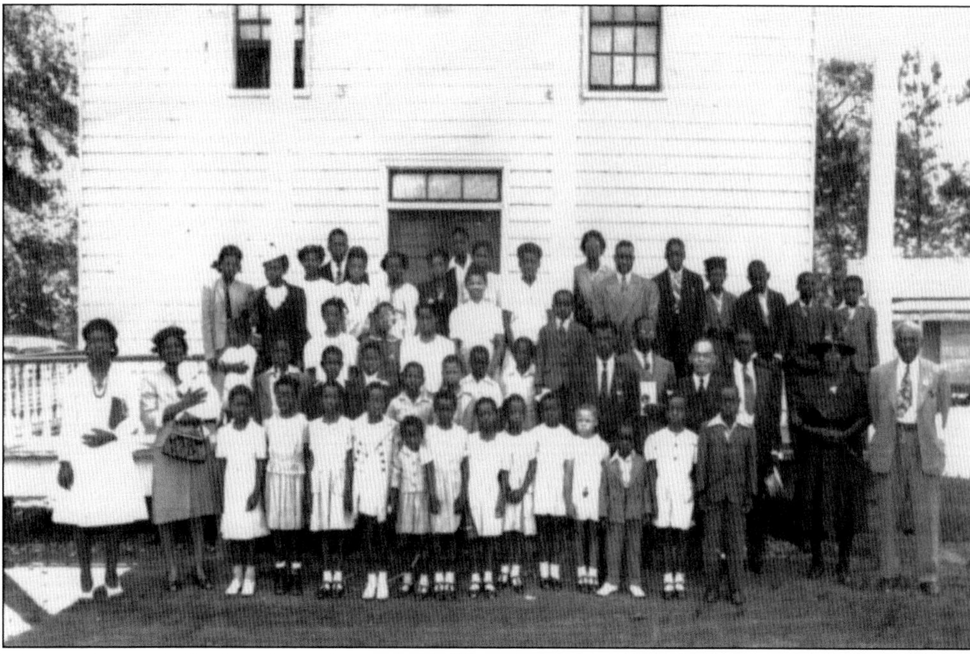

The Graham AME Church on the corner of Wappoo Road and Highway 61 was built and legally recorded in the Charleston County courthouse on September 26, 1873. The church, originally known as Stockhill, was located near Old Town prior to the move to the Pineland area at Wappoo Road. On a Sunday in 1946, the entire Sunday school poses for a photograph. "We enter to worship—We depart to serve." (Courtesy of the Archives of the late James Grant.)

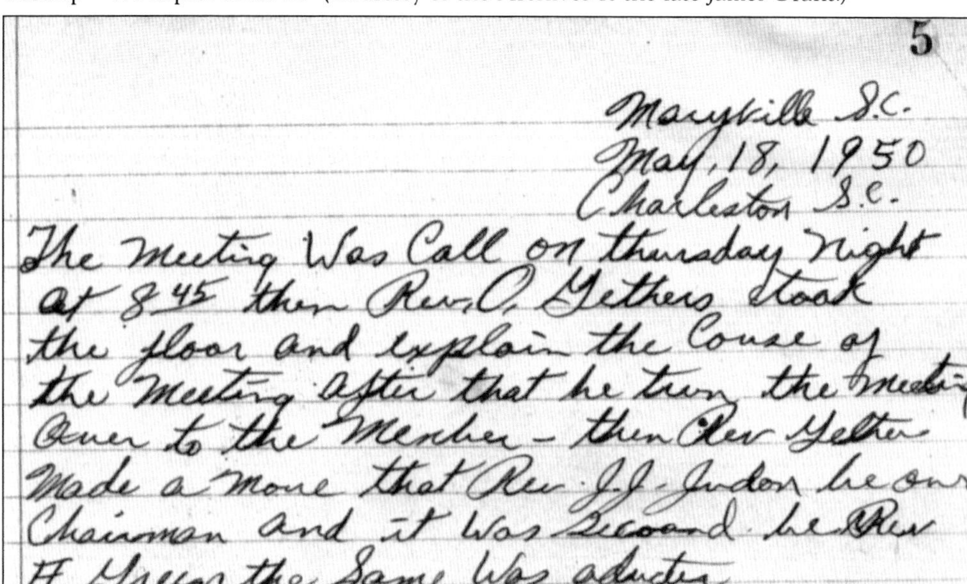

5

Maryville S.C.
May, 18, 1950
Charleston S.C.

The Meeting Was Call on thursday Night
at 8 45 then Rev. O. Gethers took
the floor and explain the Couse of
the Meeting after that he turn the meeting
Over to the Member - then Rev Gether
Made a Move that Rev. J. J. Judon be our
Chairman and it Was Second be Rev
H. Green the Same Was adupted

The Emanuel AME Church graces the corner of Fifth Avenue in Ashleyville. Many of the church records are archived at the Avery Institute. This is an excerpt from the 1950–1953 record book. In this record book is a list of church member donations. In the list are some familiar names in the community of Maryville: Brown, Carr, Green, Grant, Gethers, Hamilton, and Richardson, to name a few. (Courtesy of the Avery Institute.)

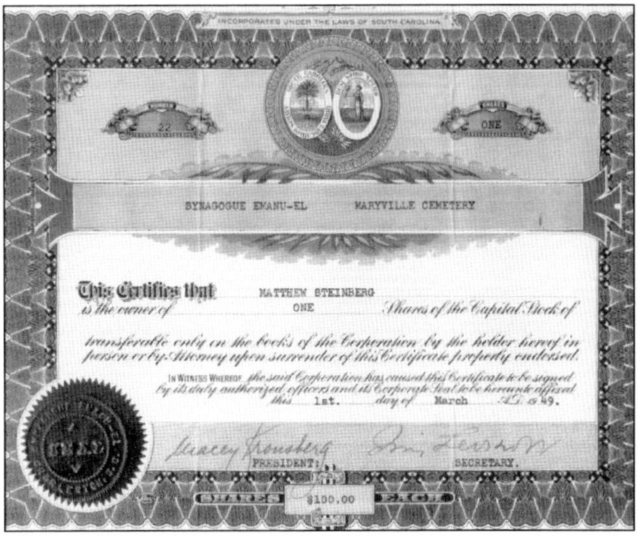

INCORPORATED UNDER THE LAWS OF SOUTH CAROLINA

22

ONE

SYNAGOGUE EMANU-EL MARYVILLE CEMETERY

This Certifies that MATTHEW STEINBERG
is the owner of ONE Shares of the Capital Stock of

transferable only on the books of the Corporation by the holder hereof in person or by Attorney upon surrender of this Certificate properly endorsed.

In Witness Whereof the said Corporation has caused this Certificate to be signed by its duly authorized officers and its Corporate Seal to be hereunto affixed this 1st. day of March A.D. 1949.

PRESIDENT. SECRETARY.

SHARES $100.00 EACH

Local treasures are hidden everywhere. This stock certificate for the Maryville Cemetery on Sycamore Road issued to Matthew Steinberg by Conservative Synagogue Emanu-El in March 1949, was discovered in Special Collections at the College of Charleston library. In 1947, Matthew Steinberg and his two brothers were among the founders of Emanu-El. (Courtesy of Special Collections, College of Charleston; gift of Joan S. Loeb.)

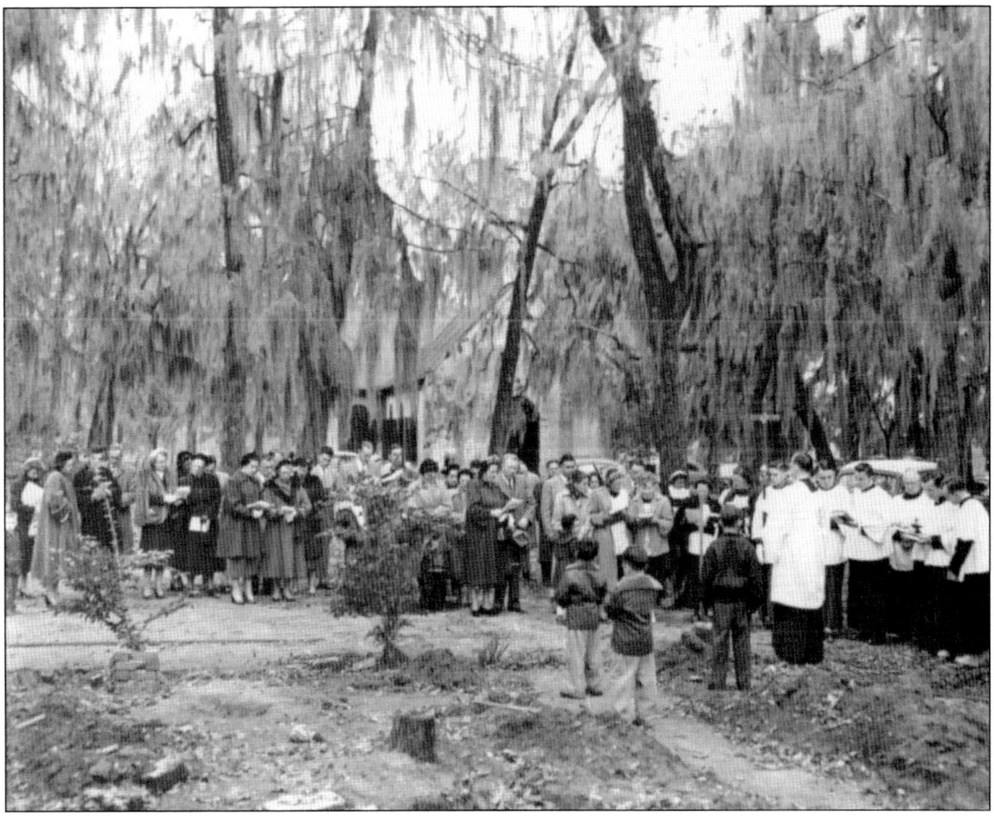

In 1948, a group of Episcopalians inquired about opening a church in West Ashley, and the bishop purposed reopening Old St. Andrew's Parish Church that had closed in 1890. The church is one of the few Colonial churches that exist in a cruciform shape. The first Easter service was held on March 28, 1948. On January 11, 1953, a ground-breaking ceremony was held for the new parish house. (Courtesy of the Old St. Andrew's Parish Church.)

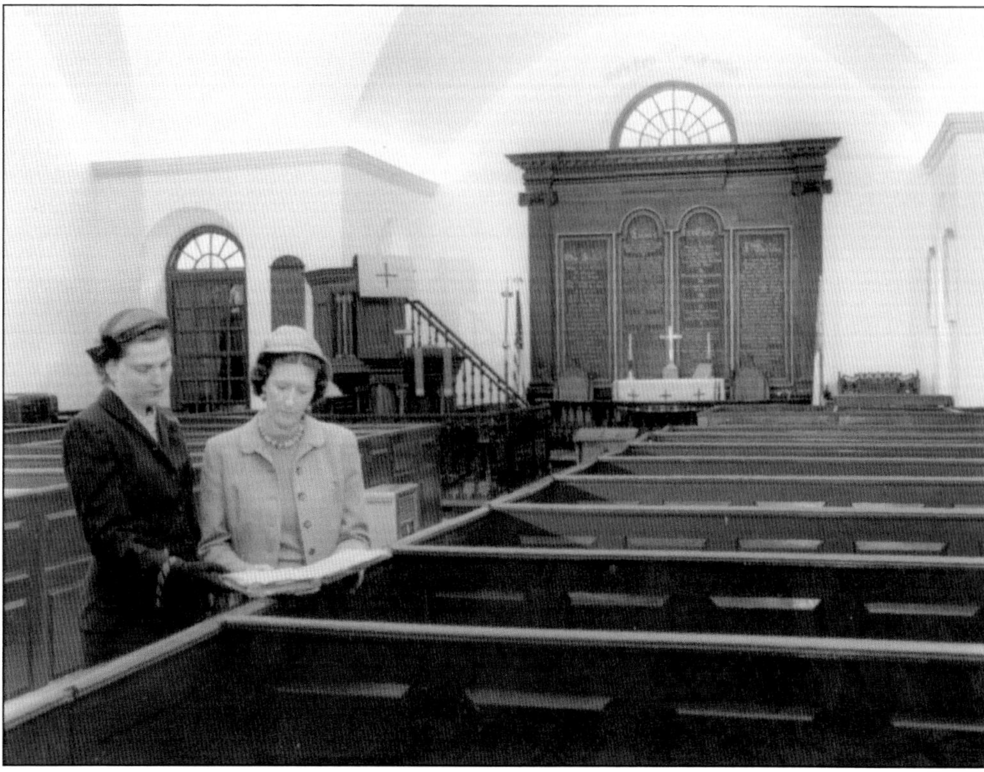

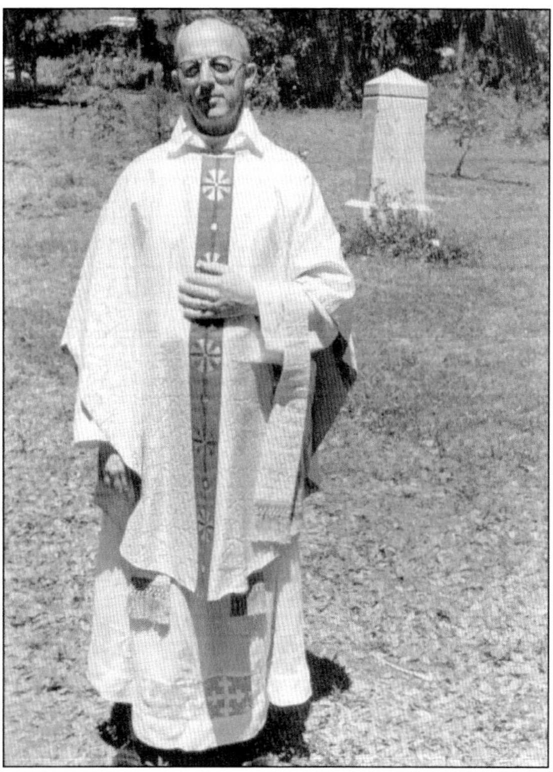

The Homecoming Day service in 1956 marked the 250th anniversary of the founding of St. Andrew's Parish and the church's construction. Rachel Butt (left) and Lila Searson are two parishioners who helped prepare for the service. In the center behind the altar is the reredos. These 18th-century, hand-hewn, black cypress tablets contain gold inscriptions of the Lord's Prayer, Ten Commandments, and Apostles' Creed. (Courtesy of the Old St. Andrew's Parish Church.)

Rev. Lynwood Magee led Old St. Andrew's Parish from 1952 until 1963. With his leadership, the church attained full parish status, a parish house and rectory were constructed, and the renovations to the main church structure continued. In 1992, Bishop Edward Salmon consecrated the parish house, Magee House, in recognition of Reverend Magee's service. (Courtesy of the Old St. Andrew's Parish Church.)

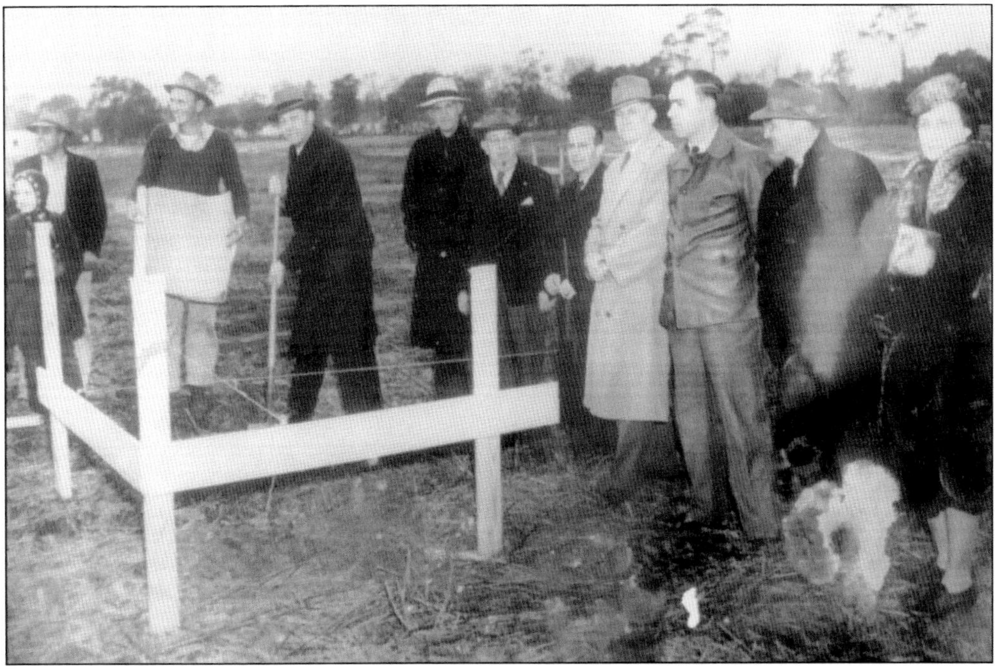

On January 10, 1946, ground was broken for the John Wesley Methodist Church Educational Building. Present for the occasion are, from left to right, Ruth Watkins, R.R. Blocker, Henry Sauls, district superintendent Shuler (Rev. H.L.F. Shuler), lawyer M.L. McCrae, architect Thomas, J.G. Altman, Rev. R.B. Shumaker (second pastor), H.E. Blocker, George Seignious, and Mrs. W.R. Richardson. From the original 34 people who attended worship service at the exchange club building on June 18, 1944, through the sanctuary construction and completion in 1950 pictured below, John Wesley Methodist Church has been a prominent figure in the West Ashley community. Rev. Ralph Shumaker conducted the first service in the new sanctuary on July 22, 1951, and performed the first wedding ceremony on September 15, 1951, for Herman M. Staubes Jr. and Hazel Myers. (Both, courtesy of John Wesley Methodist Church.)

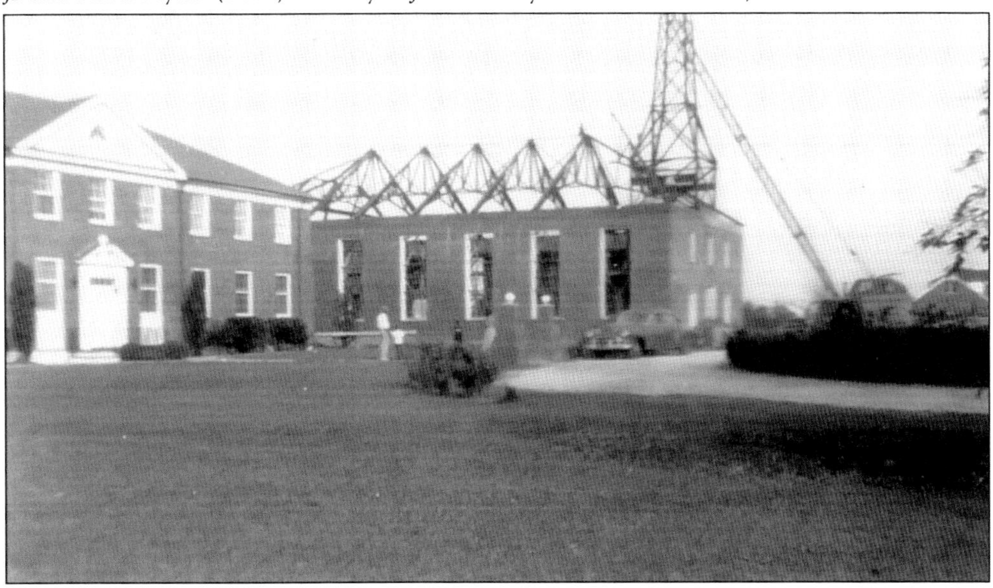

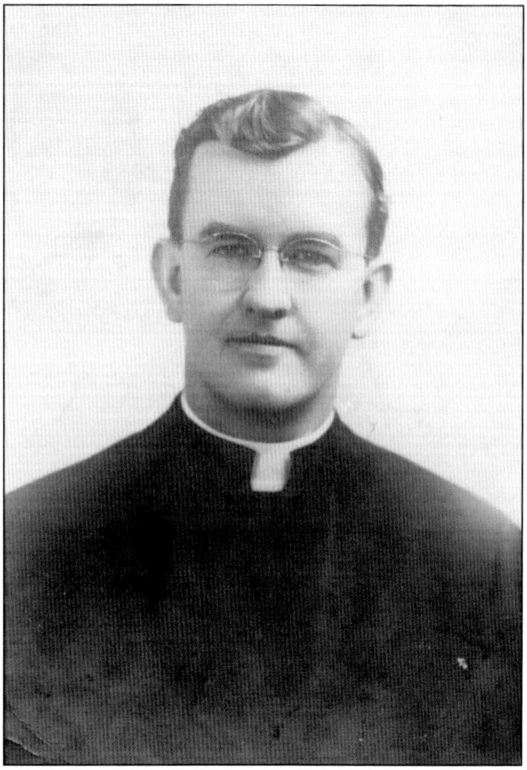

Fr. John J. McCarthy was named the first pastor of Blessed Sacrament Church in 1944. The parish began with 40 families with the rectory and chapel located at 149 Savannah Highway in Byrnes Downs. Masses were initially celebrated in the St. Andrew's Exchange Club Building until the first sanctuary was built in 1946. (Courtesy of Martha Peeples Attisano.)

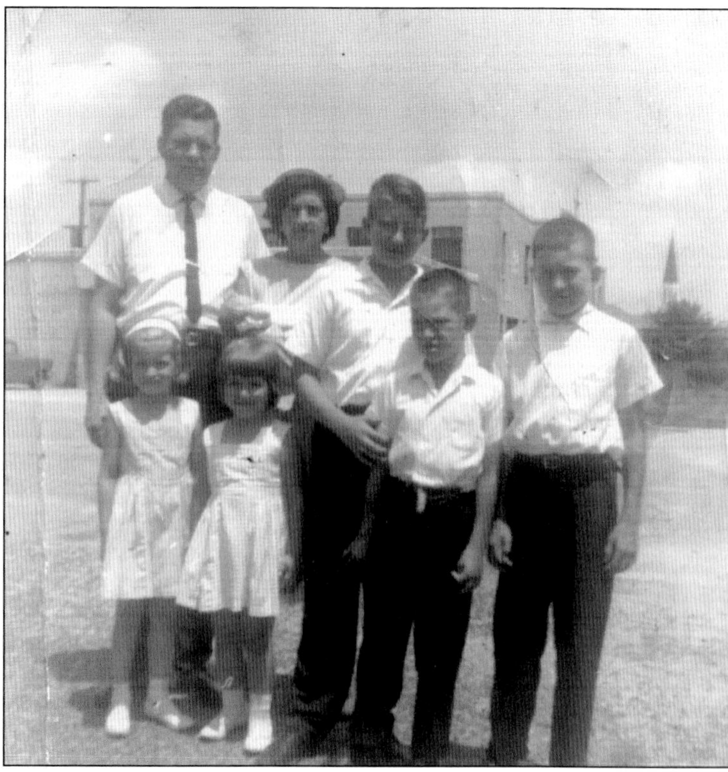

Father McCarthy married Rita Nolen and Ralph A. Peeples at Blessed Sacrament Church in 1950. The growing family poses for a picture with the first sanctuary in the background on occasion of Scott's baptism. Ralph Sr. stands next to Rita, who is holding Scott. Their other five children are, from left to right, Julie, Martha, Ralph Jr., Steve, and Mike. (Courtesy of Martha Peeples Attisano.)

Shannon Hurley stepped outside of his Byrnes Downs home on Nicholson Street to capture Blessed Sacrament Church as snow fell on March 2, 1980. This church was first used on Christmas Day in 1963 and dedicated by Bishop Ernest Unterkoefler on May 13, 1965. The two steeples of the church were destroyed during hurricane Hugo in September 1989. (Courtesy of J. Shannon Hurley.)

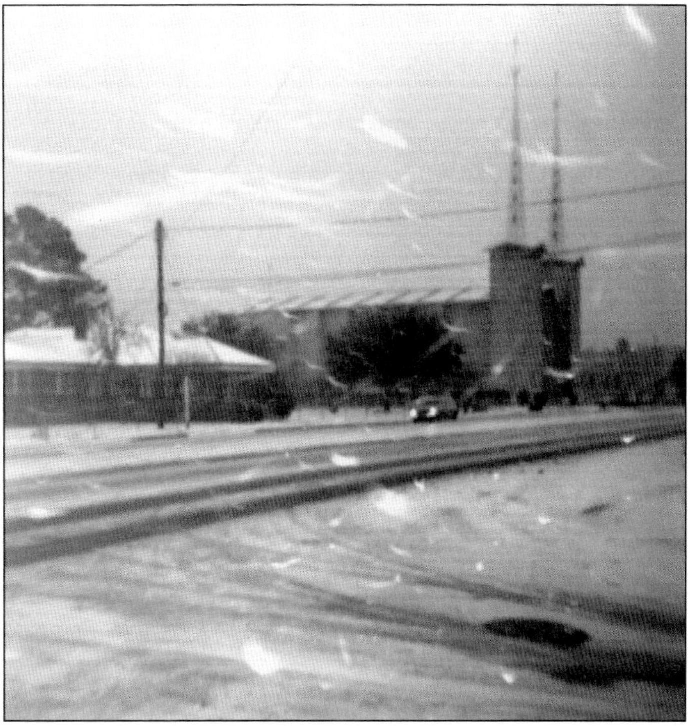

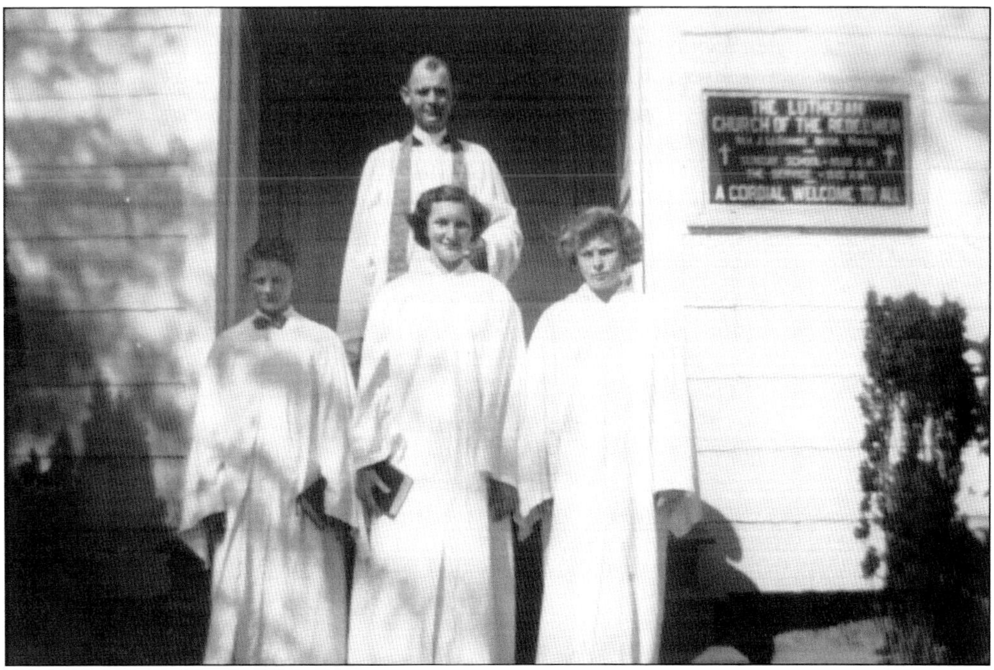

Joyce Holling (center) was confirmed into the Lutheran faith in 1950 at the Lutheran Church of the Redeemer. The Reverend J. LeGrande Mayer was the pastor of the church during this time. The church was organized in May 1943, with services held in a government surplus building located at the corner of Live Oak Avenue and Magnolia Road. In 1955, the present church was erected in Avondale. (Courtesy of Carole Clark Earhart.)

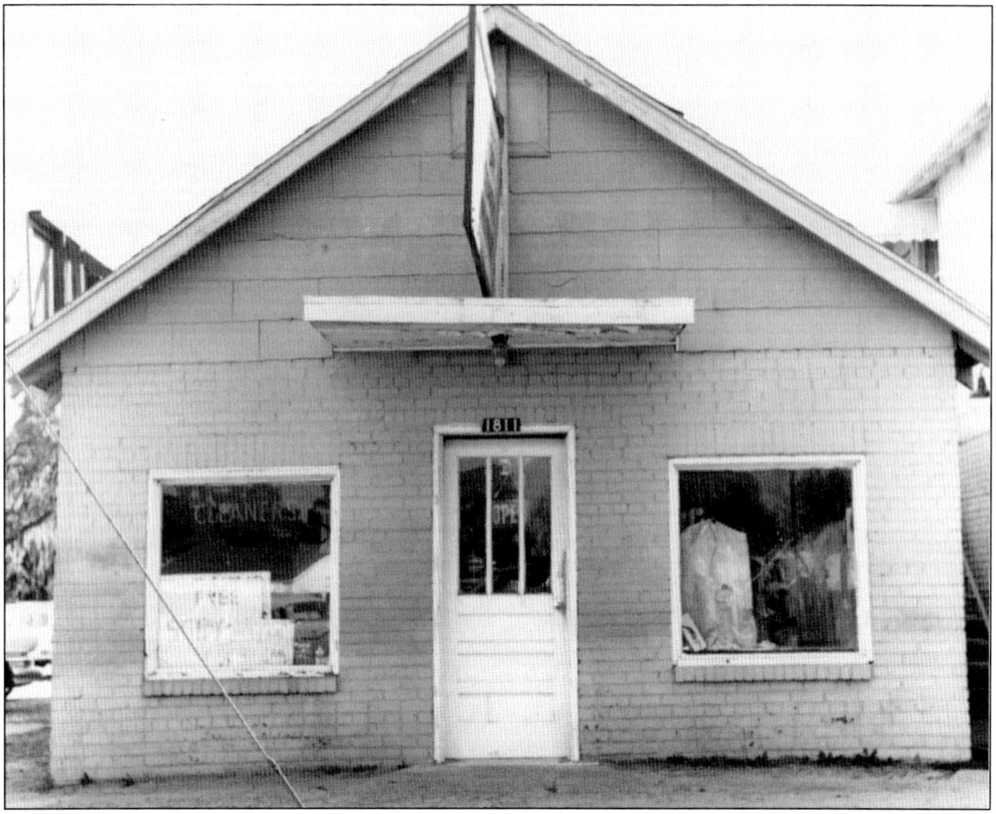

Citadel Square Baptist Church on Meeting Street in Charleston is considered the parent of the Ashley River Baptist Church. Members living west of the Ashley were interested in establishing a local place of worship. On October 8, 1942, a group of 18 met at Margiotta's on the corner of Savannah Highway and Wappoo Road to discuss holding services in West Ashley, laying the groundwork for the organization of Ashley River Baptist Church. (Courtesy of Ashley River Baptist Church.)

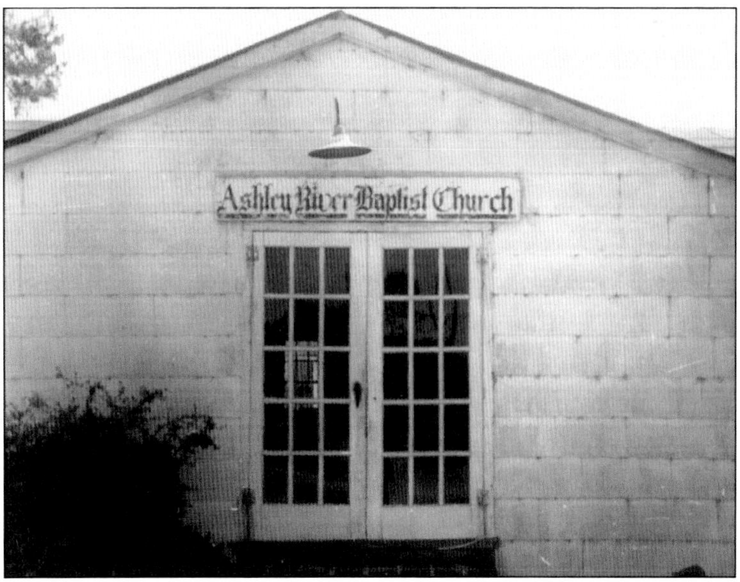

The First Sanctuary of Ashley River Baptist Church was donated by a construction company and placed on Savannah Highway near Apollo Road. On April 11, 1943, some 129 people attended Sunday school, and seven days later, 164 charter members organized the mission into the church. (Courtesy of Ashley River Baptist Church.)

Members of the congregation pose in front of the second sanctuary dedicated on April 25, 1944. Rev. John L. White was the first pastor and guided the church during its infancy. The planning and construction of the second sanctuary occurred under his leadership. The first choir director was Walter Coppedge and the first church pianist was Julian Clyburn. (Courtesy of Ashley River Baptist Church.)

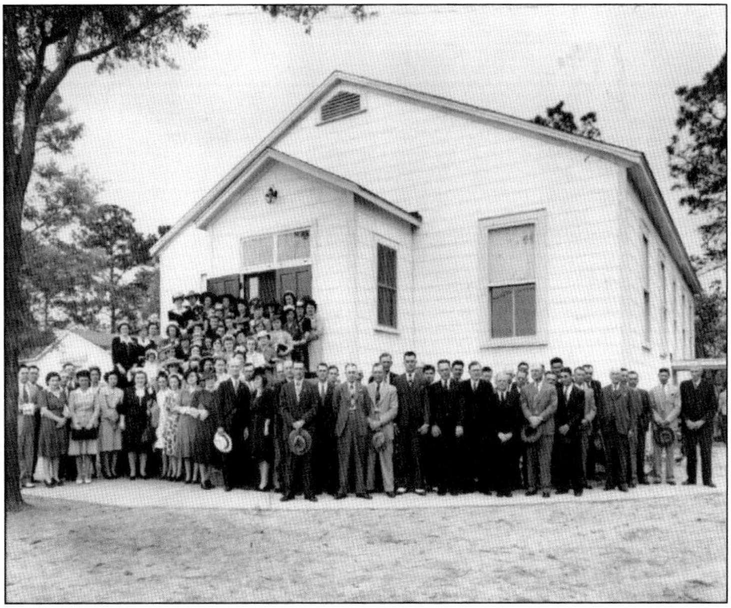

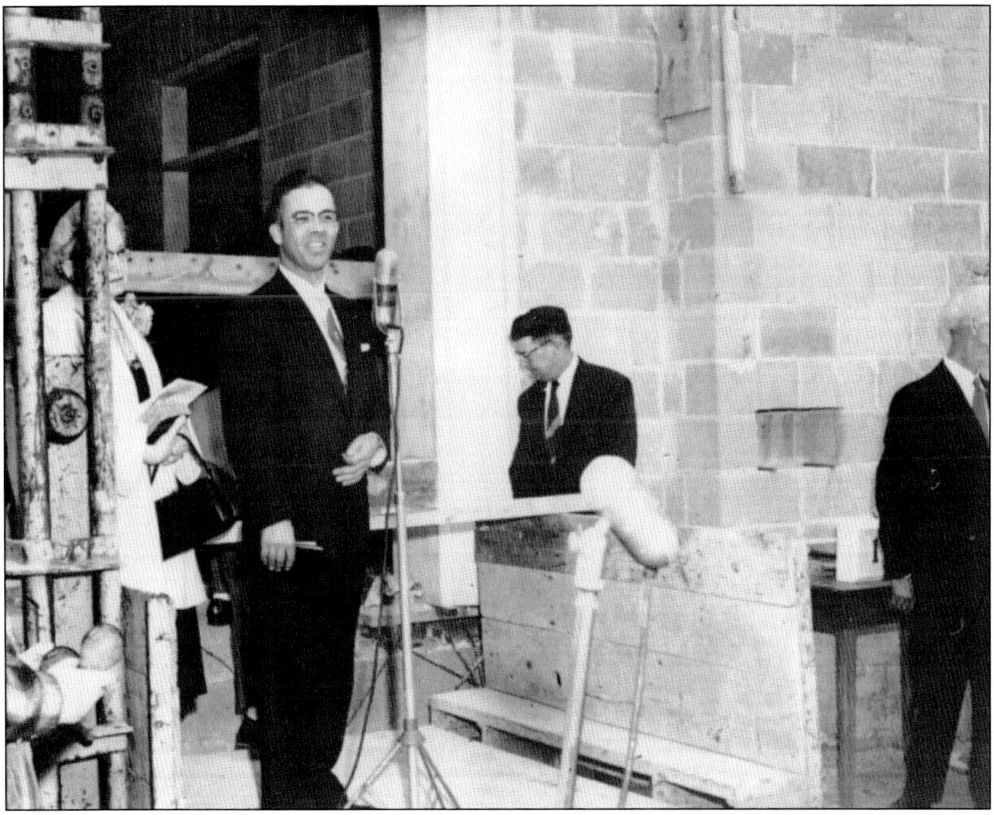

Rev. Robert W. Majors steps to the microphone at the laying of the cornerstone for the Education Building at Ashley River Baptist Church on January 9, 1955. Reverend Majors become the third pastor in October 1949. He was also an avid photographer and took many of the photographs archived in the church scrapbooks. (Courtesy of Ashley River Baptist Church.)

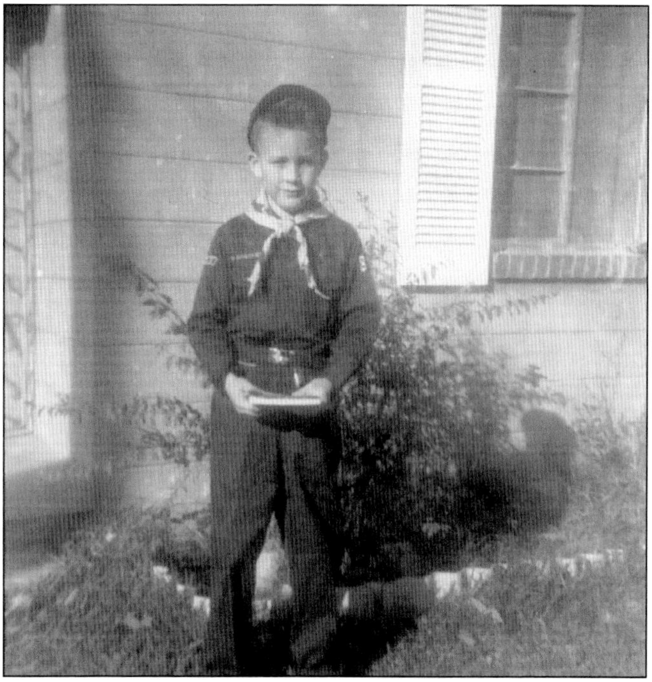

Elmer Smith, dressed in his Cub Scout uniform, stands in front of his home on Coosaw Street in West Oak Forest. After college, Elmer studied dentistry at the Medical University of South Carolina. His practice was located on Savannah Highway near Wappoo Road. (Courtesy of Mary Smith.)

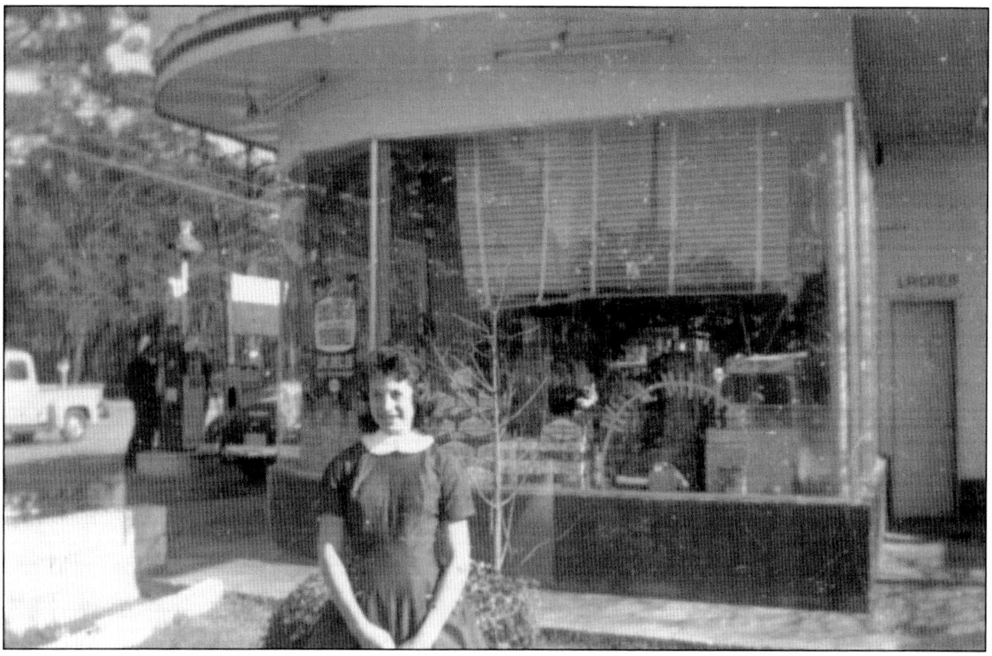

JoAnn Bunch smiles for the camera next to her father's Esso gas station. Richard M. Bunch purchased land from "Mama" Lottie Greene to open a gas station. Mama Greene worked for Dr. Waring and the story goes that he gave property to some of his help. Bunch's station was a popular hangout. Tales were told, pranks were plotted, and business was conducted at this station. The family also lived in the home adjacent to the station. Today, one can enjoy a cold beer, barbecue, and good music at Fiery Ron's Home Team BBQ where the station once stood. (Courtesy of Richard E. Bunch and JoAnn Bunch Leggette.)

Richard Bunch and T. Allen Legare Jr. (seated) were probably discussing local issues in this photograph. T. Allen Legare was a distinguished World War II veteran who pursued a career in local government. He served in both the South Carolina House of Representatives and Senate. During his tenure in the senate he was an advocate for technical education, the Medical University of South Carolina, the State Ports Authority, and transportation infrastructure. One of the Ashley River Bridges is named for him. (Courtesy of Richard Bunch.)

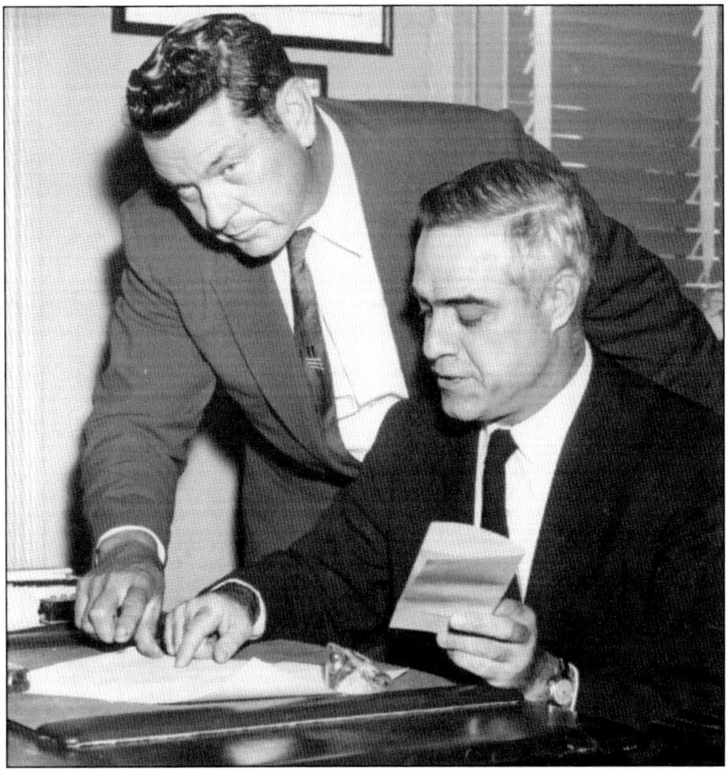

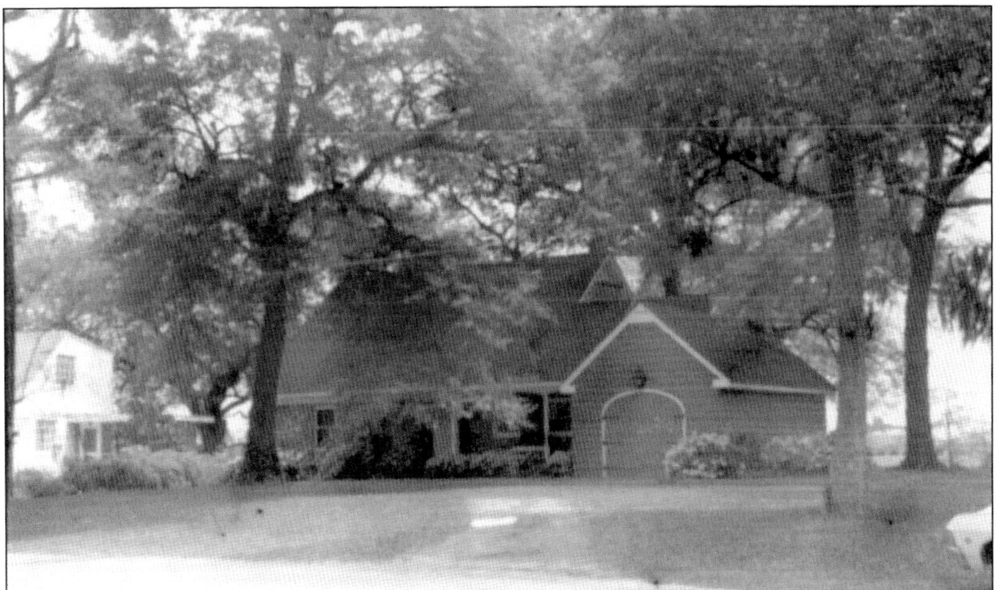

Robert (Bob) F. McNab Jr. built his home next to his parents in Moreland along the west bank of the Ashley River where he explored as a young boy. Moreland was part of Joseph Harrison's farmland prior to being sold for development. Bob recalls discovering remnants of beautiful brick front-door steps along the river near his property; perhaps the steps are remnants of the Crafts' family home. (Courtesy of Robert F. McNab Jr.)

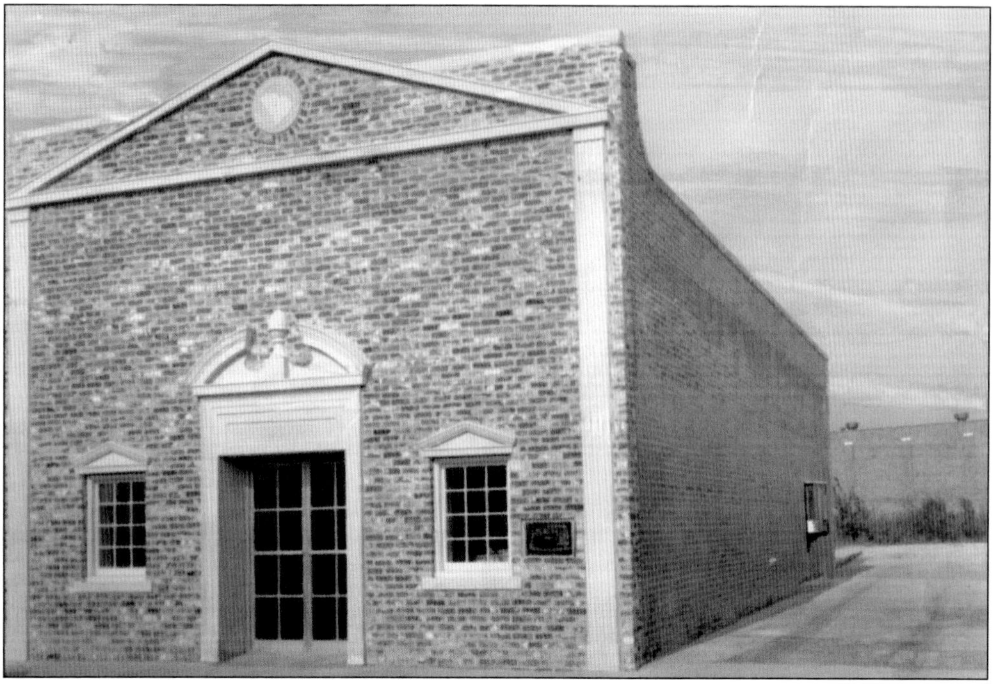

This Citizens & Southern National Bank in Avondale was the first bank in West Ashley. I.D. Peek, a prominent man in the growing community of St. Andrew's Parish and the developer of Avondale, approached Hugh Lane, the president of the bank, with this paraphrased request, "We need a bank West Ashley and I am giving C&S the first right of refusal." Hugh recruited Cecil B. Kearse in the position of cashier for the West Ashley branch office. The bank answered the needs of the residents and businesses living in St. Andrew's Parish with the "Opening of the New West Charleston Office on Wednesday February 15, 1950." In the below photograph, customers line up on opening day. Cecil is seated at the far right in the photograph. (Both, courtesy of Cecil B. Kearse.)

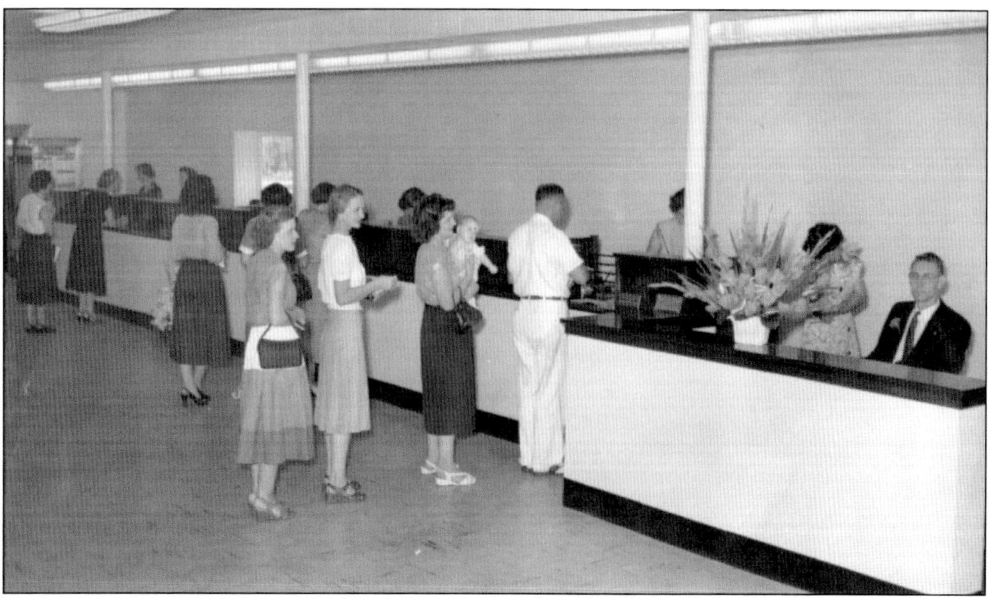

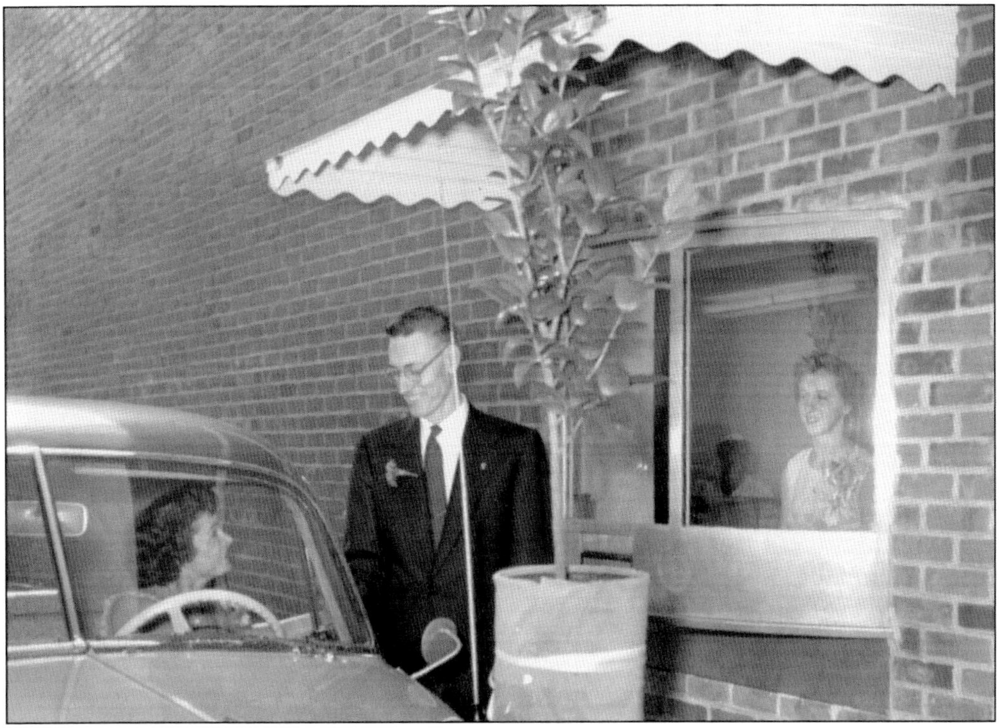

Cecil B. Kearse greets the first customer, Mrs. Lewis M. Denaux, using the new drive-in bank window service. Business at the Citizens & Southern National Bank in Avondale had grown in the two and a half years since its opening in 1950. The bank building was remodeled and a drive-in window service added. Ruth DeStefano is the teller seen serving the drive-in customer. (Courtesy of Cecil B. Kearse.)

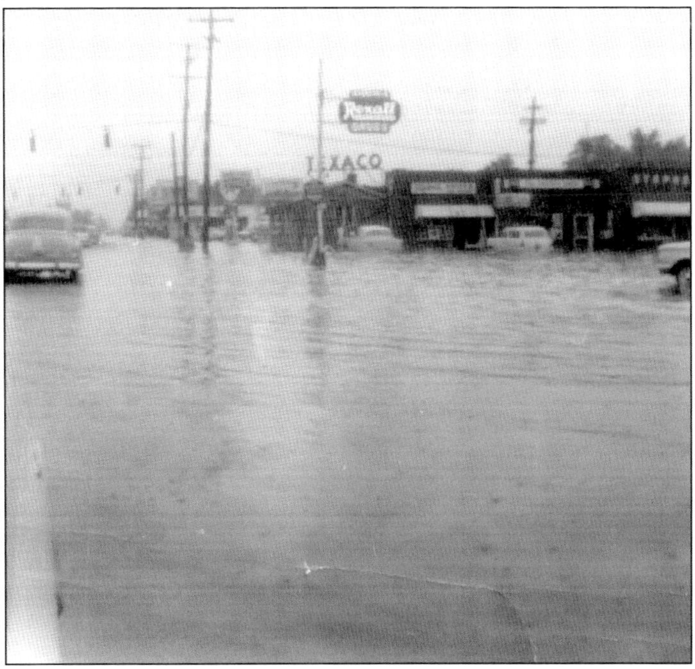

Hurricane Gracie blew through the Lowcountry on September 29, 1959. Hurricanes leave a trail of fallen trees, flooded streets, damaged homes, and permanent memories. The shops of Avondale were flooded by the storm. The view in this photograph is looking south on Savannah Highway. The Shops of Avondale can be seen on the right. Note the Texaco sign—this building today is bright orange and houses Gerald's Tires and Brakes. (Courtesy of the Mary Smith.)

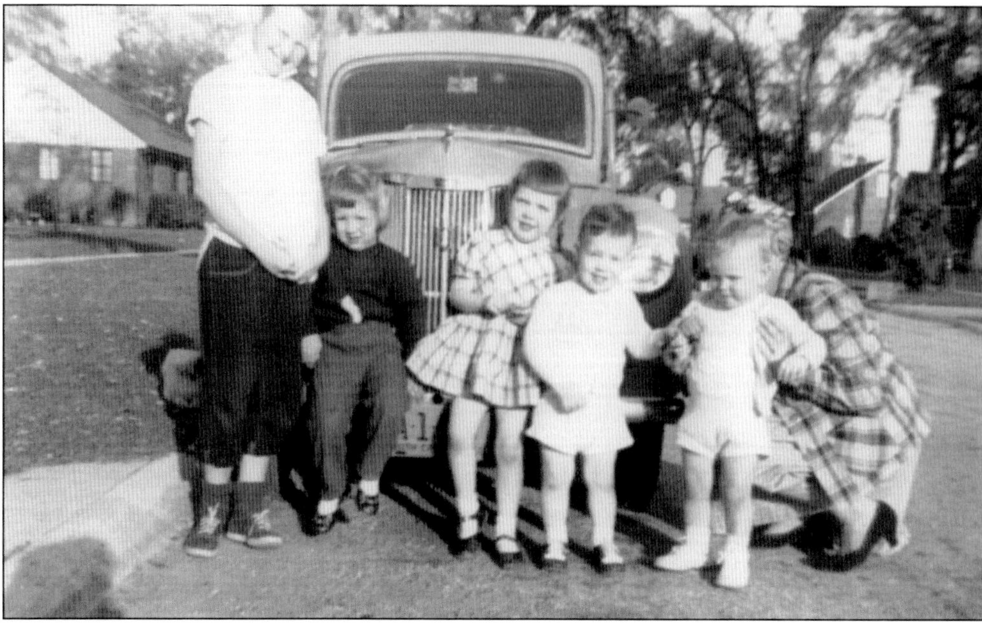

The Nelson family was one of the first families to move into Westwood in 1951. Louis August Rohde Nelson Jr. had purchased a lot on Brennon Street to build his home. Gathered in front of the car on Brennon Street are, from left to right, Marsha Nelson, Kay Kennerty, Katie Coester, Teddy Coester, and Becky Coester holding Eric Nelson. (Courtesy of Ruth Nelson.)

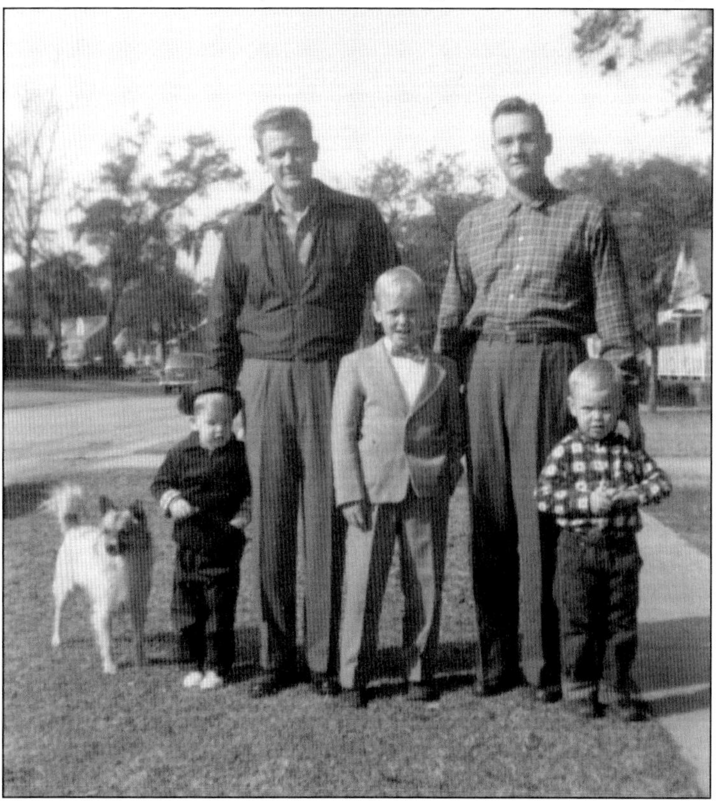

Time to pose for another photograph on Brennon Street. Pictured here are, from left to right, Sport (the family dog), George Pearce, Garland Pearce, Douglas Nelson, L.A. Rohde Nelson Jr., and Eric Nelson. L.A.R. Nelson Jr.'s family owned Nelson Printing Co. Nelson Printing Co. printed the Charleston City Directories and L.A.R. Nelson Sr. assisted the St. Andrew's Exchange Club in the publication of their 1943 and 1947 brochures on St. Andrew's Parish. (Courtesy of Ruth Nelson.)

Nancy Campbell and Jay Platte Campbell Jr. grew up in Windermere on Beverly Road. They would play in this sandbox in the backyard of their home adjacent to the Atlantic Coast Line Railroad. The trees in the background grew on the land that would become South Windermere Shopping Center. (Courtesy of Nancy Campbell Vick.)

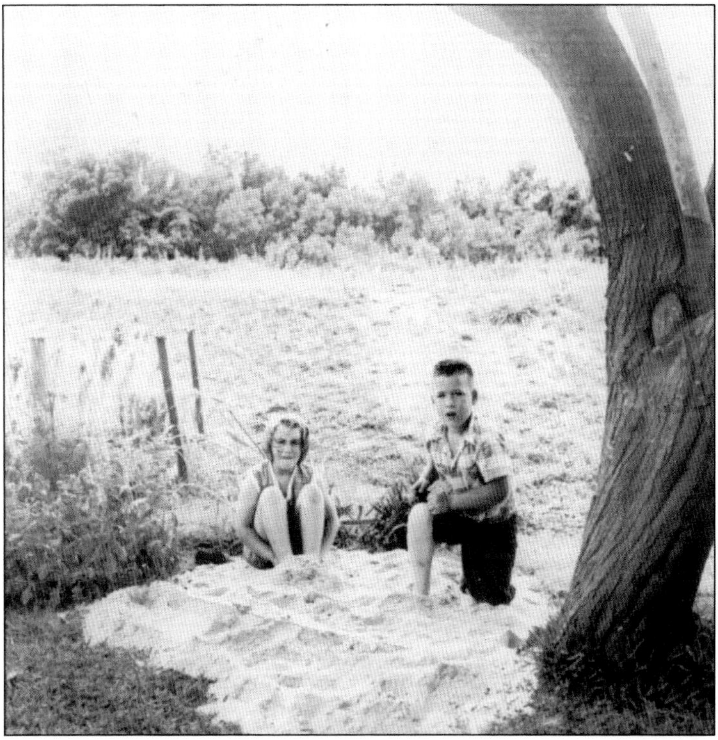

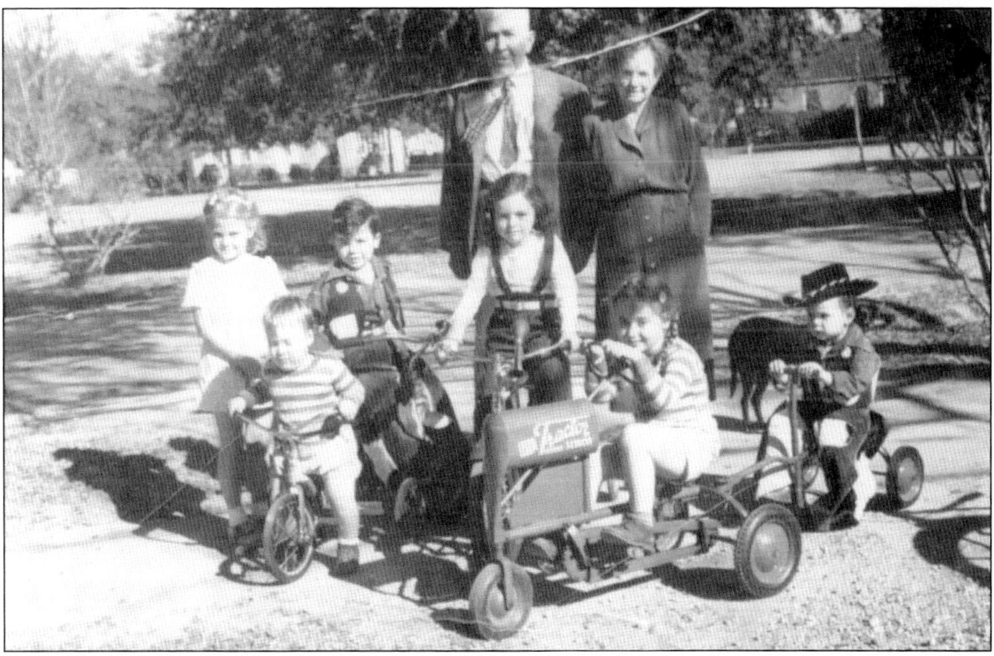

The Windermere neighborhood kids are ready to ride, but they pose first for a photograph with Mr. and Mrs. Mills (standing in back). Seen here are, from left to right, Jeanne Thomas, Jay Campbell Jr. (on tricycle), Bucky Morris (on bicycle,) Paula Dawson (on bicycle), and Nancy Campbell on the tractor pulling David Morris on the tricycle hooked to the tractor. (Courtesy of Nancy Campbell Vick.)

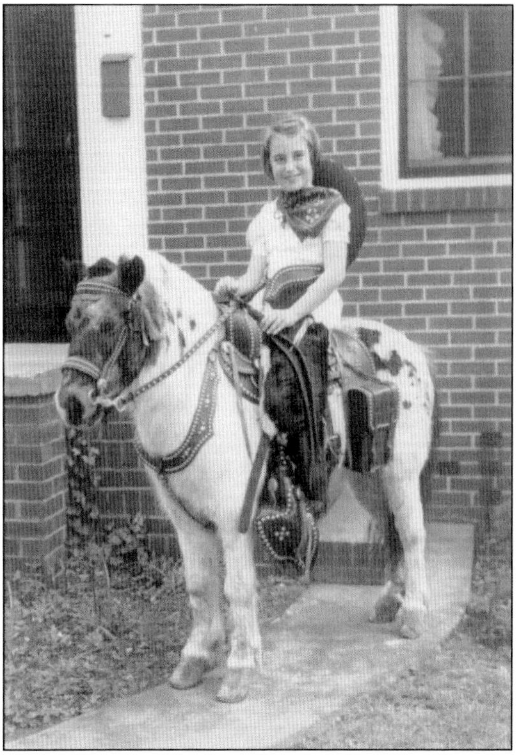

In the early 1950s, the traveling photographers are still on the circuit, but this time traveling with a pony through Windermere. Nancy Campbell sits proudly in the saddle complete with chaps, cowgirl hat, and scarf. (Courtesy of Nancy Campbell Vick.)

Barbara and Virginia "Ginny" Blank posed with their maternal grandmother, Gertrude Mixson Ostendorff, in the front yard of 9 Stocker Drive in Windermere. Homes were still being built in the neighborhood, established in 1926 by James Simmons, as the two homes across the street are under construction. (Courtesy of Barbara Blank Gilchrist.)

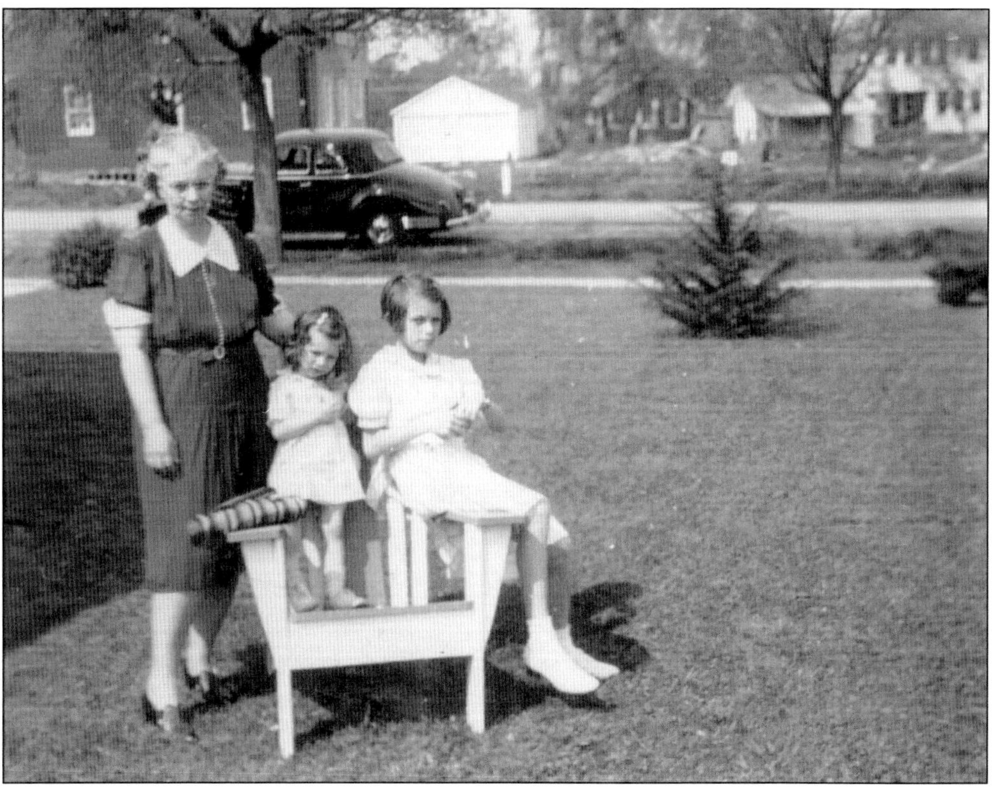

Caroline Ostendorff Blank and Barbara Blank are ready to take Leonard, the baby of the family, on a walk in his baby carriage. Leonard Blank serves on city council for James Island. Barbara Blank would later be an active member of both the St. Andrew's Constituent School Board and Charleston County School Board. (Courtesy of Barbara Blank Gilchrist.)

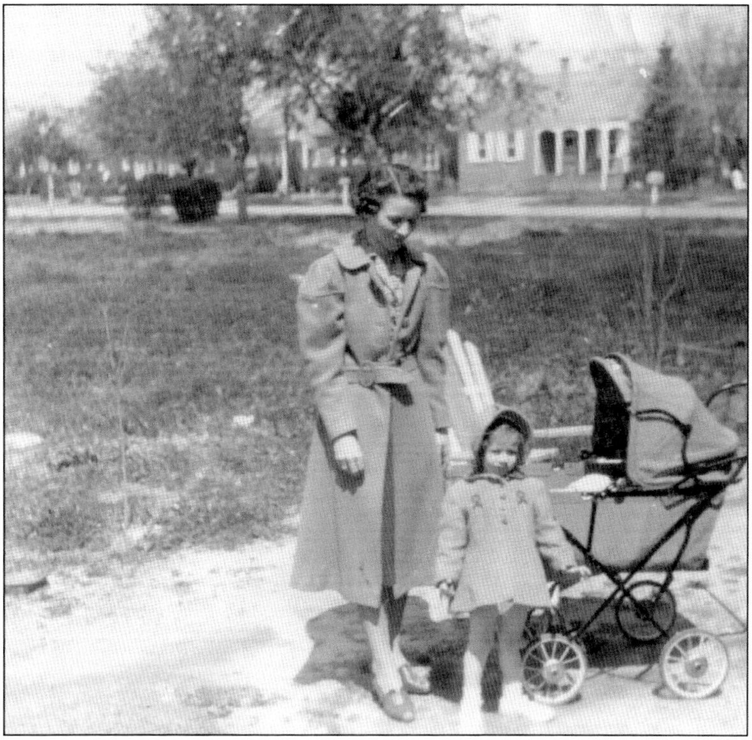

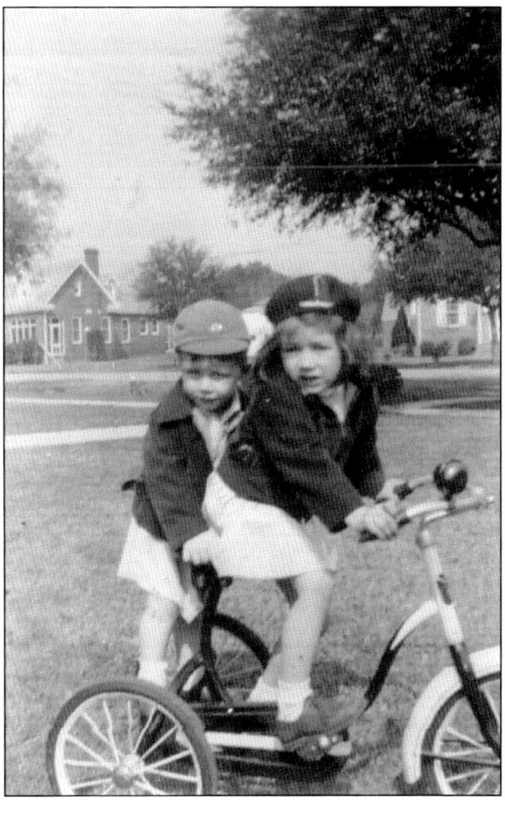

Lloyd Blank Jr. (Butch) catches a ride on the back of his sister Barbara's tricycle. Windermere was built with sidewalks encouraging the families to walk, ride tricycles, and push strollers. The residents would also plant trees, and today, the streets of Windermere are canopied and even more enticing for a stroll. (Courtesy of Barbara Blank Gilchrist.)

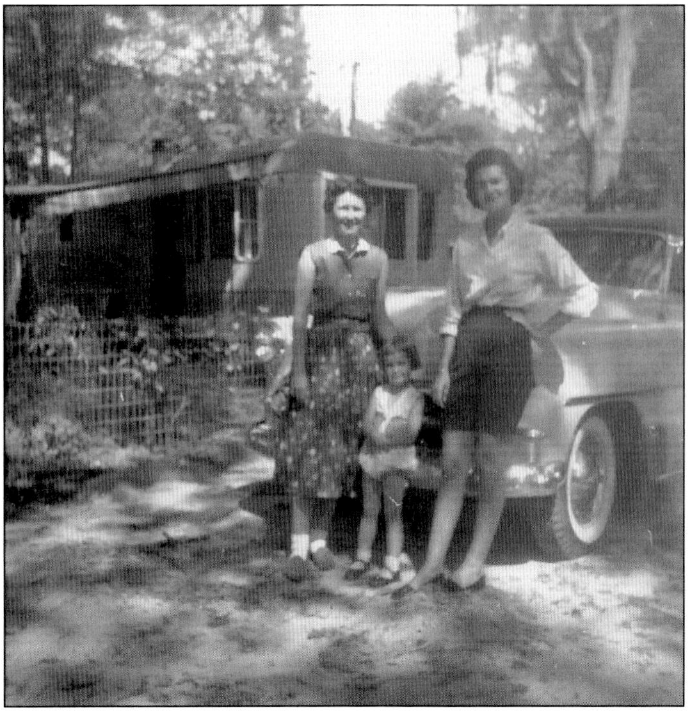

Shirley Parker (right) has traveled from Kershaw, South Carolina, to the Oak Lane Trailer Park for a visit with her older sister, Susie Parker Fender. Susie, her daughter Becky, and Shirley record the moment on film in 1956. The Oak Lane Grocery Store was located in front of the trailer park. Becky recalls hours of hula-hooping fun at the store. Later, Susie married Jack Eades, the developer of Sylvan Shores. (Courtesy of Becky Fender Weigand.)

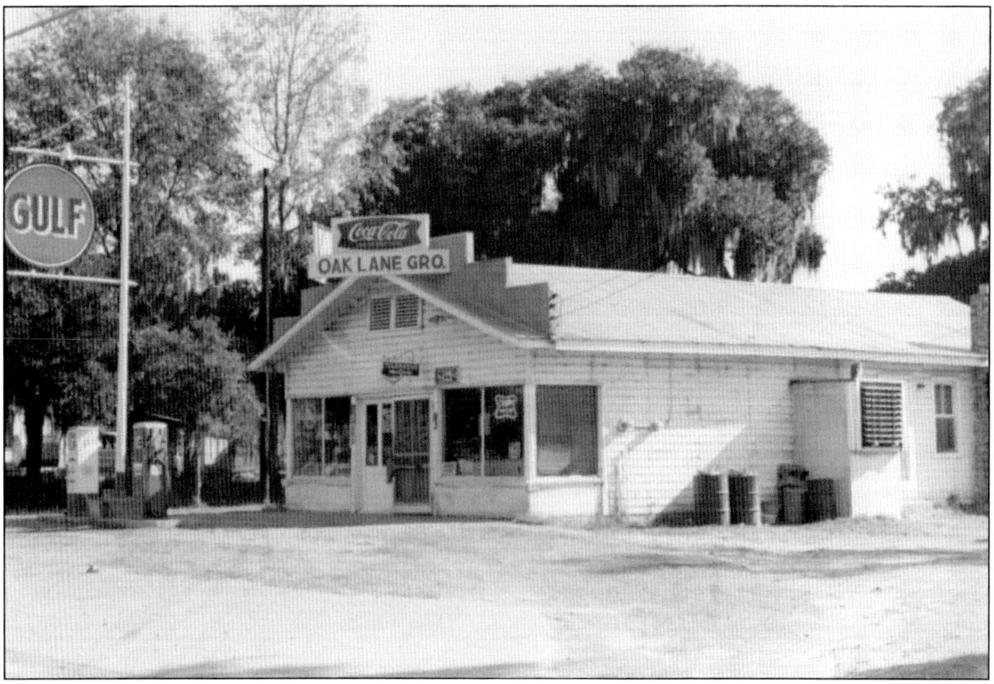

Grace E. and Philip Luther Bootle divorced in 1945, and Bootle's Grocery at Pleasant Grove closed in the fall of that year, according to a letter she wrote to her son P. Luther Jr. Grace later married George Long, who traveled in the Southeast working the produce markets. In 1955, Grace E. and her daughter Grace opened the Oak Lane Grocery on Savannah Highway near the Oak Lane Trailer Park. (Courtesy of P. Luther Bootle Jr., Ina Bootle.)

Jack Eades studied Botany and Ecology at Fort Hays State University prior to working for the USDA Federal Research Laboratory on Savannah Highway. Originally from Kansas, he was a "product of the Dust Bowl," he recalls. He started acquiring land in St. Andrew's Parish during the 1950s, where he raised show Tanmarque collies and Charolais cattle. He built his first home by himself (below) at the end of the avenue of oaks next to Oak Lane Trailer Park. His wife, Lorraine, was ill when he opened Sylvan Shores in 1956. The name Sylvan, meaning "wooded area," was Lorraine's choice. After Lorraine passed away, Jack courted Susie Fender by cutting a new road, Eades Lane, to his home and building a tennis court. Susie liked to play tennis and his efforts proved successful. They married in 1978. Even though Susie passed away in 2007, Jack continues to enjoy life in Sylvan Shores. (Both, courtesy of Jack Eades.)

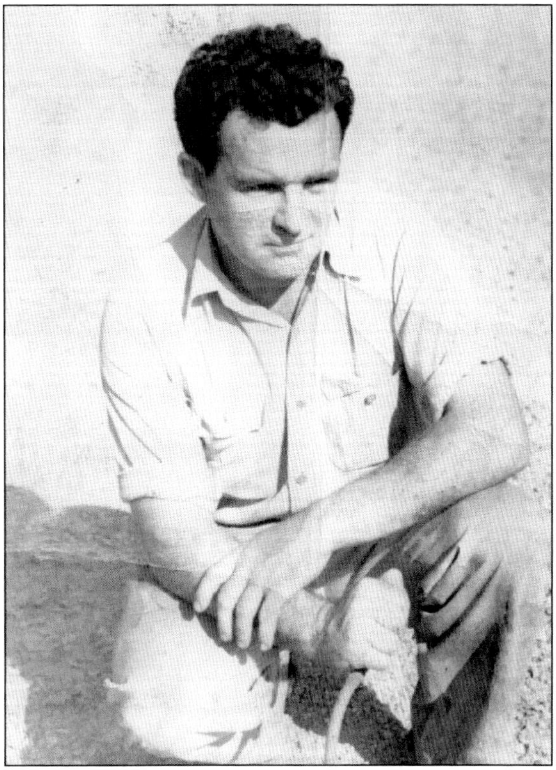

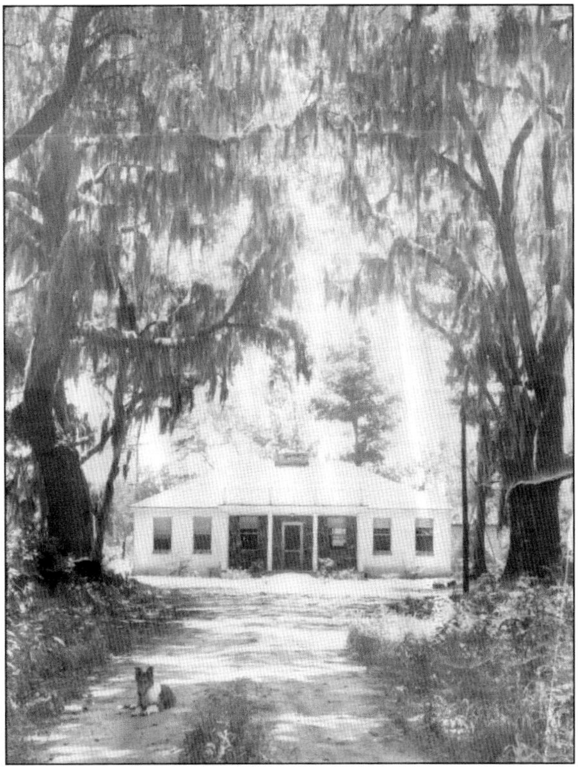

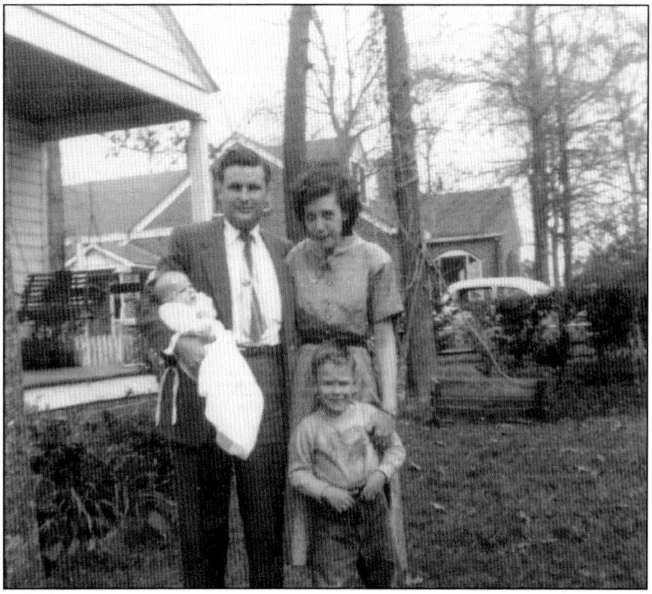

George W. Seignious III, holding his daughter Jane, and Virginia Blocker Seignious, holding her son Bill, pose at her family home on Savannah Highway Pleasant Grove in March 1953. Virginia recounts that she was sitting on the porch swing, which can be seen to the back left of the photograph, when the newspaper boy came down the street shouting "Extra, Extra!" with news of the beginning of World War II. (Courtesy of Virginia Blocker Seignious.)

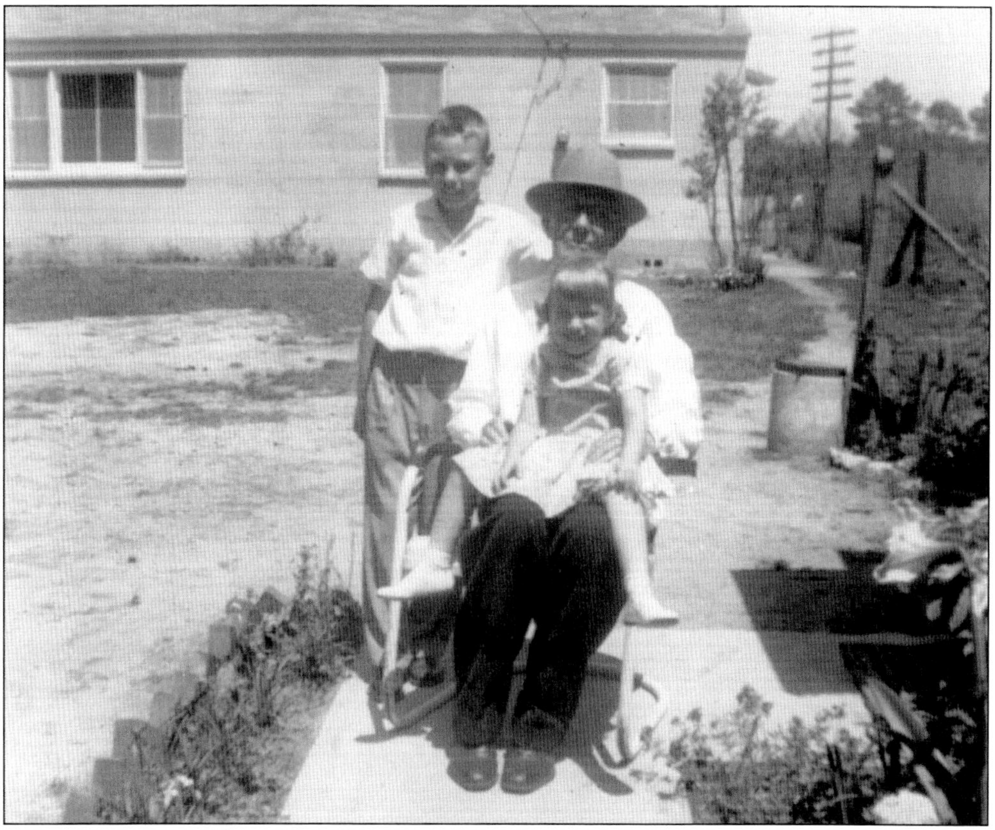

Jane Seignious sits on her maternal grandfather's lap and her brother, Bill, stands behind Richard Riley Blocker on Pleasant Grove Lane in April 1957. Richard Riley Blocker (known affectionately as "RR" or "railroad") moved his family to Charleston in the early 1930s and worked briefly as a carpenter and a guard for the Woodstock Company. (Courtesy of Virginia Blocker Seignious.)

George W. Seignious III and Virginia Blocker Seignious met at John Wesley Methodist Church. They were charter members. One of their first homes was on Magnolia Road in Ashley Forest. Bill sits in the rocking chair and Jane stands close by as the camera catches them in February 1954. The shops of Avondale can be seen in the background. (Courtesy of Virginia Blocker Seignious.)

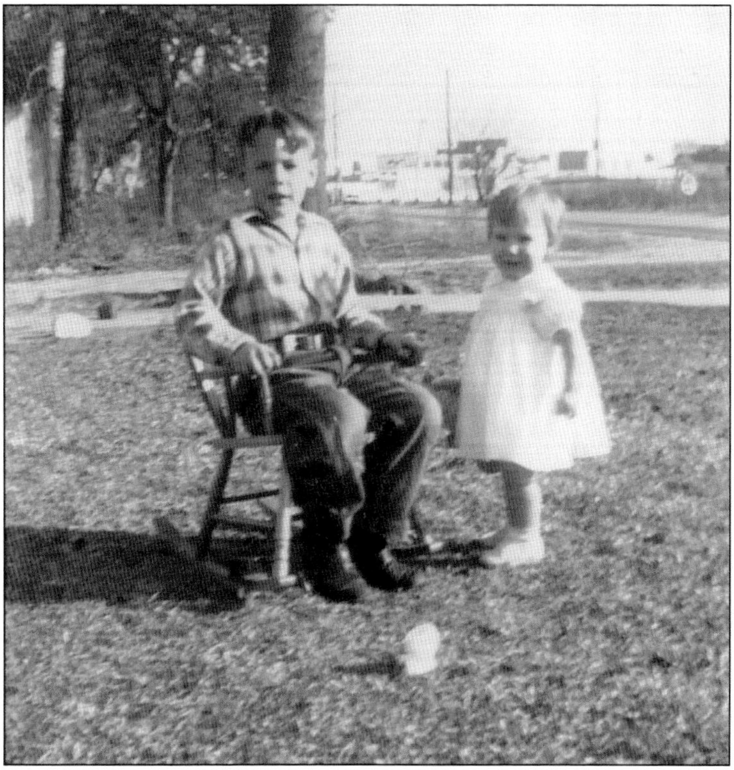

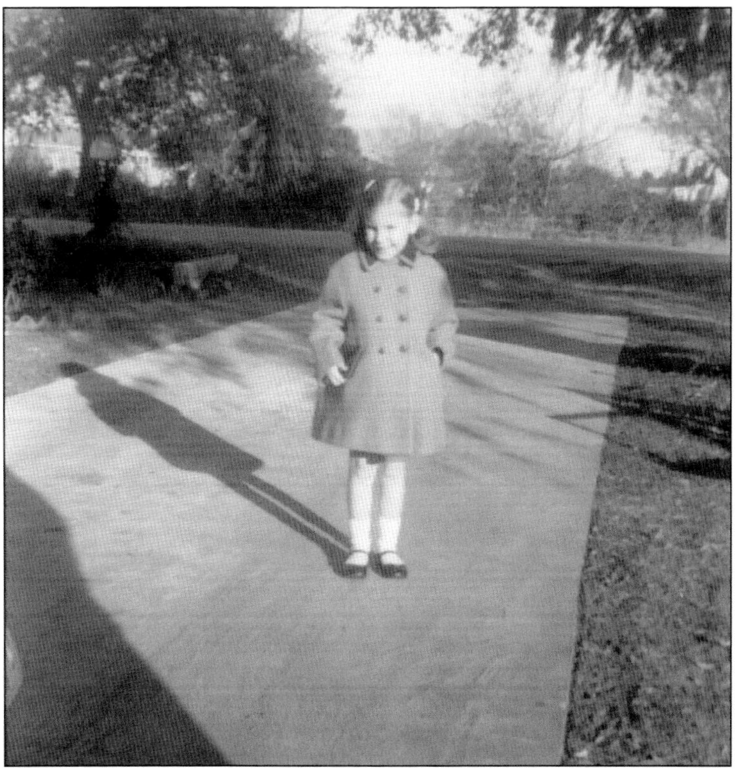

The Seignious family built their new home on Wappoo Road near the intersection of Savannah Highway to be close to family and to Stono Park Elementary School, which had a good reputation. The wooded area around the home provided great entertainment for the children. It is winter in 1957 and Jane is smiling and warm in her blue winter coat. Later, George would build "their dream home" on Coleridge Street in Charlestowne Estates III. (Courtesy of Virginia Blocker Seignious.)

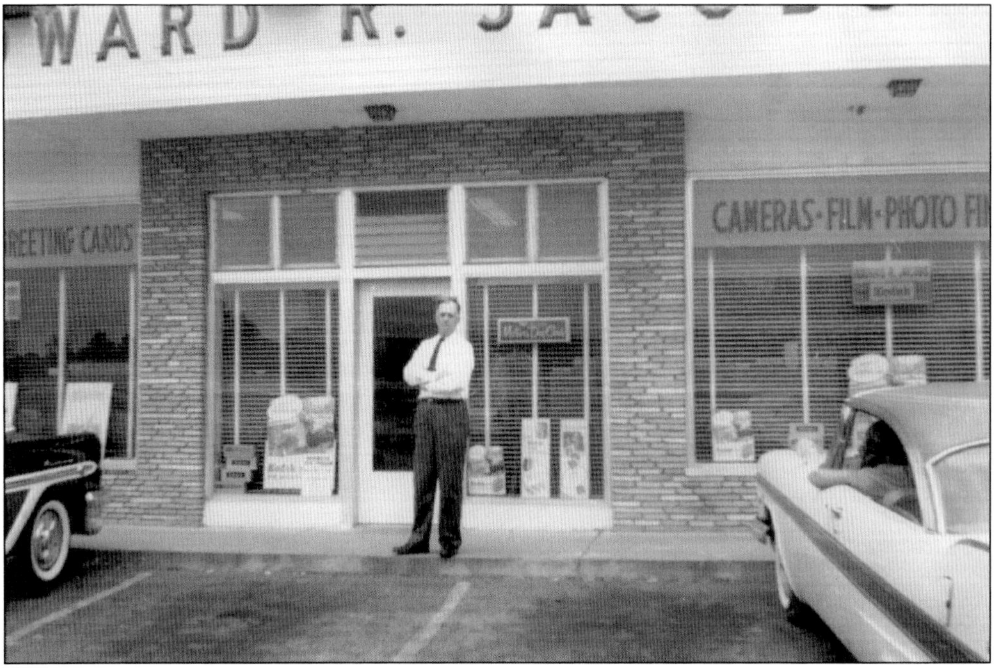

Howard R. Jacobs poses in front of his photography store in the South Windermere Shopping Center. Howard developed a passion for photography at an early age opening a photofinishing store on Liberty Street in downtown Charleston for $65. Two of his aunts ran the business while he served during World War I in Mexico. His career in commercial photography was curtailed by the onset of cataracts. In 1953, he built his home (below) on Tarleton Drive in South Windermere, known then as the "up and coming" subdivision being developed by William H. Ackerman. (Courtesy of Howard Rivers Jacobs Jr.)

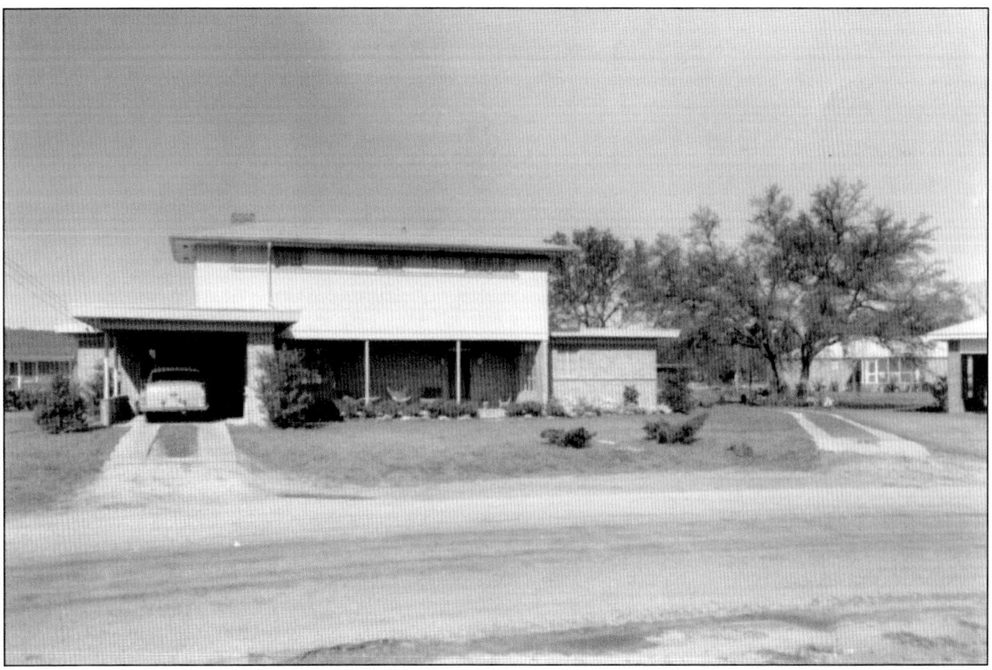

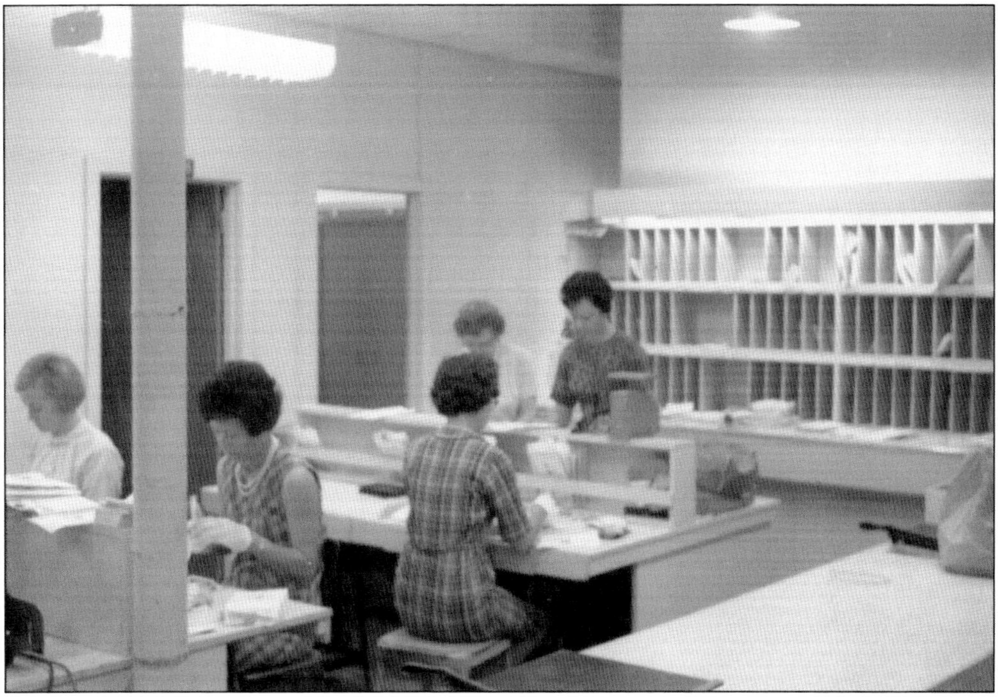

Photographic processing in the plant behind the storefront was a major part of the operation at the South Windermere location. Initially, 12 employees processed film, reviewed orders for print quality, and assisted with billing. Cameras, film, and photographic supplies were sold in the store. Howard R. (Rivers) Jacobs Jr. assisted his father in opening this location after he returned from his service during the Korean War. (Courtesy of Howard Rivers Jacobs Jr.)

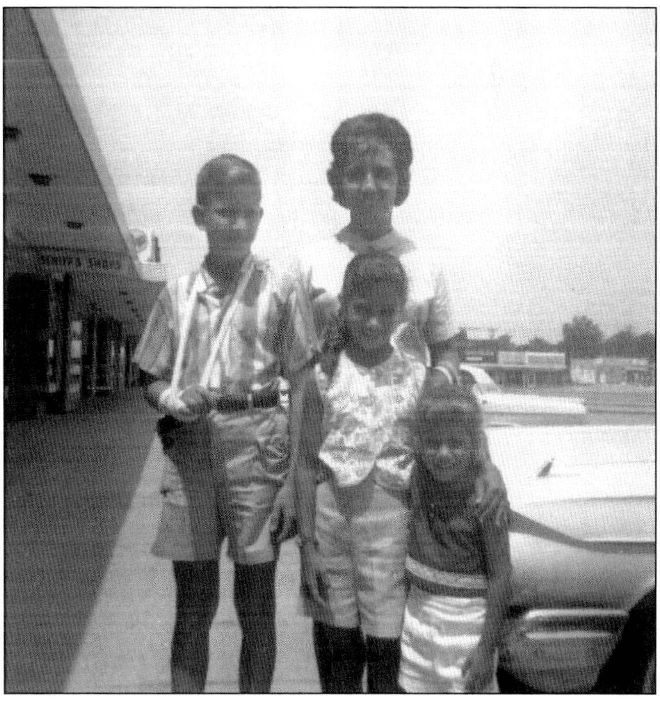

Helen Goldberg, with her children Alan, Cheryl, and Susan, pose before they go shopping at the South Windermere Shopping Center in August 1963. Possibly they were getting ready to go back to school. The South Windermere Shopping Center was the brainchild of William H. Ackerman and the first of its kind in South Carolina when it opened in 1953. Notice the store signs: Schiff's Shoes, A&P, Lesser Tanenbaum, and the gas station located on the corner. (Courtesy of Herb and Helen Goldberg.)

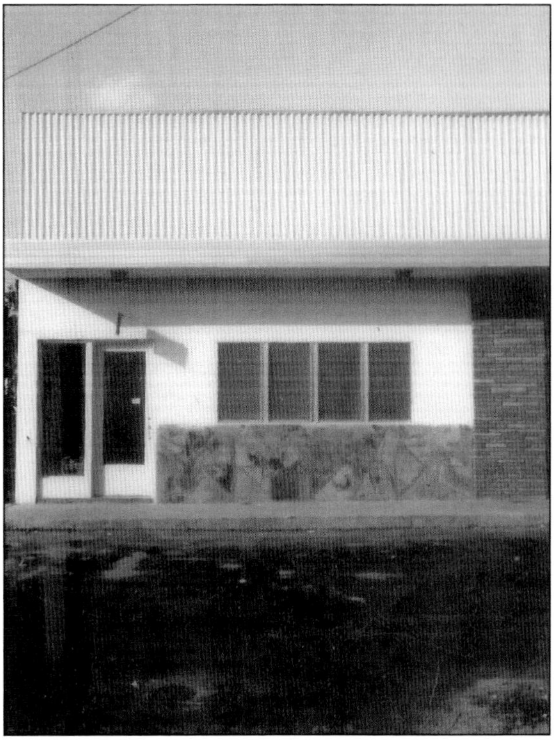

Felix Nepveux served as a naval dental surgeon for nine years prior to opening his practice in the South Windermere Shopping Center on May 22, 1954. His naval career included serving with the Fleet Marine Force in the Pacific and with the First Marine Division where he participated in the Inchon Landing and Battle for the Chosin reservoir. Felix retired from his dental practice in 1982, at which time he turned his attention to volunteer work, winning the Ann D. Edwards Volunteer of the Year award in 2000. (Courtesy of Ethel Nepveux.)

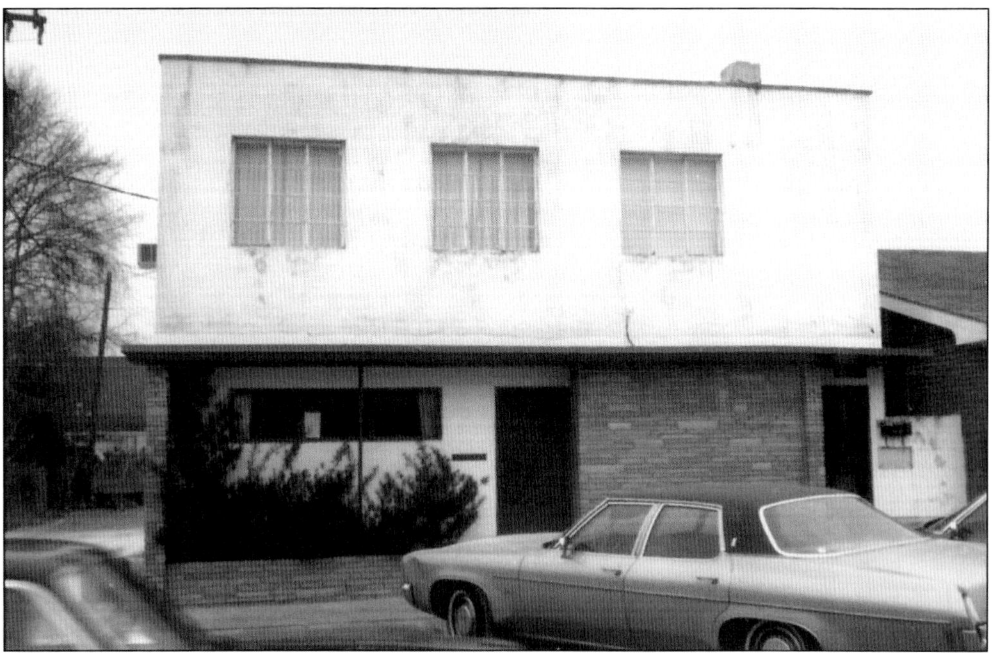

In 1953, Dr. Leon Feldman purchased land on Daniel Street in Byrnes Downs from Jack Vane for $7,500. "A good investment," recounts Dr. Feldman. He built this building for his dental office and made the claim that it was the first true dental office built in West Ashley. He practiced dentistry at this location until he retired in 1990. Today, the building houses Dr. Chen's Skin Therapy Center. (Courtesy of Leon Feldman.)

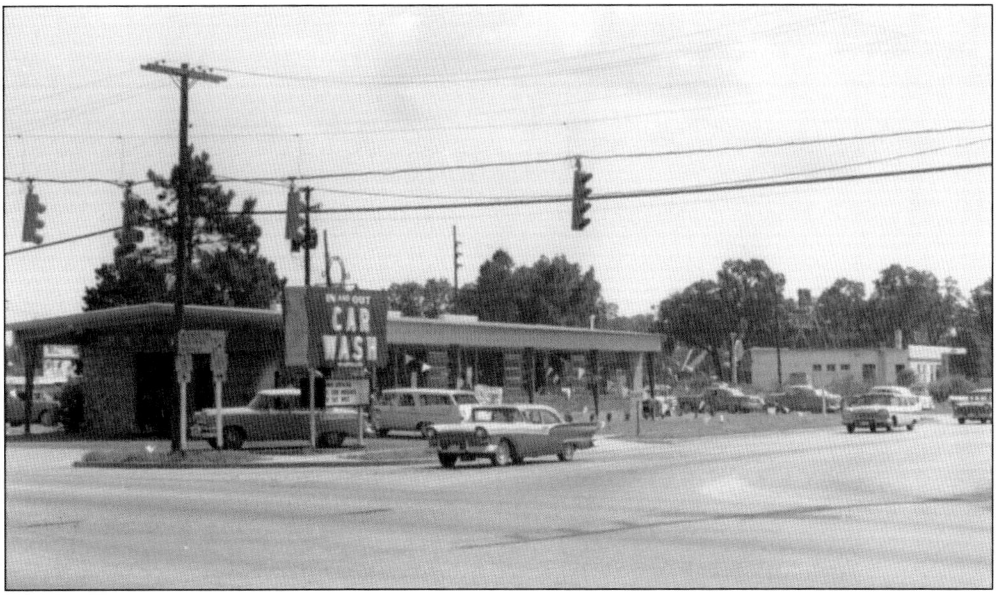

Patrick N. McGinnis opened the In and Out Car Wash on St. Andrew's Boulevard in 1960 with $300 and a lot of help from his father. Moving to the suburbs and owning cars was becoming popular and Patrick capitalized on the trend. The surrounding farm fields have turned to shopping centers and the roads have been widened, but the In and Out Car Wash continues to serve the West Ashley community today. Customer loyalty and employee longevity are two hallmarks of this establishment. (Courtesy of Sandy McGinnis Ellett.)

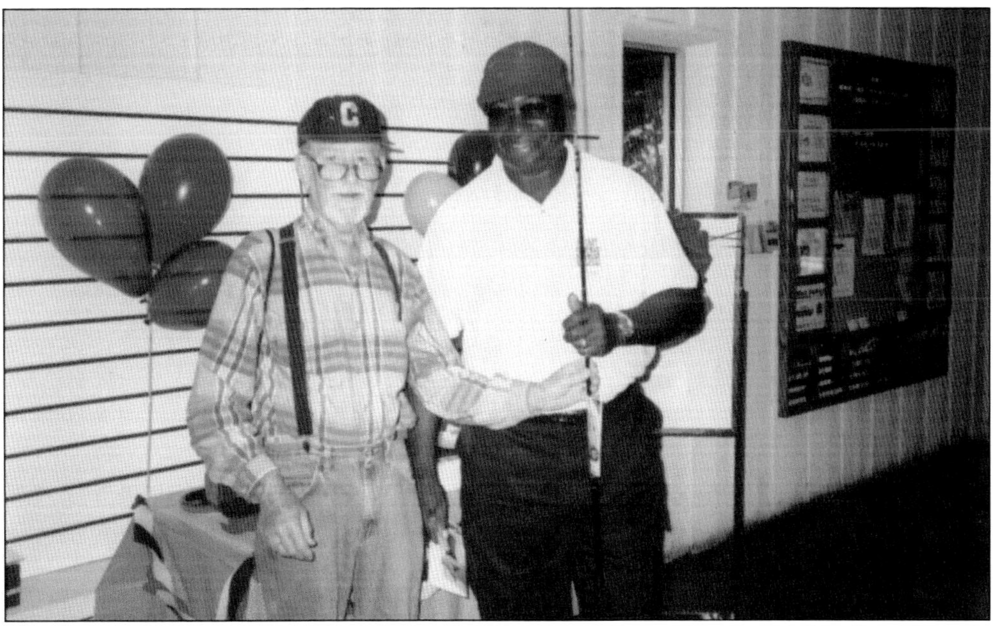

Perry Capers (right) has worked for Patrick McGinnis (left) at the In and Out Car Wash for over 50 years. Today, he is the manager and on any given day, Perry is keeping a close eye on the detailing of the cars, the work ethic of his crew, and the satisfaction of his customers. He offers a smile and a kind greeting to all of his friends waiting on a shaded bench for the cars to be detailed. (Courtesy of Sandy McGinnis Ellett.)

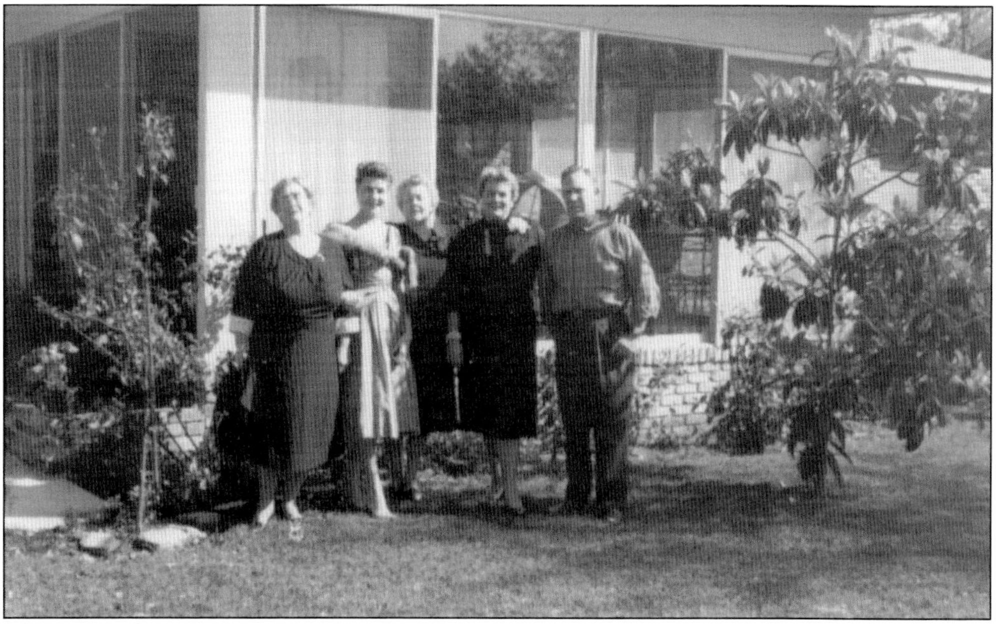

The Napier home at 1617 Carterett Avenue was one of the first homes built in section I of Charlestowne Estates in the late 1950s. Floyd and Hilda Napier were Anna Wireman's aunt and uncle. Anna recalls being raised by four mothers. They are, from left to right, Lillie Reeves (her grandmother), June Wireman (her mother), Lucille Bunch (her great aunt), and Hilda Napier (her aunt). Floyd Napier is seen on the right. (Courtesy of Anna Wireman McAllister.)

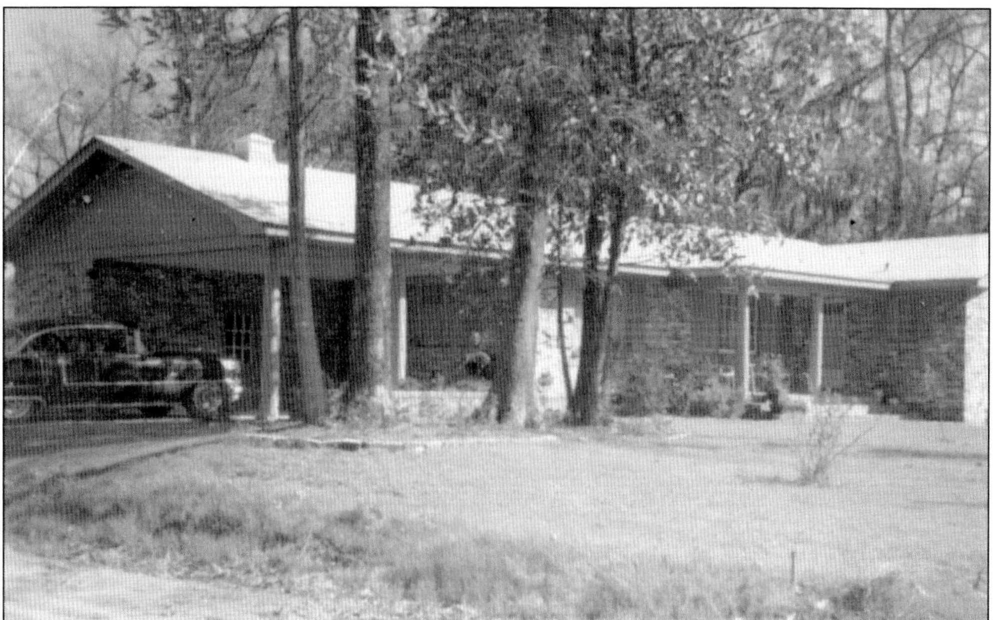

Anna Wireman's mother was anxious to move closer to her family in Charlestowne Estates. In the early 1960s, her parents, Charles L. Wireman, and his wife built the first home in section II of the subdivision at 1582 Teague—the first home in Charlestowne Estates II. Their 1956 Cadillac sits in driveway. (Courtesy of Anna Wireman McAllister.)

Four

Going to School

One of the hallmarks of a growing community is the organization of a formal education structure. Schools provide this structure as well as social interaction for the community. Scrapbooks, photographs, memorabilia, and stories about going to school are some of the most delightful memories people will share. Students attending St. Andrew's Parish Schools are no exception to this. The segregated schools of St. Andrew's Parish School District No. 10 had their beginnings in the late 1800s on the plantation of Edward T. Legare and in the new African American town of Maryville. Mary Mathews Just, attributed with the founding of Maryville, had a strong belief in the importance of education. The Deming School was founded by Mary to serve the children of Maryville. Her son Ernest embraced his mother's passion for education and went on to have a distinguished career in developmental biology. St. Andrew's Parish High School traces its history to the school organized in a slave church on the Legare Plantation in 1898. The location of this school was not convenient for all of St. Andrew's Parish, and a second school opened on land granted by G.D. Dupont Sr. In 1909, the two schools consolidated and moved to a location on Savannah Highway. In 1918, the school moved to the geographical center of the school district on Wappoo Road, and was known as the Little Brown School House. By 1928, the enrollment had grown and construction of a new modern school building was the topic of discussion for the Parent Teacher Association (PTA). In 1940, a new wing opened on the school to accommodate the high school grades, from eight to eleventh grade. Prior to this time, Parish students attended high school in Charleston. Wallace Consolidated School opened in 1953 to serve the African American students of the district under principal John W. Carr Sr. The school was named for Mattie Wallace, who owned the land where the school was constructed. Wallace Consolidated School closed in 1969 due to integration and the student population was sent to the various elementary, middle, and high schools in the district. By 1963, more than 10 public and private schools existed in the Parish.

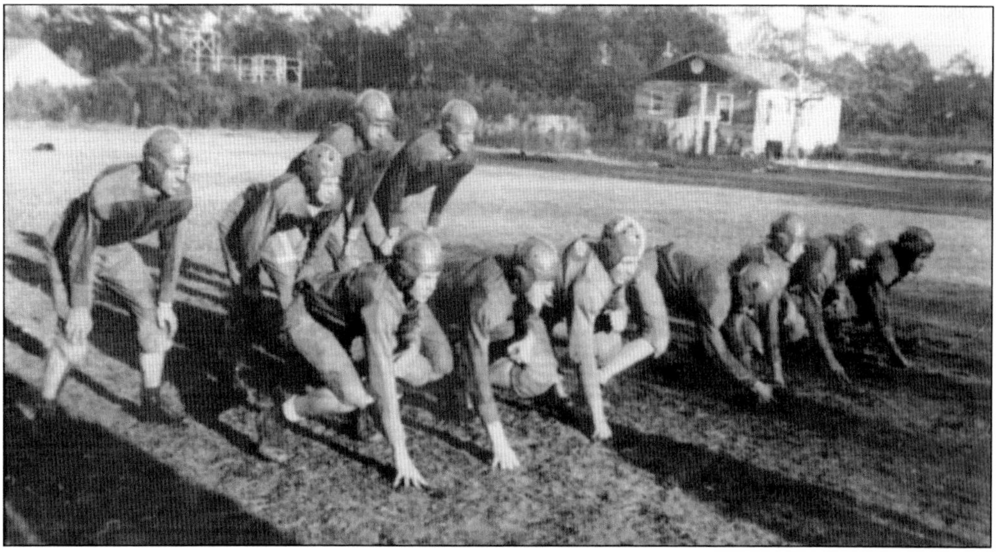

The 1944 to 1945 high school football team practiced on the field beside the school. Bill Brockenfelt played for the Rocks and identified a few of his teammates: Milton Almedia (full back), Louis Bowen (running back), Henry Schaffer (end), and William Patrick (center). Henry Hassselmeyer coached that year and the team hung on his every word. In the background is the Little Brown School House. During this time, Mr. Robinson, the curator, lived there, and the football team used the building. (Courtesy of Bill Brockenfelt.)

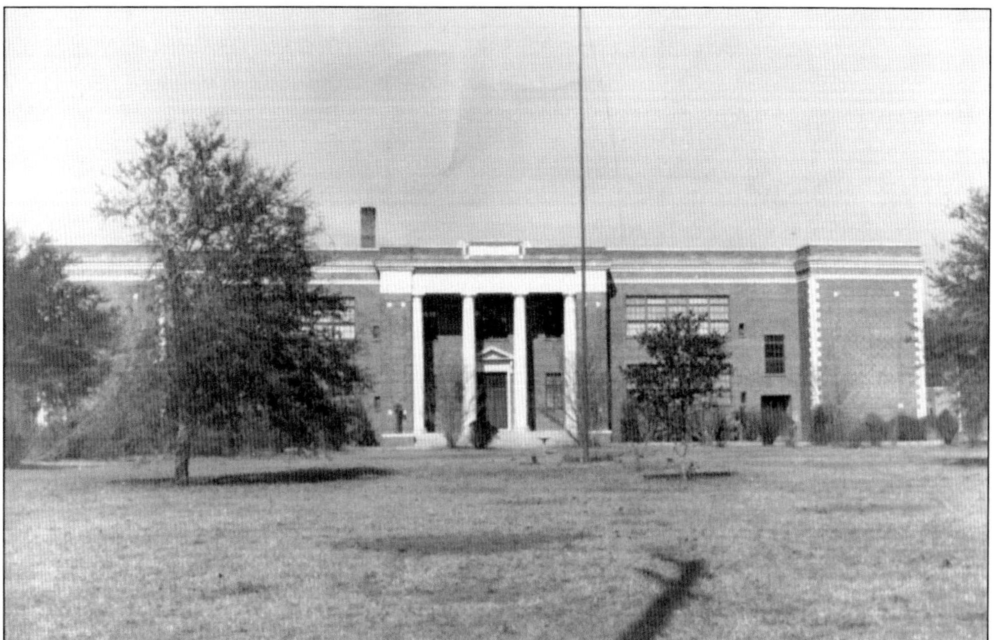

St. Andrew's Parish High School was familiar to everyone from when it was built in 1939, until a fire consumed it in December 1978. Alumni only need to see a bit of the structure and the memories come flooding back. After the fire, it was necessary to demolish the remaining structure. During the demolition, Mr. Hester's scrapbooks from 1941 until the 1960s were discovered in the rubbish. (Courtesy of Bill Brockenfelt.)

Mary Ruth Carr poses for her graduation photograph in front of her home in Maryville. She received her baccalaureate degree from the Avery Institute in 1930. Mary's mother, Mary Ellen Green Carr (Mamie), was a midwife to the women in Maryville and delivered many of the town's children. Mary Ruth later married Charles Irving Houston Sr. (Courtesy of the Avery Institute.)

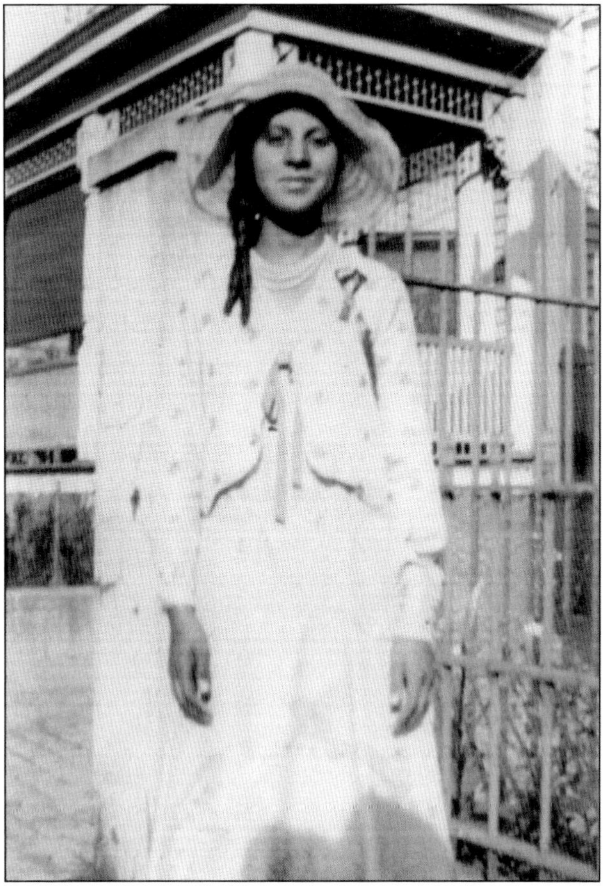

When the Wallace Consolidated School originally opened, it only went to the 11th grade, like the other schools in the district. Diane Hamilton, the historian at Graham AME Church on Wappoo Road, graduated from Wallace in 1962. She delivered the graduation speech titled "Worlds Beyond" to her class. The graduation exercises were held in the auditorium on the school grounds. (Courtesy of Yvonne Groves Gilreath.)

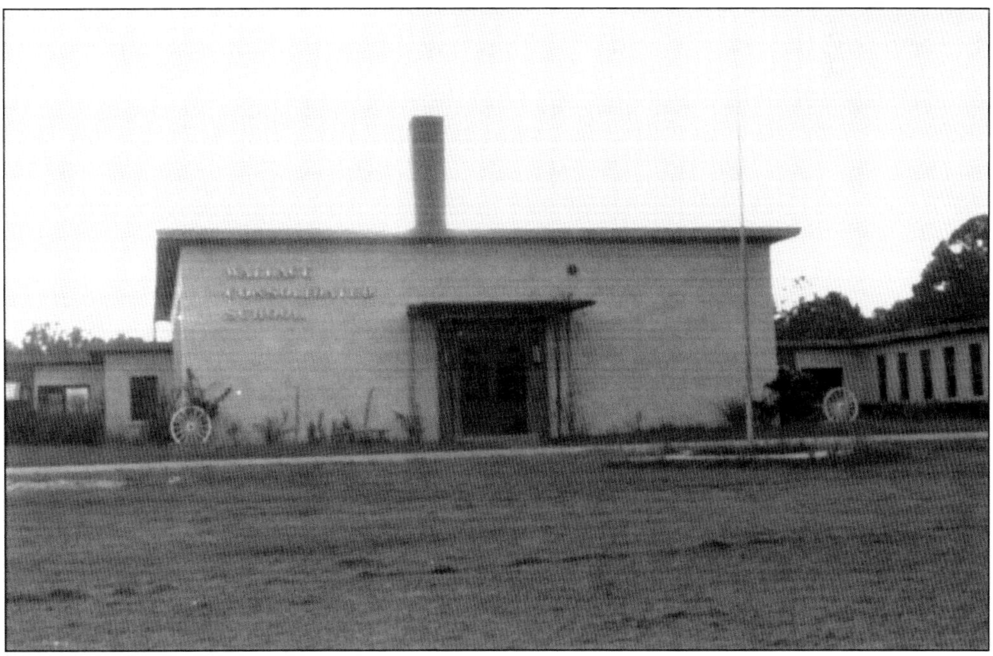

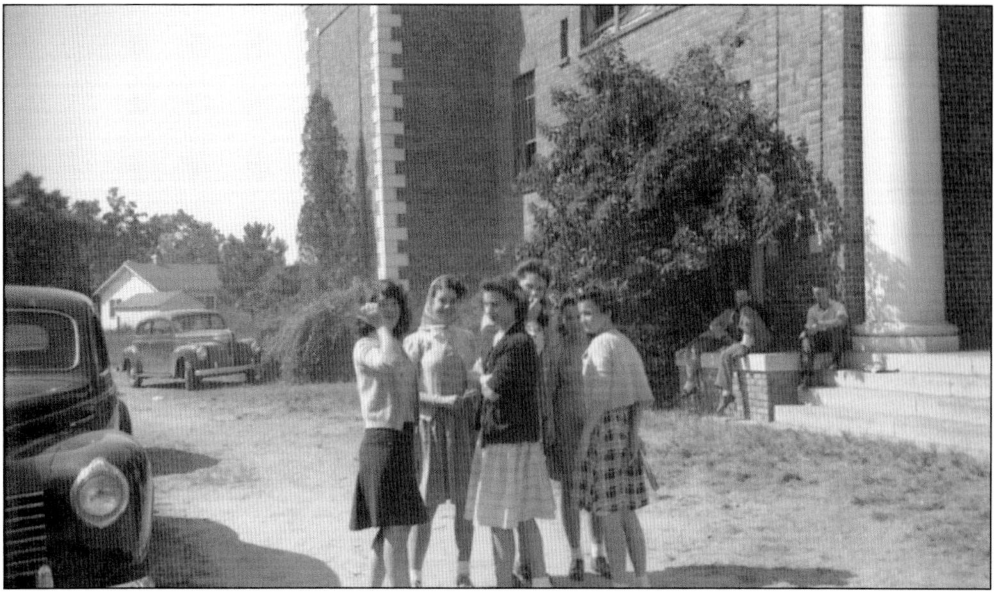

For the school year 1942 to 1943, P. Luther Bootle Jr. was the school photographer for the *Pelican*, St. Andrew's Parish High School yearbook. This photograph is reproduced from one of the 300 negatives that were in his archives. It captures life at the school from a student's point of view. (Courtesy of P. Luther Bootle Jr., Ina Bootle.)

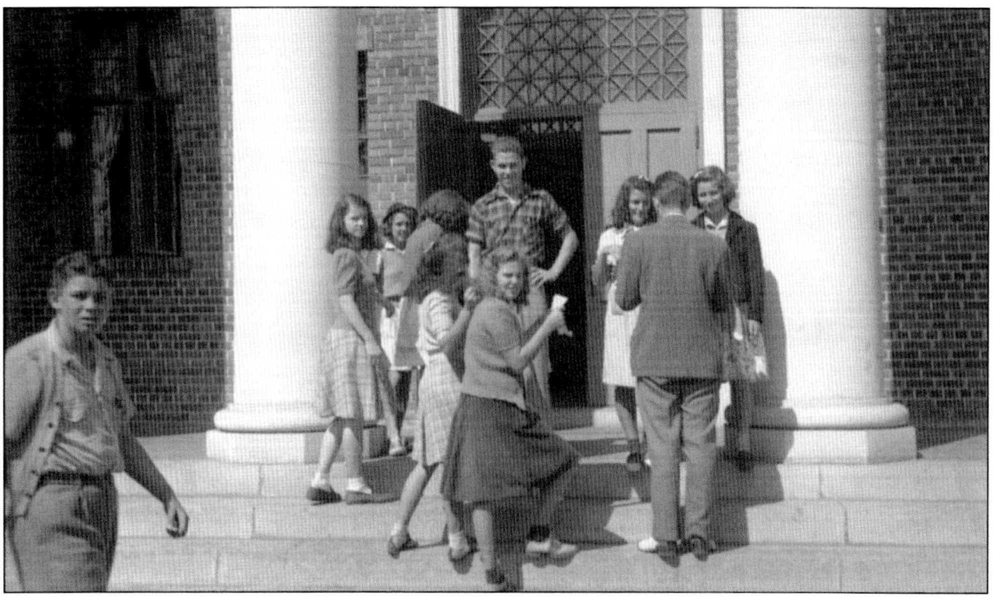

The steps at the entrance of St. Andrew's Parish High School were known as the senior steps, and only seniors were allowed to hang out on them. Most students' names have been lost with time, but J.E. Thames (far left), Paul Graham (smiling in the center), and Rosina Kennerty (next to Paul) were identified by Arthur Ravenel Jr., who graduated from the high school in 1944. (Courtesy of P. Luther Bootle Jr., Ina Bootle.)

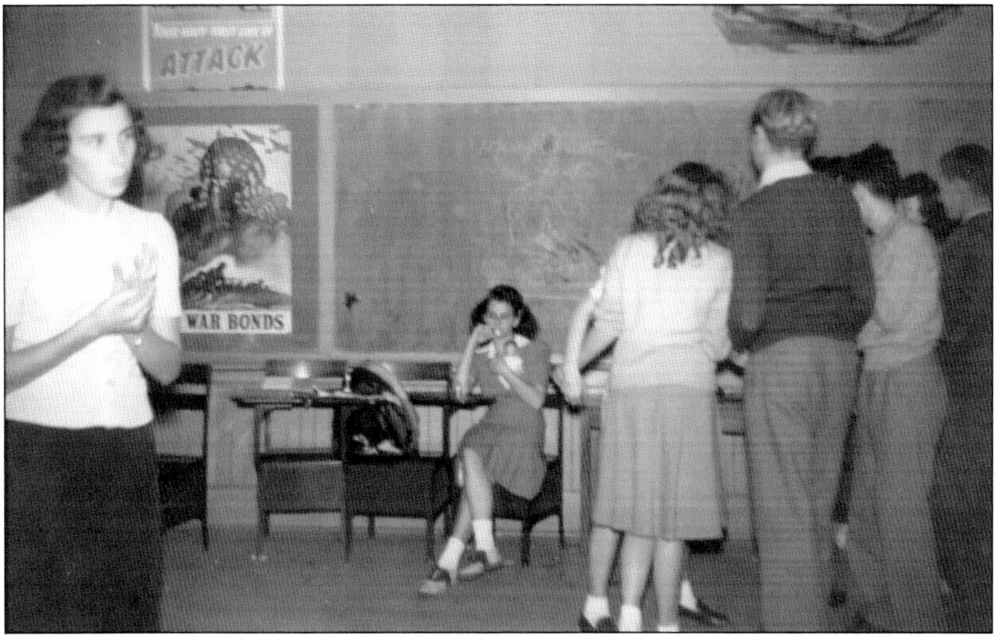

"Merry Christmas, Mr. Hester" is written on the blackboard of the classroom at St. Andrew's Parish High School. Mr. Hester inspired many generations who attended the school with his love for the school, the students, and his passion for theater. He is remembered as an outstanding performer with ties to the Dock Street Theater. The War Bond posters on the wall reminded us that the time is 1942 to 1943. (Courtesy of P. Luther Bootle Jr., Ina Bootle.)

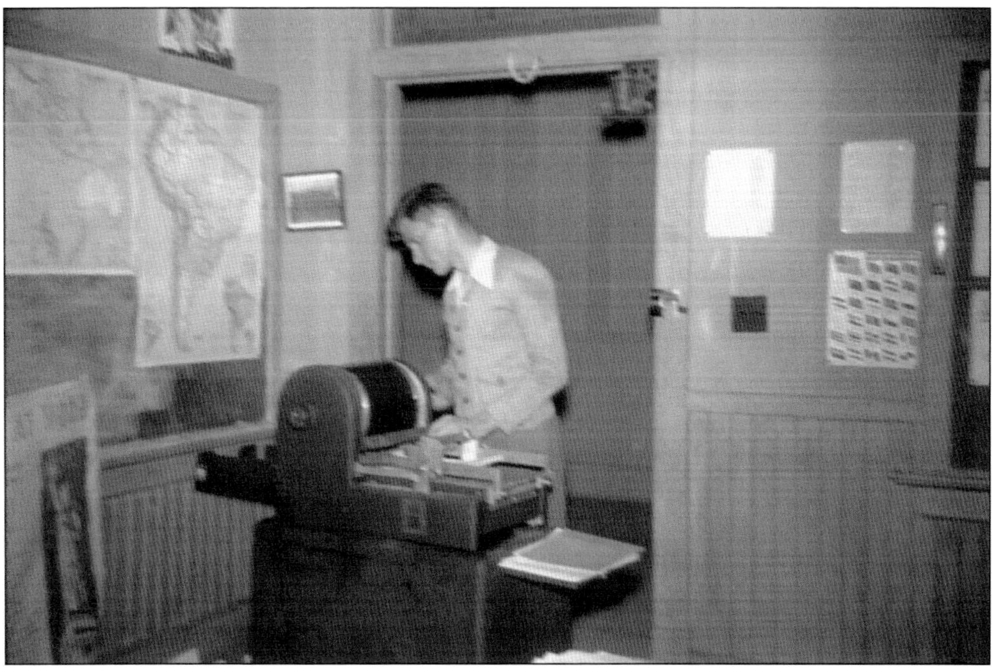

Who remembers mimeographs, the printing press machines that pressed ink through a stencil onto paper? Luther Bootle recorded the everyday life of school, including mimeographing. Notice the maps on the wall of the classroom. (Courtesy of P. Luther Bootle Jr., Ina Bootle.)

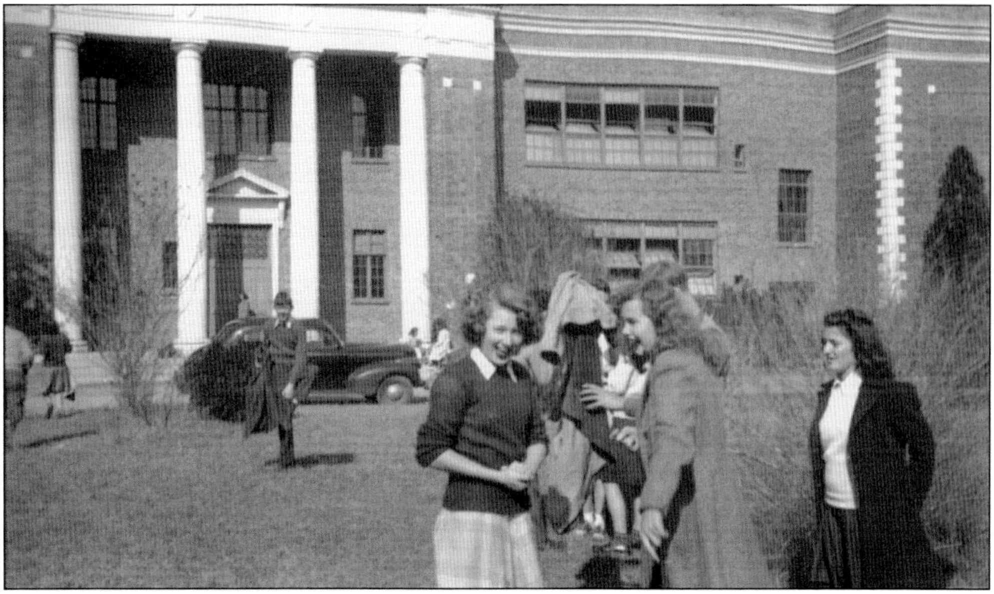

Alberta Hartnett Busch, class of 1944, identified Betty McKenzie (smiling), Jackie Smith (center), and Rosina Kennerty (right) on the grounds in front of St. Andrew's Parish High School. The photograph captures the spirit of the school. Today, the alumni hold regular reunions, retell their school stories, and maintain websites, thus keeping the spirit captured in this photograph alive. (Courtesy of P. Luther Bootle Jr., Ina Bootle.)

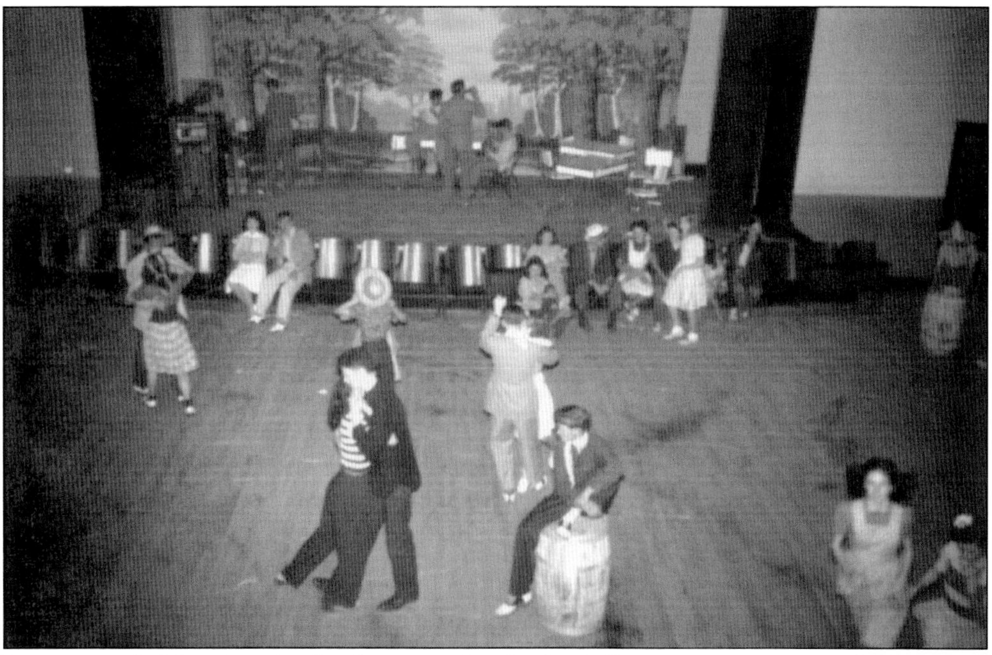

Dances were held in the school auditorium after the football games to raise money for the junior and senior prom. Mr. Hester's musical revues were also held in the auditorium. Later when the gymnasium was built, the dances were held there. They were called sock hops. The students removed their shoes and danced in their socks so they would not destroy the gym floor. (Courtesy of P. Luther Bootle Jr., Ina Bootle.)

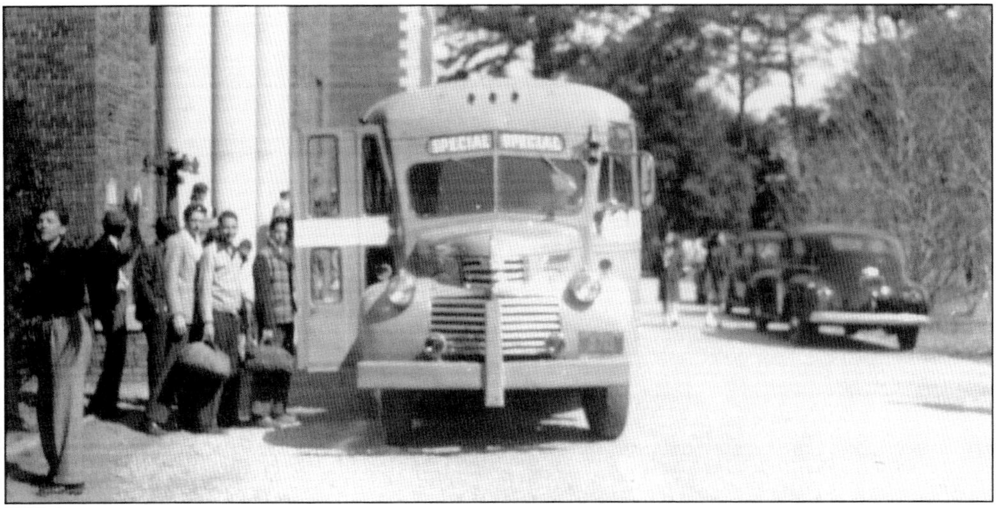

Lewis Bowen, known as "Louis" throughout his school years, learned of the correct spelling of his name when he entered the service. Lewis was another photographer for the school annual. He captured students loading onto the special bus used for transporting football and basketball teams to out of town games. In 1955, transportation to games east of the Ashley River changed to railroad due to the destruction of the Ashley River Bridge by the tanker *Fort Fetterman*. (Courtesy of Lewis (Louis) and Ginny Blank Bowen.)

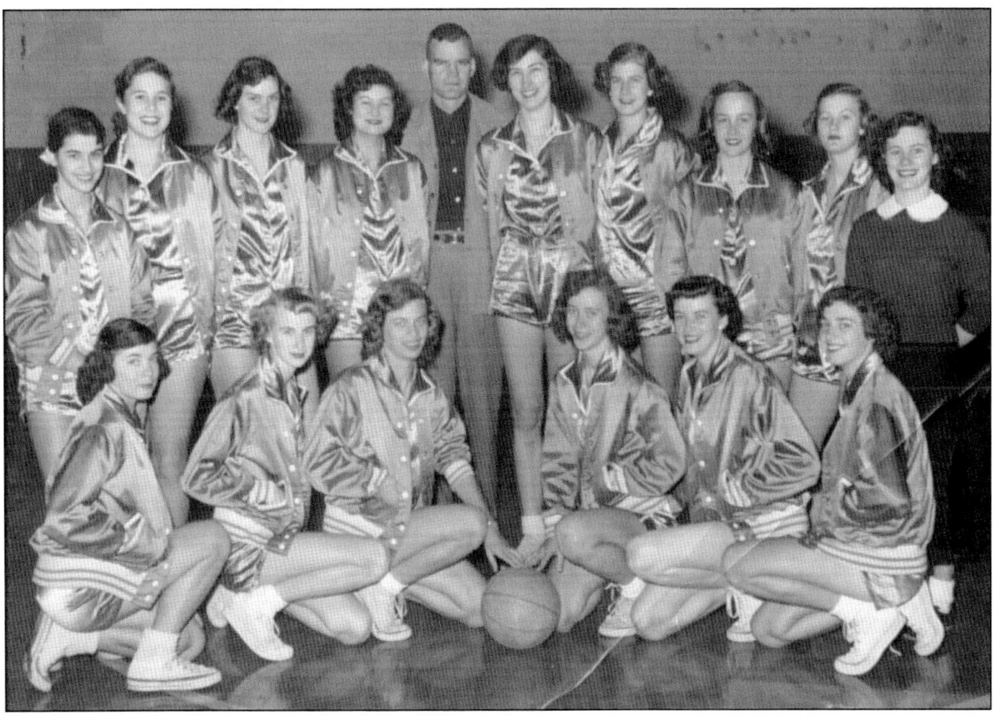

Coach Hazel Gilstrap proudly poses with the St. Andrew's Parish High School girls' basketball team as they celebrate the district championship of 1952. Stella Milton, in street clothes, was the manager for the team. Joanne Newberry, No. 9, wrote on the back of the photograph, "To the best coach in the world. Please don't leave us. You're the only one that could ever put up with us noisy bunch of basketball girls and we really appreciate it." (Courtesy of Bill Brockenfelt.)

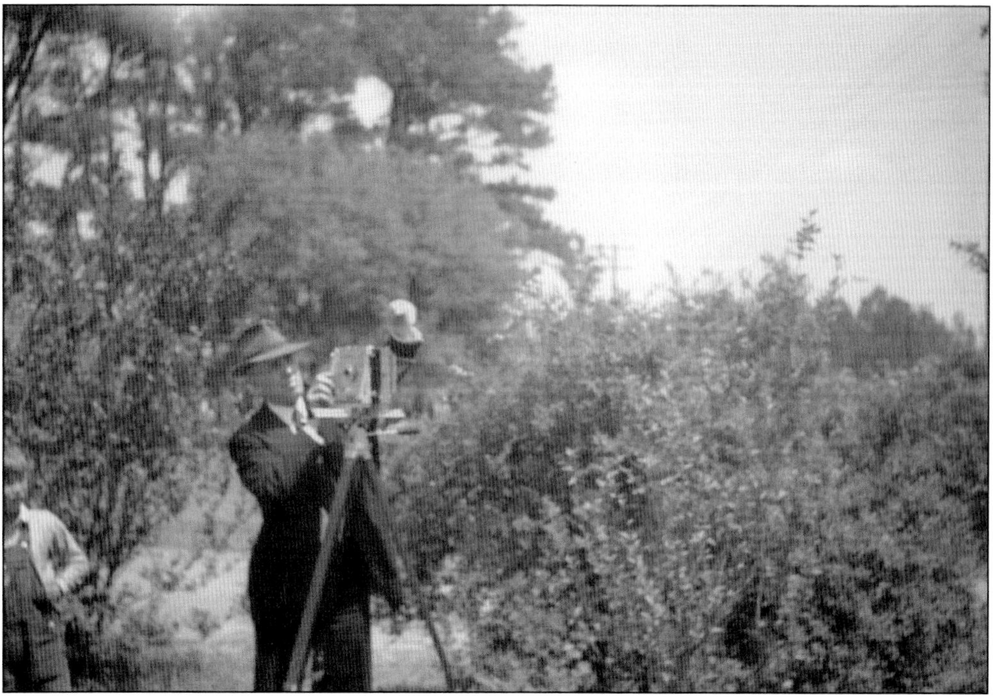

In this rare photographic composition, the photographer is captured at his trade. Howard R. Jacobs was widely known as a commercial photographer. Fortunately, Luther Bootle snapped him in action. (Courtesy of P. Luther Bootle Jr., Ina Bootle.)

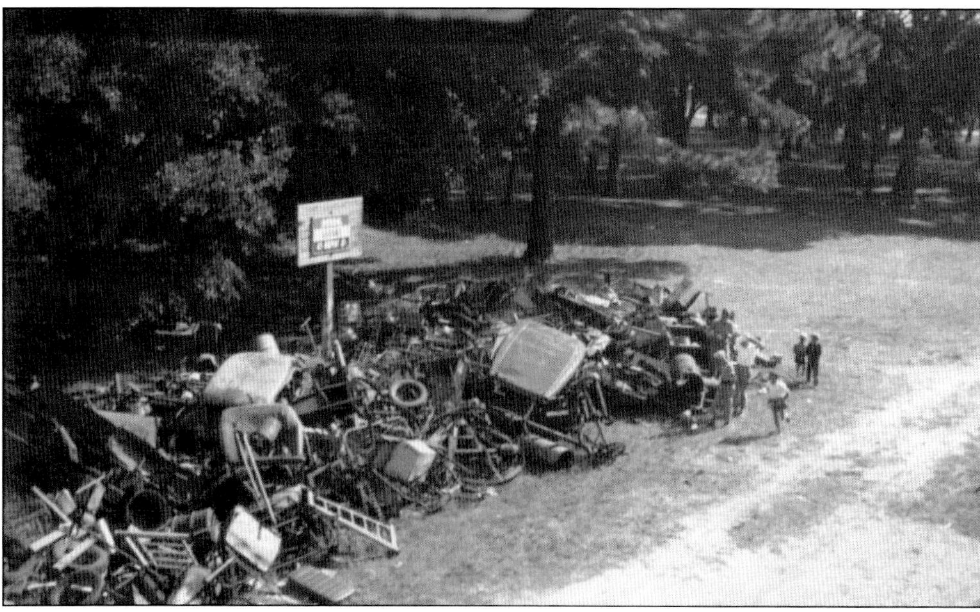

Who remembers this large pile of trash? The sign in the middle says "Official Salvage Depot." It must have been significant because Luther Bootle took several photographs of this pile and even included it in the collage of photographs for the 1943 *Pelican*. There are six young men on the right of the pile. Maybe they are going to find a treasure. (Courtesy of P. Luther Bootle Jr., Ina Bootle.)

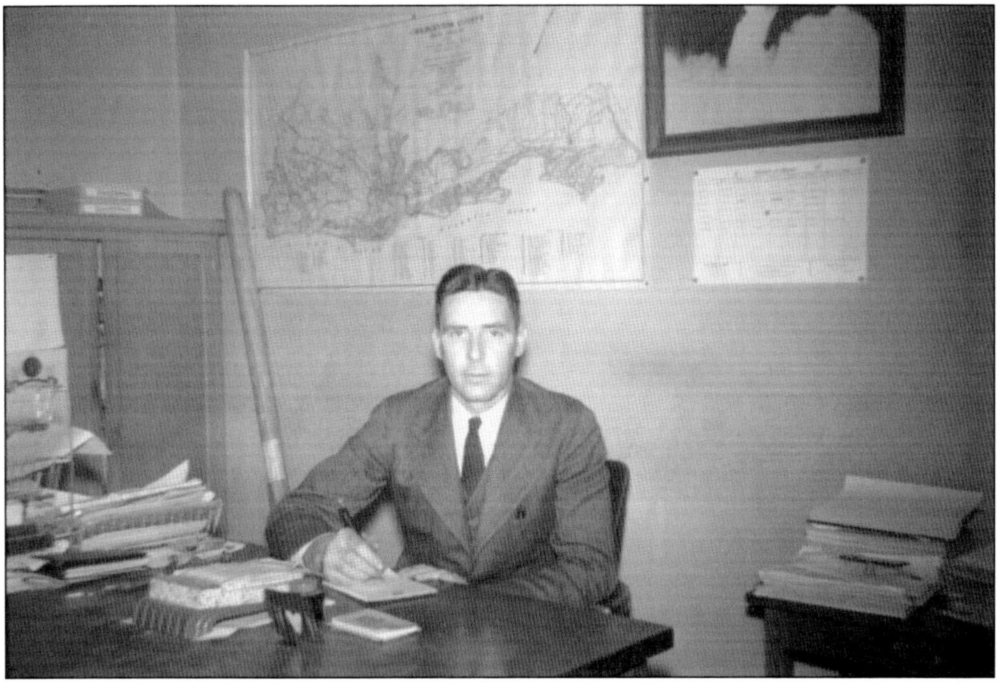

C.E. Williams was the principal of St. Andrew's Parish High School from 1941 until 1943, when he became the superintendent according to the class of 1945's history published in the *Pelican*. He was a loyal fan of the Rocks and attended all of the football games. Stella Milton recalls when she was injured at recess and he waited with her on the senior steps until her mother arrived. C.E. Williams Middle School bears his name. (Courtesy of P. Luther Bootle Jr., Ina Bootle.)

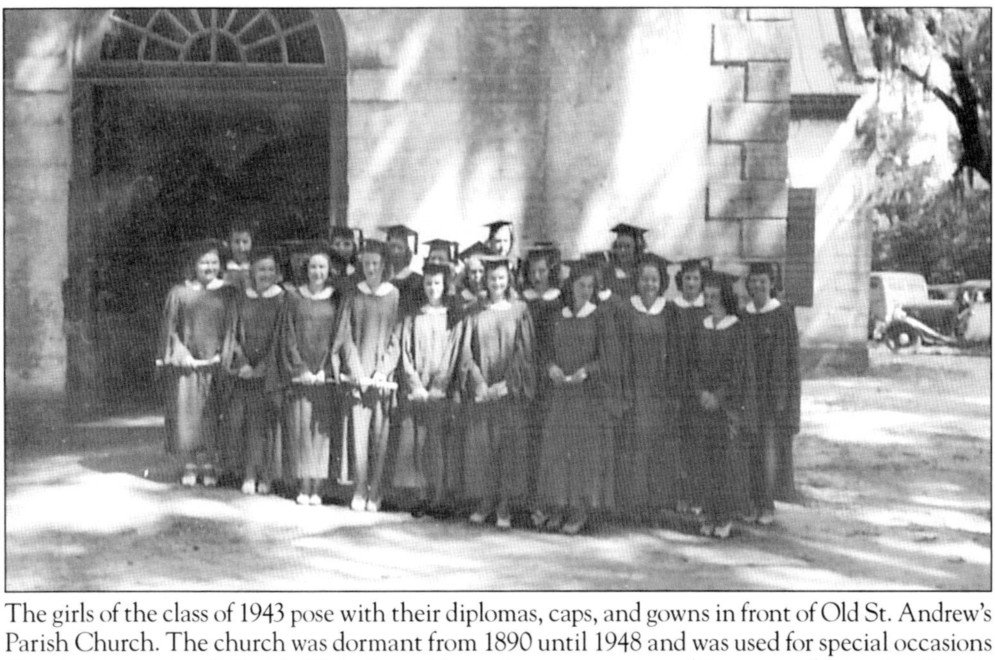

The girls of the class of 1943 pose with their diplomas, caps, and gowns in front of Old St. Andrew's Parish Church. The church was dormant from 1890 until 1948 and was used for special occasions like the St. Andrew's Parish High School baccalaureate services. (Courtesy of P. Luther Bootle Jr., Ina Bootle.)

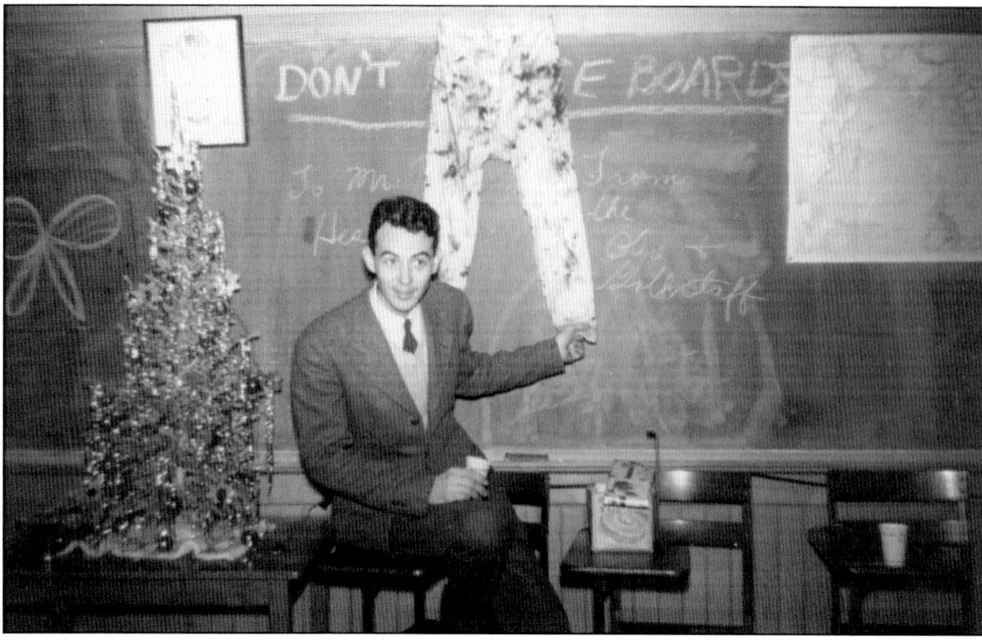

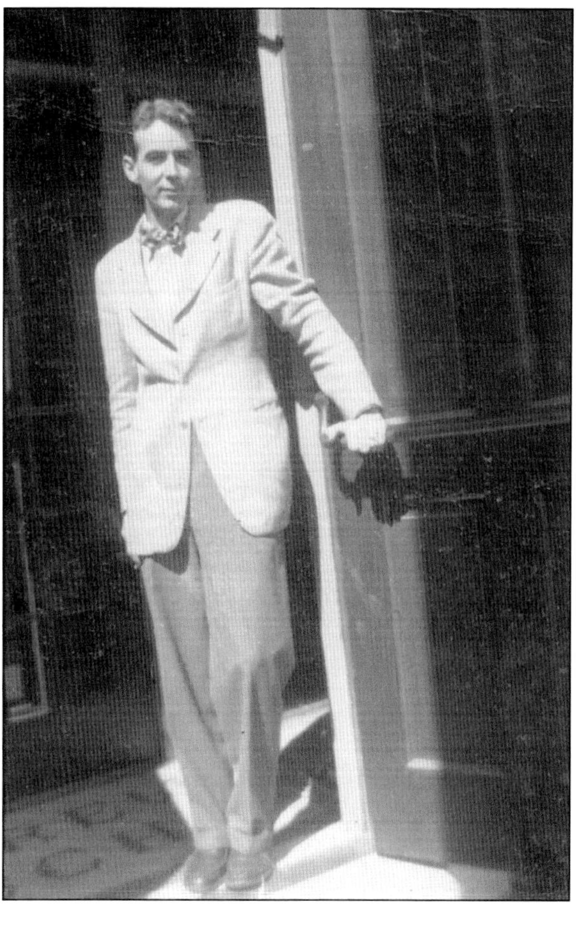

In addition to teaching English and history, E. Bernard Hester was the faculty advisor for the St. Andrew's Parish High School Dramatic Club. Each year, Mr. Hester would visit New York City and take in the Broadway shows. His enthusiasm for these productions was infectious and most of students participated in the annual musical revues that he directed. He also maintained scrapbooks of all the school's and students' activities. (Courtesy of P. Luther Bootle Jr., Ina Bootle.)

E. Bernard Hester became the principal of St. Andrew's Parish High School in 1943 according to the class history published in the 1945 edition of the *Pelican*. He was extremely popular among the students, and they called him "Fess," short for professor. Some of the most popular memories of Mr. Hester are of the school revues that he directed every year. (Courtesy of Carole Holling Earhardt.)

Frances Comar Hartnett was the president of the St. Andrew's Parish Elementary School Parent Teacher Association when her family lived in the Parish. She was recognized for her devotion to both community and church service when, in 1959, the Federation of Woman's Clubs named her "Woman of the Year." (Courtesy of Alberta Hartnett Busch.)

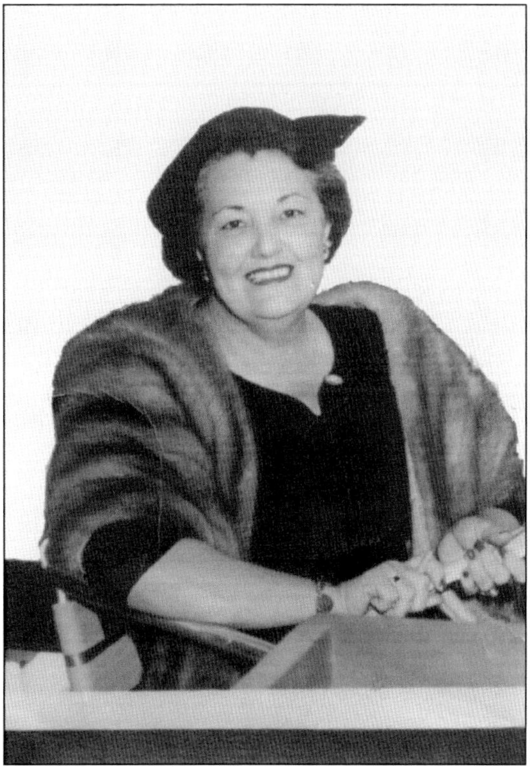

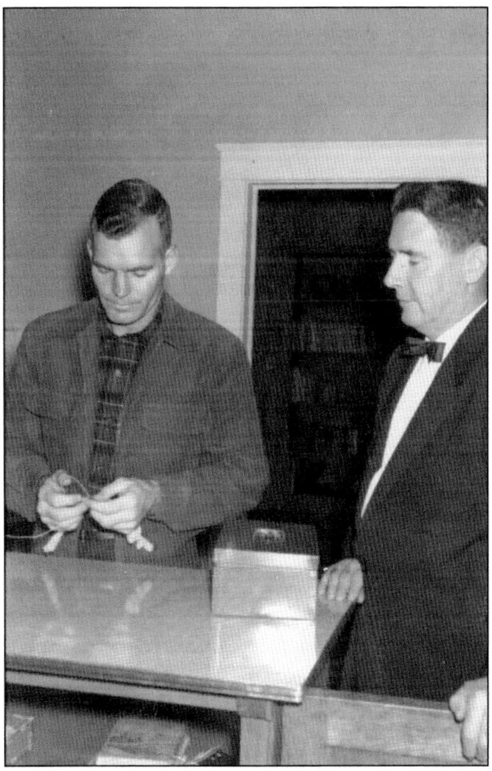

Hazel Gilstrap (left) and C.E. Williams have a moment in the school front office. Hazel Gilstrap attended Furman on a football scholarship. He became the coach at St. Andrew's Parish High School in 1948, coaching all the sports teams for both the boys and girls. The 1952–1953 *Pelican* was dedicated to him recognizing his coach of the year honor. All the students adored him and he coached several teams to state championships. (Courtesy of Barbara Blank Gilchrist.)

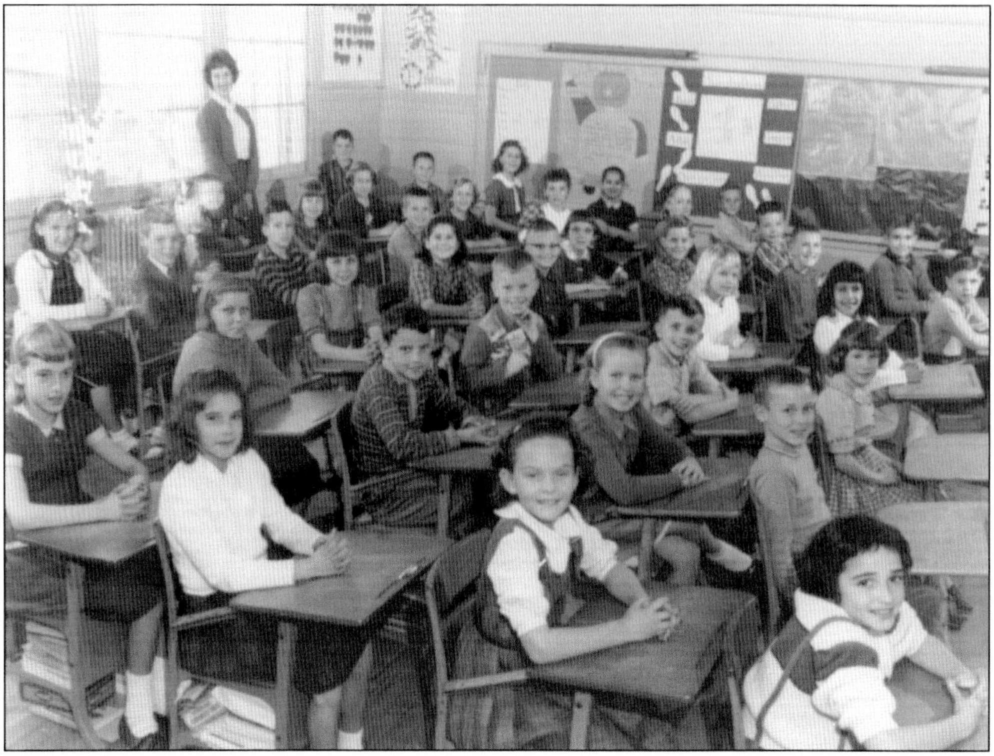

Charlie Wireman attended the fourth grade at Albemarle Elementary in 1961 when this class photograph was taken. Constructed in 1943, Albemarle Elementary was the first school to branch from the central school on Wappoo Road. The enrollment had grown to the point that a separate elementary school was required. The school building still exists on the corner of Magnolia Road and Sycamore Drive. (Courtesy of Anna Wireman McAllister.)

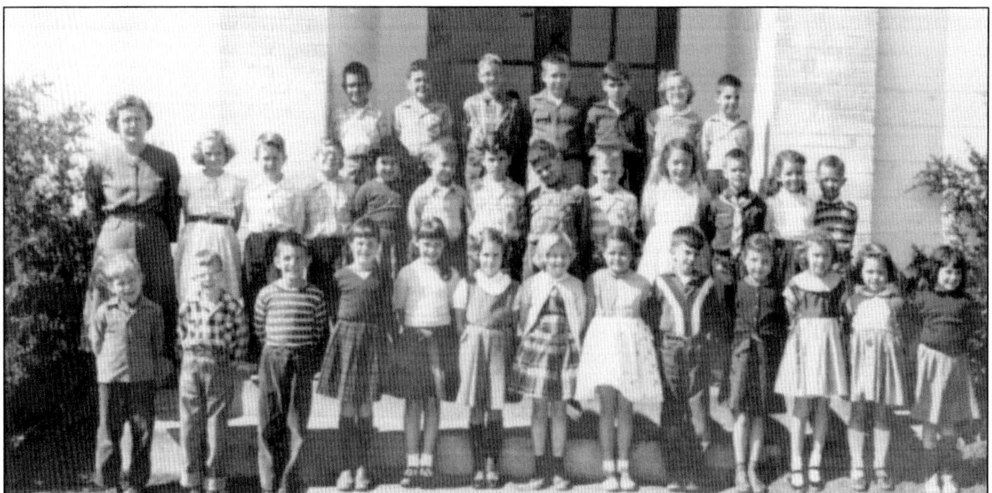

Jay Platte Campbell Jr. (third row, fourth from the left) was a member of Mrs. Walton Smith's second-grade class at St. Andrew's Elementary in 1956. Mr. Charles B. Culbertson was the principal of the school and lived at 35 Campbell Drive in Byrnes Downs. St. Andrew's Elementary was built in 1950 on land acquired from the estate of James S. Simmons. (Courtesy of Nancy Campbell Vick.)

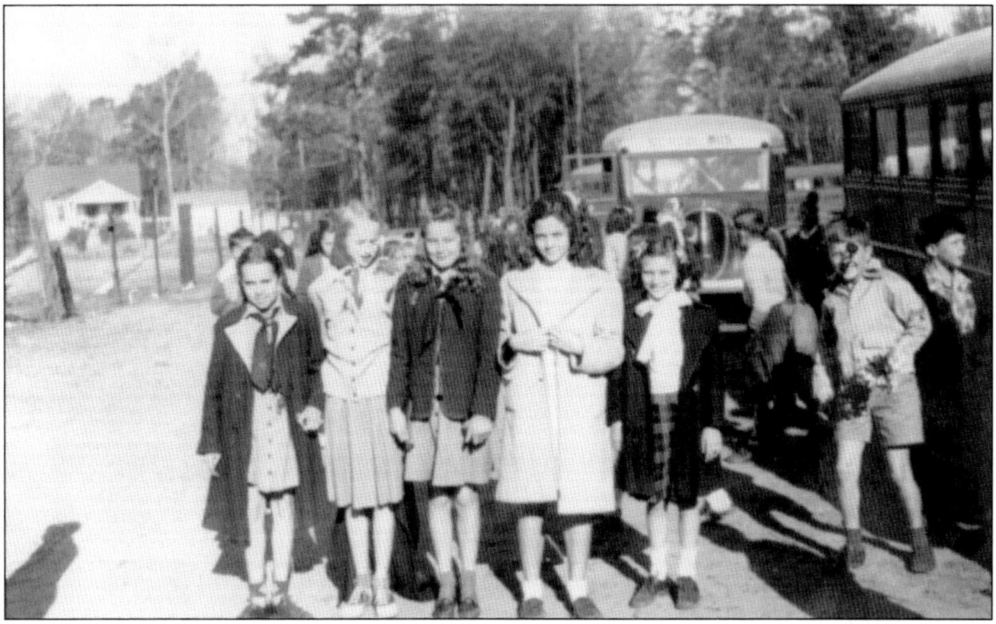

Patsy Peters, Joyce Harris, Marilyn Smith, Trigger Hogan, and Stella Milton are in the seventh-grade class at St. Andrew's Parish High School. At this time, the school went from the first grade to the eleventh grade all in one building. Their smiles might suggest that school is out for the day. (Courtesy of Stella Milton Kearse.)

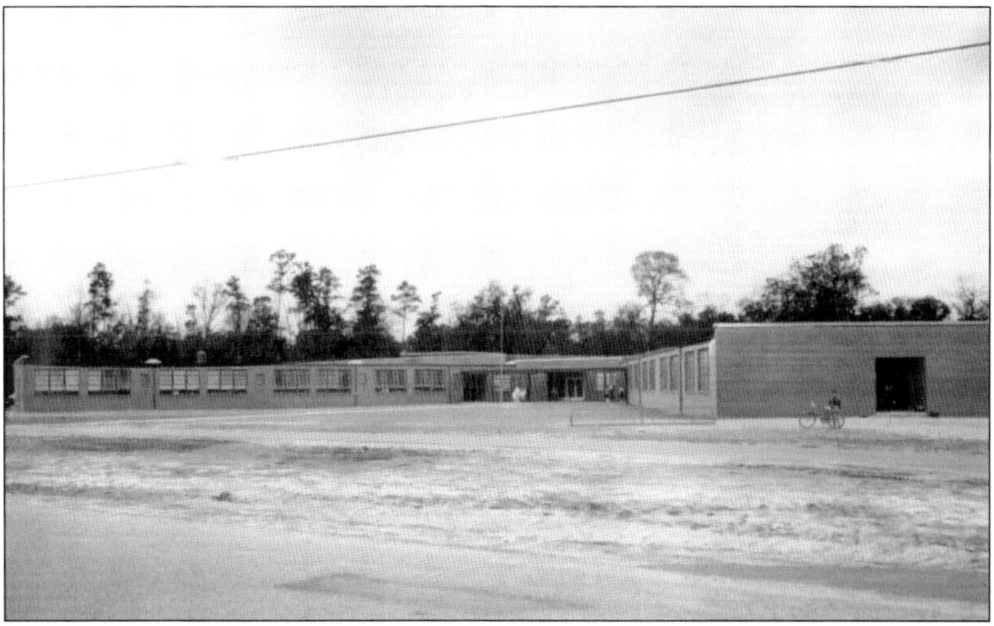

Orange Grove Elementary opened in 1963 on Orange Branch Road. J.C. Reames of Albemarle Elementary was asked to be the first principal. The school's Parent Teacher Association (PTA) held a carnival as an annual fundraiser. Stella Kearse Milton was the PTA president for the term from 1969 to 1970. She recalls one year that Jim Fowler of *Wild Kingdom* brought a puma to the carnival. Jim was in town designing the animal forest for Charles Towne Landing. (Courtesy of Orange Grove Elementary.)

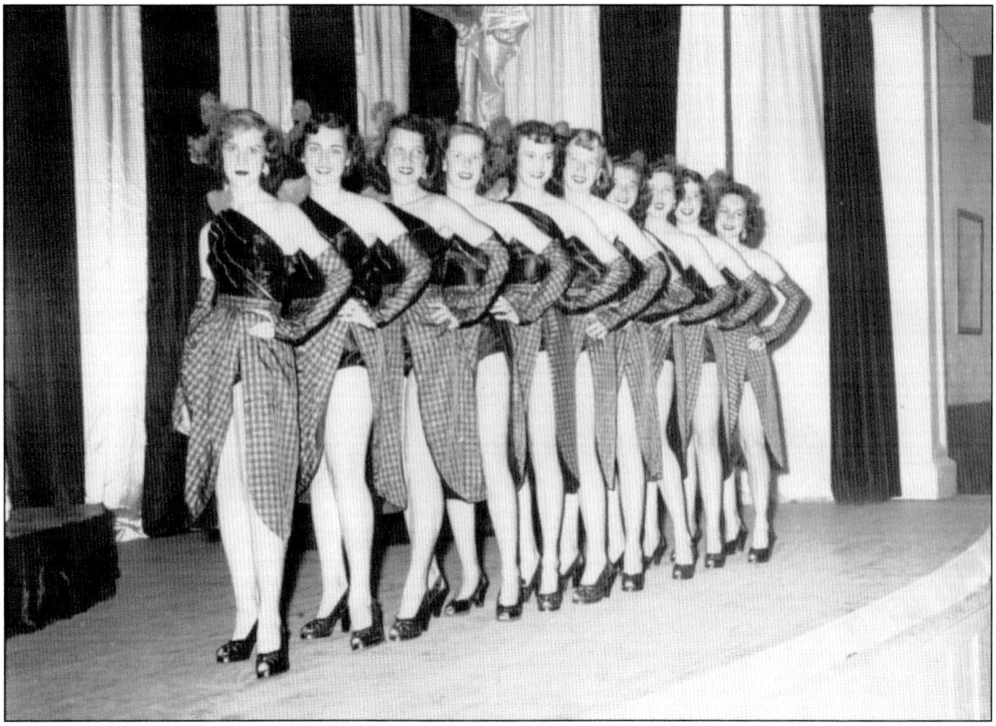

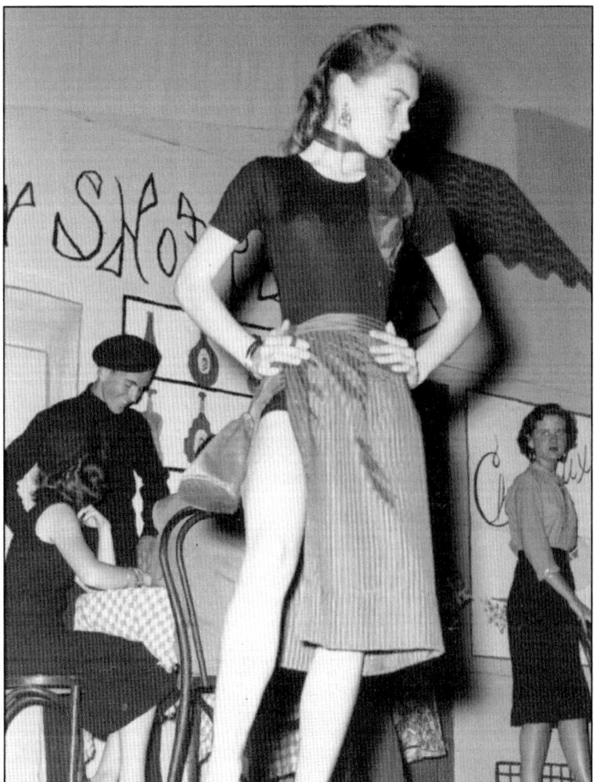

The girls of the short chorus line in the 1954 *Great Day* revue strike a pose for the annual photograph. One alumnus observed that St. Andrew's had *Glee* before there was a *Glee*. The St. Andrew's Parish High School Players Club was originally called the Dramatic Club and was the most popular club at the school according to Barbara Blank, who was a member of the tap chorus that danced in the Players Club Musical Revue. (Courtesy of Barbara Blank Gilchrist.)

Delores Pearson strikes a pose during the dance routine "Paris After Dark" in the 1955 *Road Show* revue. The students, under Mr. Hester's direction went to elaborate detail in costumes, staging, and choreography. Everyone at the school loved the football and basketball games, but the revues were the highlight of each school year. (Courtesy of Barbara Blank Gilchrist.)

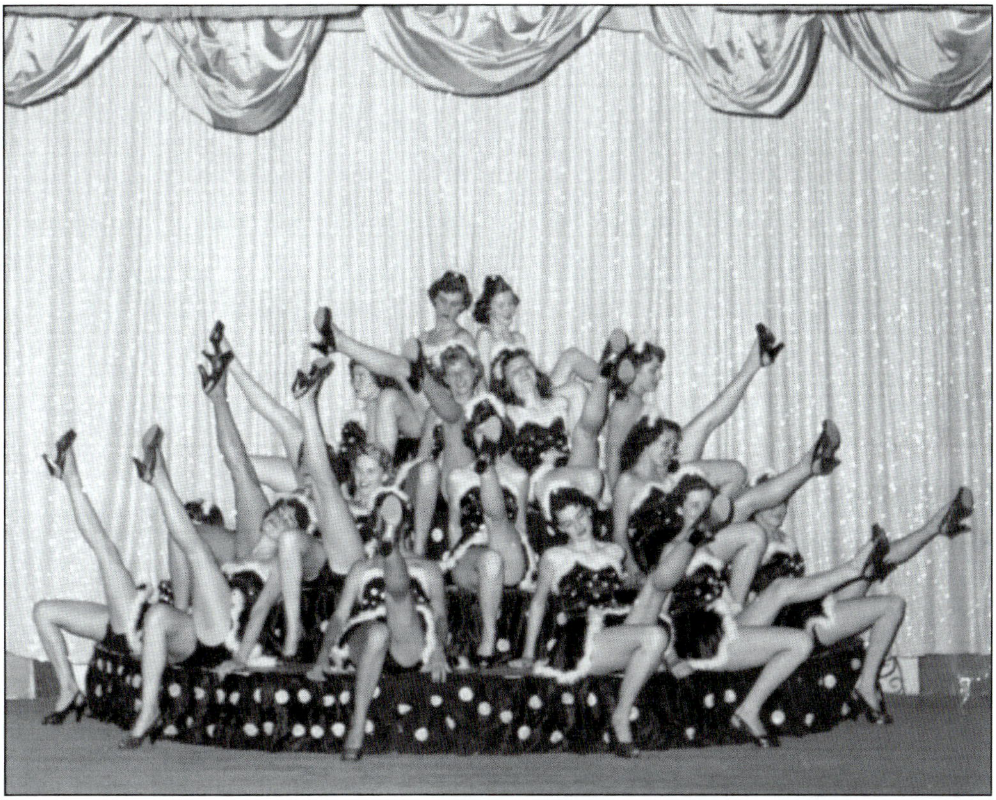

The dancers, dressed in costumes decorated with mirrors, kick up their heels in "Broadway Melody," one of the dance routines from the 1955 revue *Road Show*. The first musical revue produced by Bernard Hester and his dramatic club was *Blitzkreig* in 1941. (Courtesy of Barbara Blank Gilchrist.)

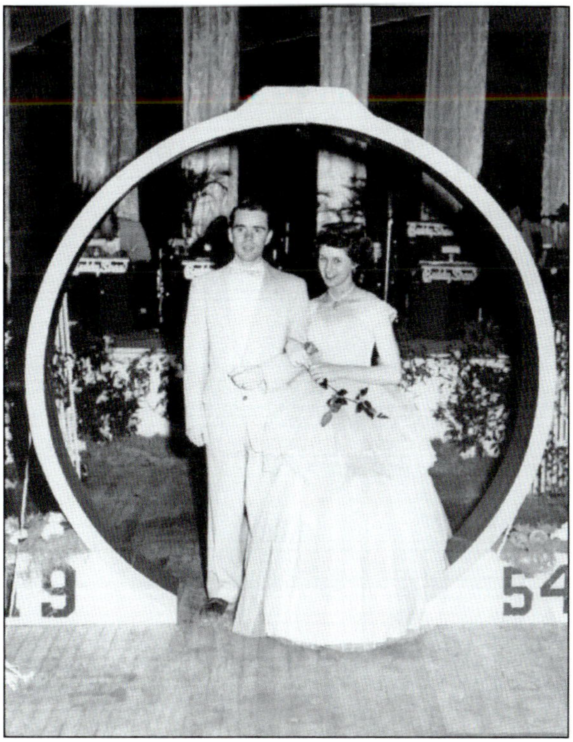

John Gilchrist escorted Barbara Blank to the 1954 ring hop held in the school auditorium. The Buddy Shaw Band played for the hop. Barbara and John later married, and John studied to become an Episcopalian Priest. Their courtship included stopping for sodas at Red and Bertha's on Savannah Highway. They returned after seminary school when John was appointed the Rector at Old St. Andrew's Parish Church. (Courtesy of Barbara Blank Gilchrist.)

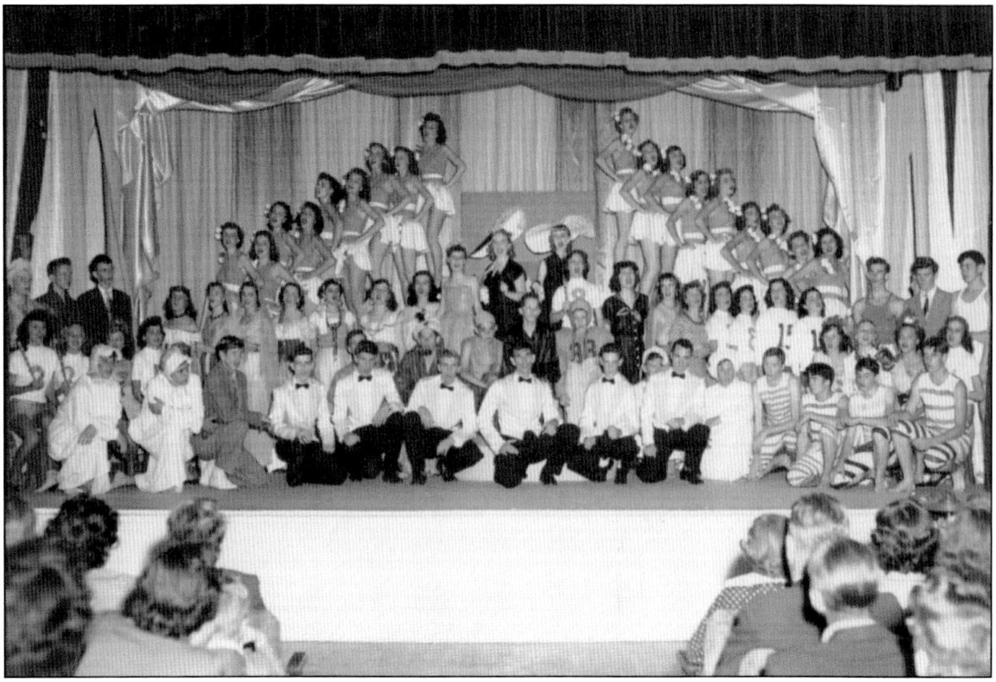

It is spring of 1952 and the entire cast of *Get Happy* gathers on the stage for the finale and final applause. After the show, Mr. Hester hosted a party for the students at his home on Elliott Street in downtown Charleston. Mr. Hester was known as a well-dressed individual and on occasion, the students would purchase clothes from Berlin's on King Street as a thank you for his commitment to them. (Courtesy of Stella Milton Kearse.)

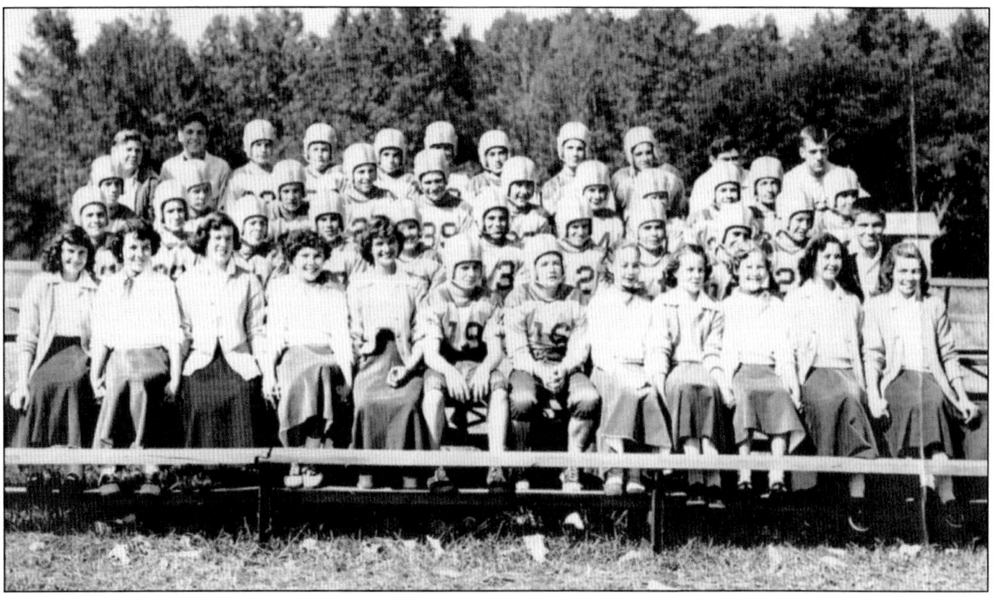

The cheerleaders of St. Andrew's Parks and Playground pose with the 1952 football all-stars on the playground bleachers. These all-stars were chosen from the middle school teams of St. Andrew's Parish. Delores Pearson was one of the cheerleaders. She continued cheerleading in her high school years and became head cheerleader her senior year. (Courtesy of Delores Pearson Rogers.)

Delores Pearson danced with Kenneth Gilliam in "Temptation," one of the numbers in the 1955 musical revue *Encore*. Delores recalls Mr. Hester's devotion to his students and these productions. He would often pick her up from her home in Byrnes Downs on his way to rehearsals from his home downtown. Kenneth would later work for his father at the ABC Awning Company. (Courtesy of Delores Pearson Rogers.)

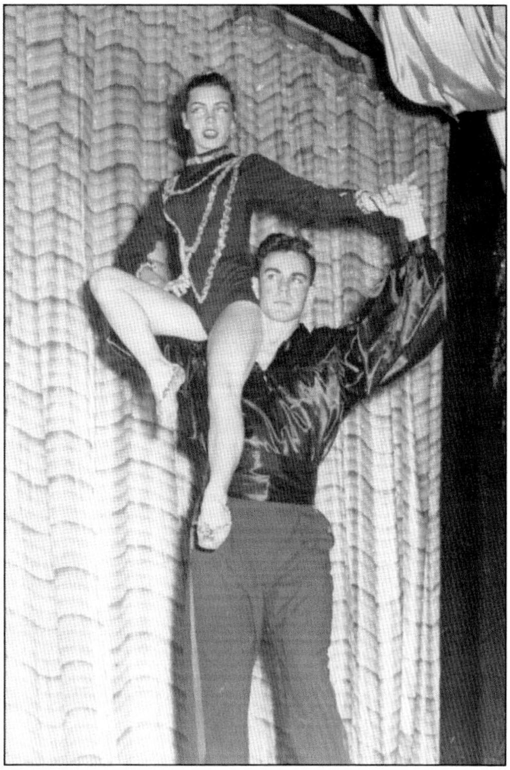

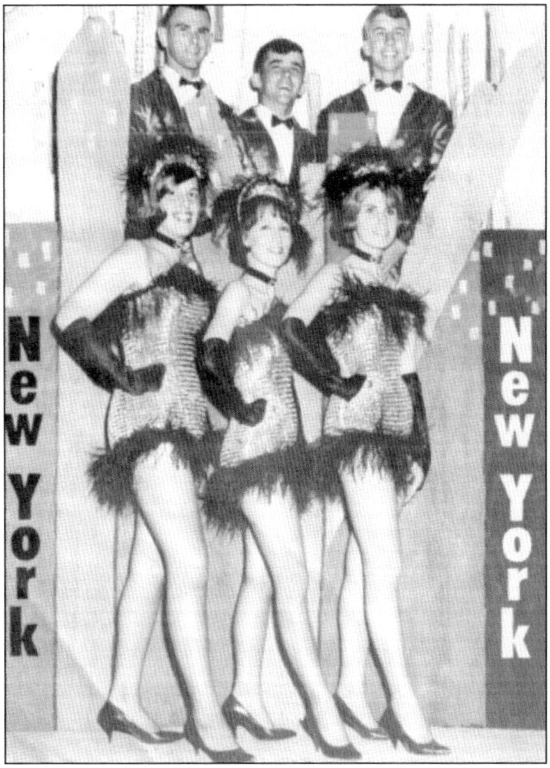

The St. Andrew's Parish High School Players Club's production of *New York, New York* was held in the auditorium in the spring of 1965. Mr. Hester's involvement in these shows was obvious, but he wanted the students to be responsible for the choreography. "New York, New York," "We'll Take New York," and "Manhattan Themes" were just a few of the numbers in the show. The cover of the *Playbill*, shown here, illustrates the costuming, staging, and fun that went into the revue. (Courtesy of Nancy Campbell Vick.)

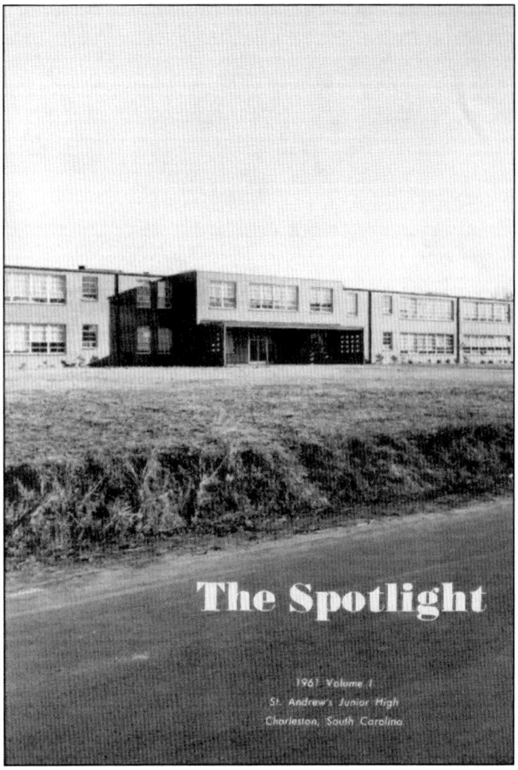

Saint Andrew's Junior High School was built in 1959. The annual, the *Spotlight*, celebrates the first graduating class of 1961 (notice Vol. 1). In 1963, C.H. Gilstrap was the principal and Lucius E. Platt was the assistant at the junior high school. Enrollment was recorded at 1,337 students. (Courtesy of Richard Bunch.)

Anna Wireman, the "Queen of Hearts" of all the students, was caught by surprise at the announcement crowning her Miss St. Andrew's for the 1964–1965 school year. The runner-ups were Hope Morris (No. 7) and Susan Odom (No. 8). Al Westerlund, senior class president, presented her with the traditional silver cup. Anna and her best friend, Cele, can regale for hours with their stories of growing up and going to school in St. Andrew' Parish. (Courtesy of Anna Wireman McAllister.)

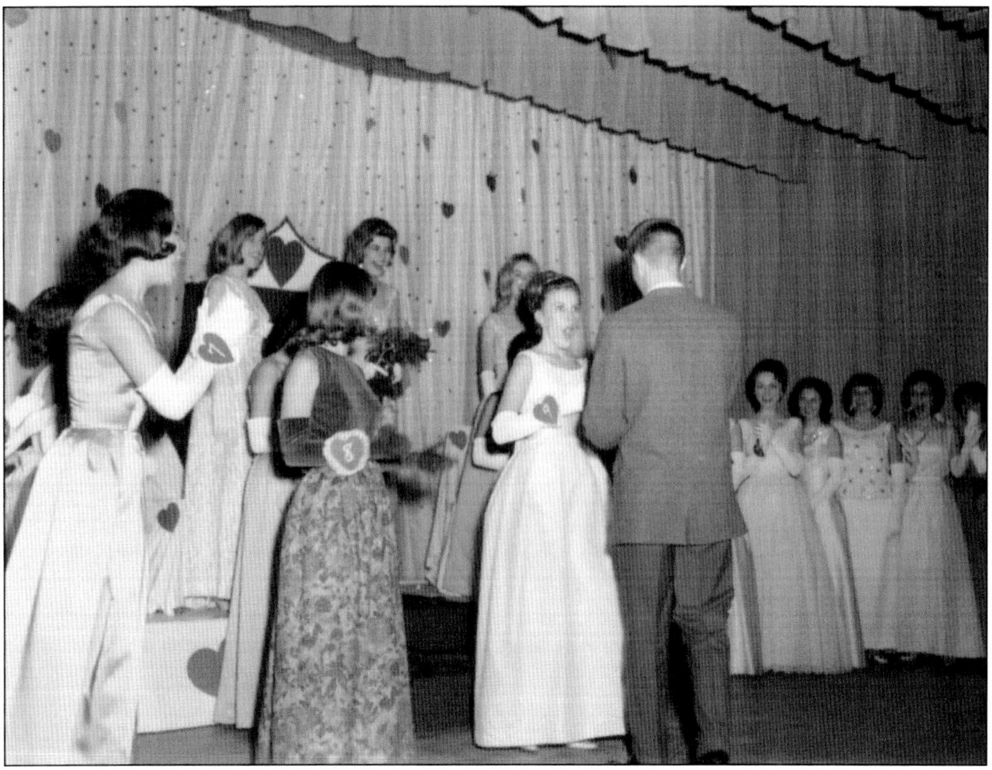

Five

Gathering Places

Open the door to a memory of having fun and people can enchant a listener with stories for hours. Soon, going to the movies at the Ashley Theater or Magnolia Drive-In, playing ball at St. Andrew's Parks and Playgrounds, dancing at the Cavallero, listening to Big Band music at Club 17, getting a red star on the receipt at Roy Hart's, gathering at Carter's or Bunch's gas station to catch up on the local buzz, planning hunting events, shooting in skeet competitions along the Ashley River, or just walking to the corner store for a soda are alive like it was yesterday and people are having fun west of the Ashley. The places to gather offer this opportunity and are forever etched in the memory fabric of the community. If one wanted to see friends, he or she went to these places and hung out. Many of the gathering places are gone or have been converted to other uses. Bunch's gas station, now Fiery Ron's Home Team BBQ; Bill's Holly House, now a golf cart store; Bootles Guest House, now a law firm; Cavallero, now a car dealership—but with a little prompting it can be like yesterday, when one enjoyed the barbecue, conversation out front, or dancing and a delicious steak. When asked, "Remember Roy Hart's?" the descriptions of chili, ham salad sandwiches, barbecue, milk shakes, and hot dogs create a delight in the voice and the face that is timeless. The location of a Roy Hart memory changes with each person. Come to find out, Roy Hart was affiliated with several establishments during his time in the restaurant business, delighting generations with his food and places to meet. And just about everyone will mention Roy Hart and Virginia, the lady who made the delicious chili, in the same breath. One gathering place has not been lost with time: the Owls' Roost on Bender Street in Ashleyville. The Roost still functions as the home of the Owls Whist Club. Soon, the club will celebrate its 100-year anniversary.

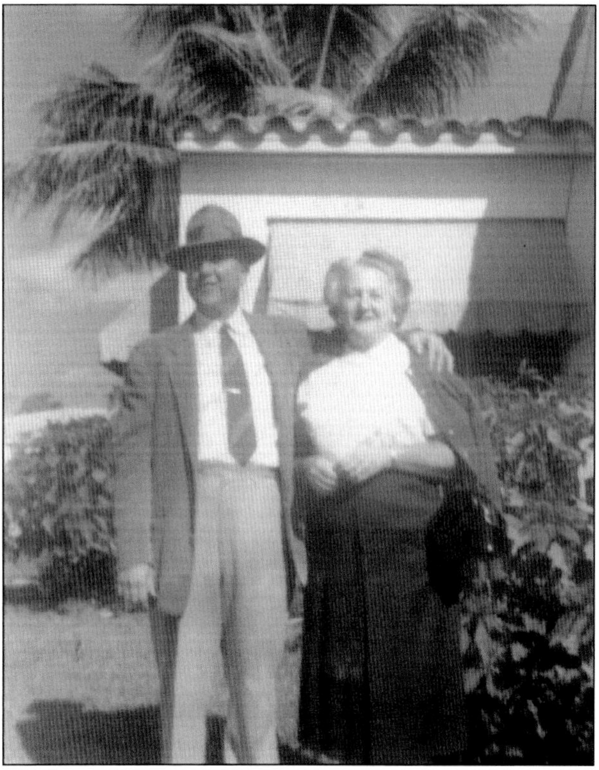

The 1961 Charleston City Directory lists Roy J. and Alma B. Hart on Lindendale Avenue in Avondale. Roy Hart memories would fill this book. Everyone has a unique perspective of the man, a distinct memory of his establishments, or affection for a particular menu item. Hot dogs with Virginia's chili, barbecue, milk shakes, or ham salad sandwiches are just a few. He was good to his employees and his customers, serving everyone with an equal attitude. Roy Hart served the community from three different sites: a drive-in on the south side of Savannah Highway near Coburg Road, a walk-up diner car located behind what is now the Triangle Char and Bar restaurant, and the soda fountain in the drugstore at South Windermere Shopping Center. (Courtesy of Ann Marie Holling Griffin.)

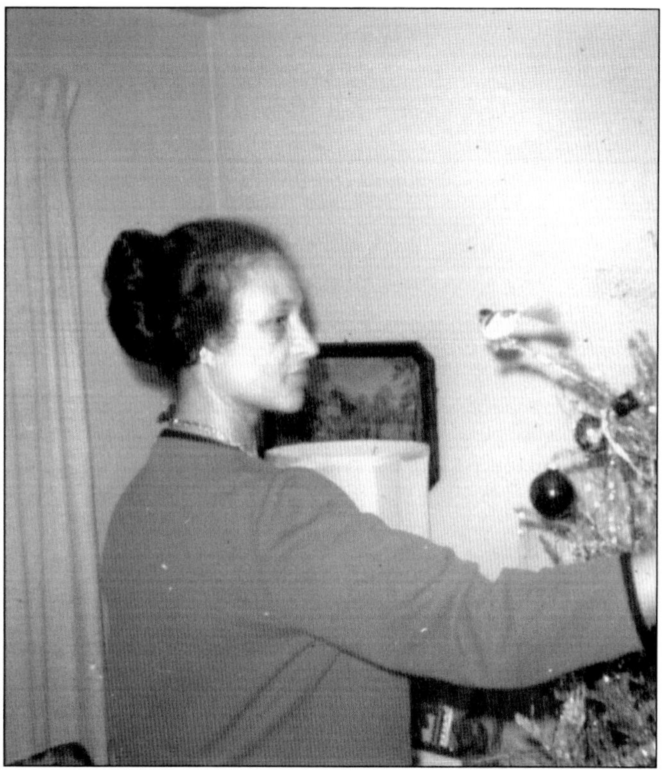

Virginia Wright Rouse worked for Roy Hart at his West Ashley location. According to the Charleston City Directory, the official name for his establishment was the Dairy Royal, but everyone called it Roy Hart's. Patrons and past employees speak of Roy Hart and Virginia in the same breath. Virginia lived in Maryville and loved to cook for her family on Sunday. However, in this photograph, she decorates her tree for Christmas. (Courtesy of Tony Wright.)

Tony Wright, known in the greater Charleston community as "the Peanut Man," is the son of Virginia Wright Rouse. Spicing food with love and care must run in the family. Virginia's chili was legendary. She shared this recipe with a patron who asked if she would give it to her. It contains simple ingredients, so the key secret ingredient must be in Virginia's touch. Maybe that same secret ingredient has found its way into the Peanut Man's boiled and roasted peanuts. (Right, courtesy of Tony Wright; below, courtesy of Delores Pearson Rogers.)

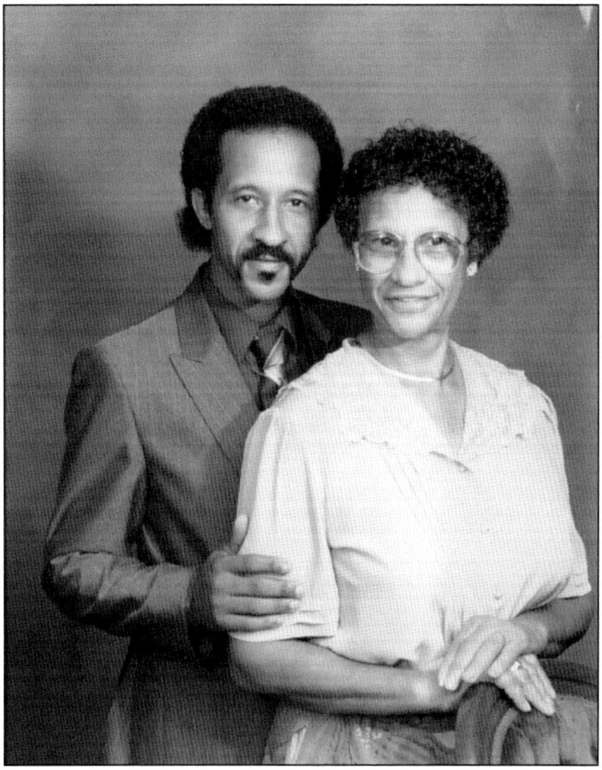

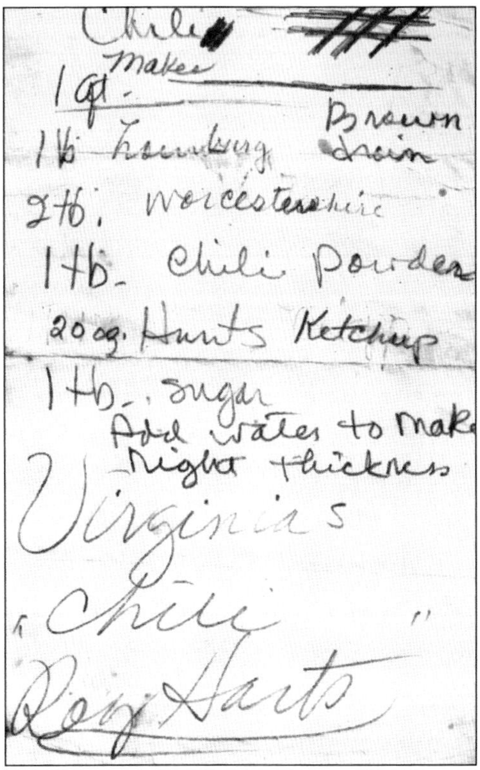

Chili
Makes
1 qt.
1 lb hamburg Brown drain
2 tb. Worcestershire
1 tb. Chili powder
20 oz. Hunts Ketchup
1 tb. sugar
Add water to make right thickness
Virginia's
"Chili"

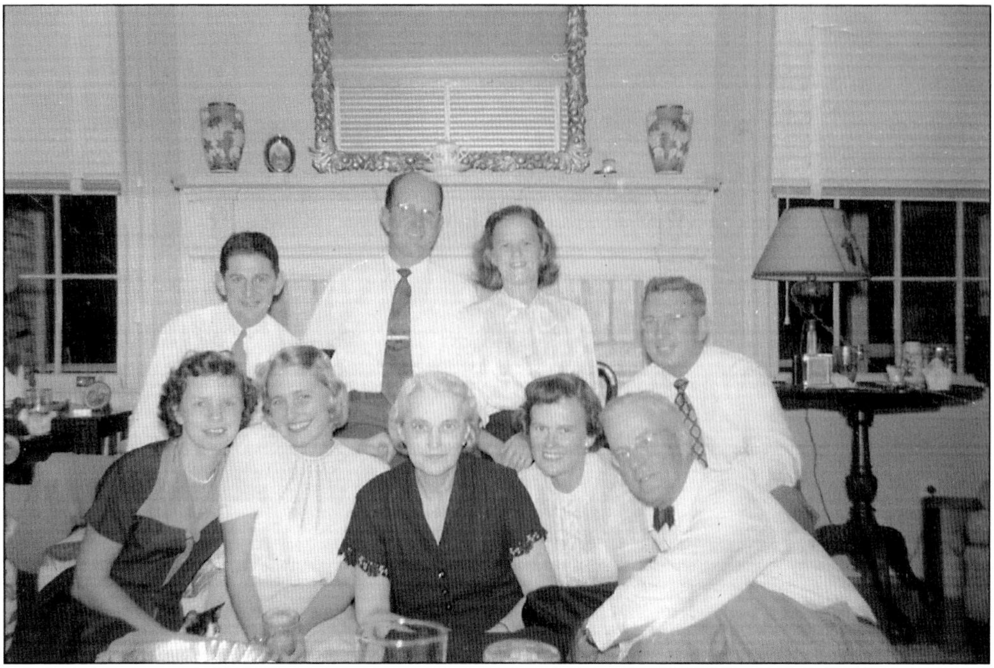

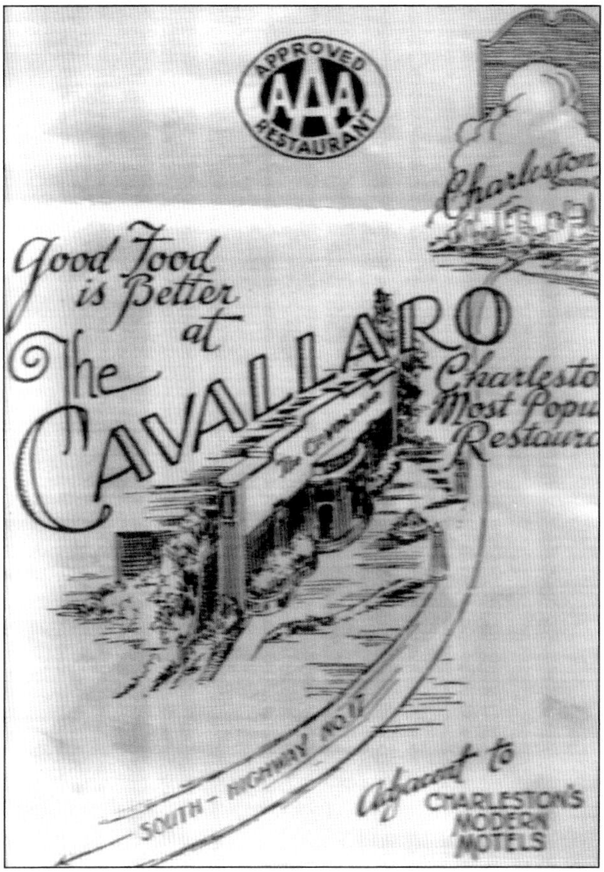

The occasion is T. Lesesne "Lit" Wilson's birthday. Having come to celebrate are, from left to right, (first row) Ruth Ellison, Anne Smith, Trudi Smith (Betty's mother) Mary Aitmar, and Bill Smith (Betty's father); (second row) Bill Ellison, "Lit" Wilson, Betty Smith Wilson, and Gene Johnson. Betty, Lit, Ruth and Bill were members of "The Supper Club" that began in 1944. After the end World War II, they would meet at the mess hall of the old POW camp on Colony Drive. (Courtesy of Betty Smith Wilson.)

The Cavallero was known as "the South's Finest and Most Modern Dining and Dancing Club." It was the place to go for great steaks prepared by Marcus Bloom and to enjoy live music and to dance. For New Year's Eve celebrations, prom nights, anniversaries, or special dates, people went to the Cavallero. (Courtesy of Sears Saul.)

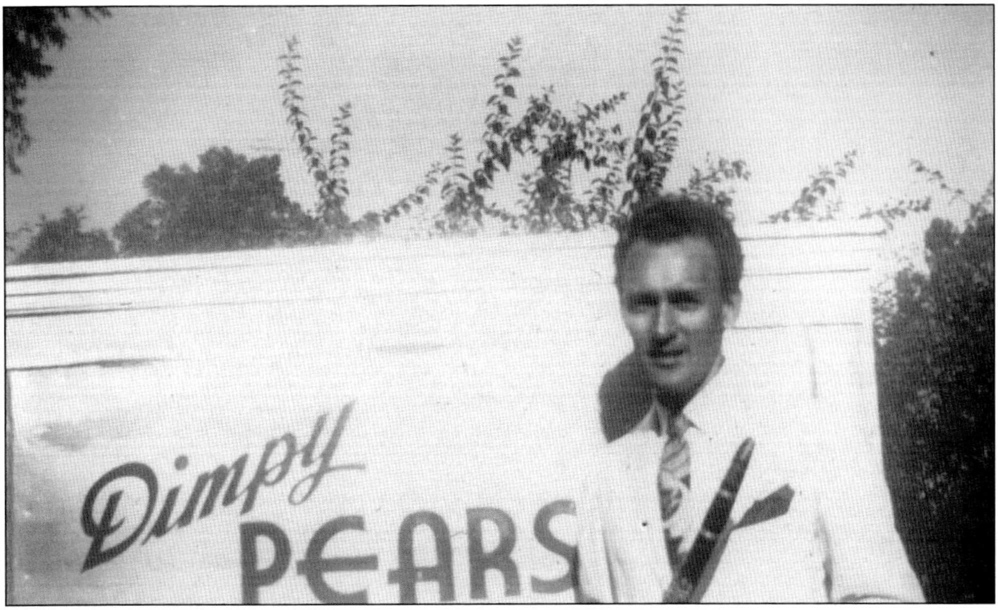

Dimpy Pearson poses with his clarinet next to his music trailer. Music was Dimpy Pearson's passion. He worked at Seigling's Music House, and played the clarinet in his dance orchestra, providing live music for school dances, weddings, and social functions. He was a Board Member of the Charleston Jazz Society. The Jazz Society mission was "to promote jazz and live music." (Courtesy of Delores Pearson Rogers.)

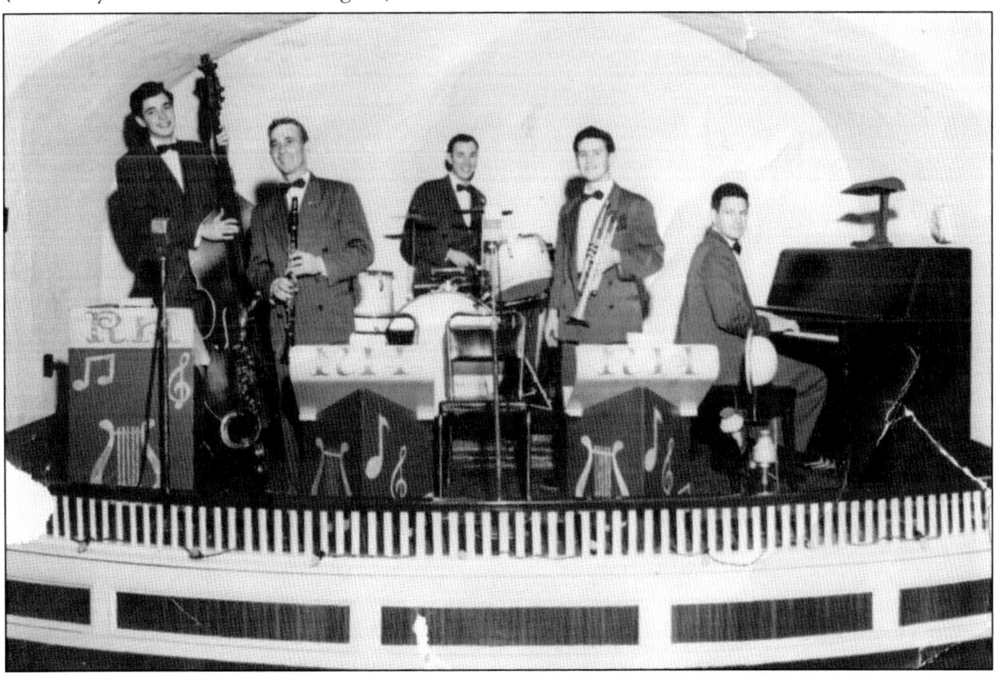

This image could be of a Friday night with Roy Heissenbuttle's band on stage in the band shell at the Cavallero. Lee Patillo is on the bass, Roy Heissenbuttle is on the saxophone, Wesley Mallard is on the drums, Willard Bolchoz is on the trumpet, and Ralph Peeples is on the piano. Ready to dance? (Courtesy of Martha Peeples Attisano.)

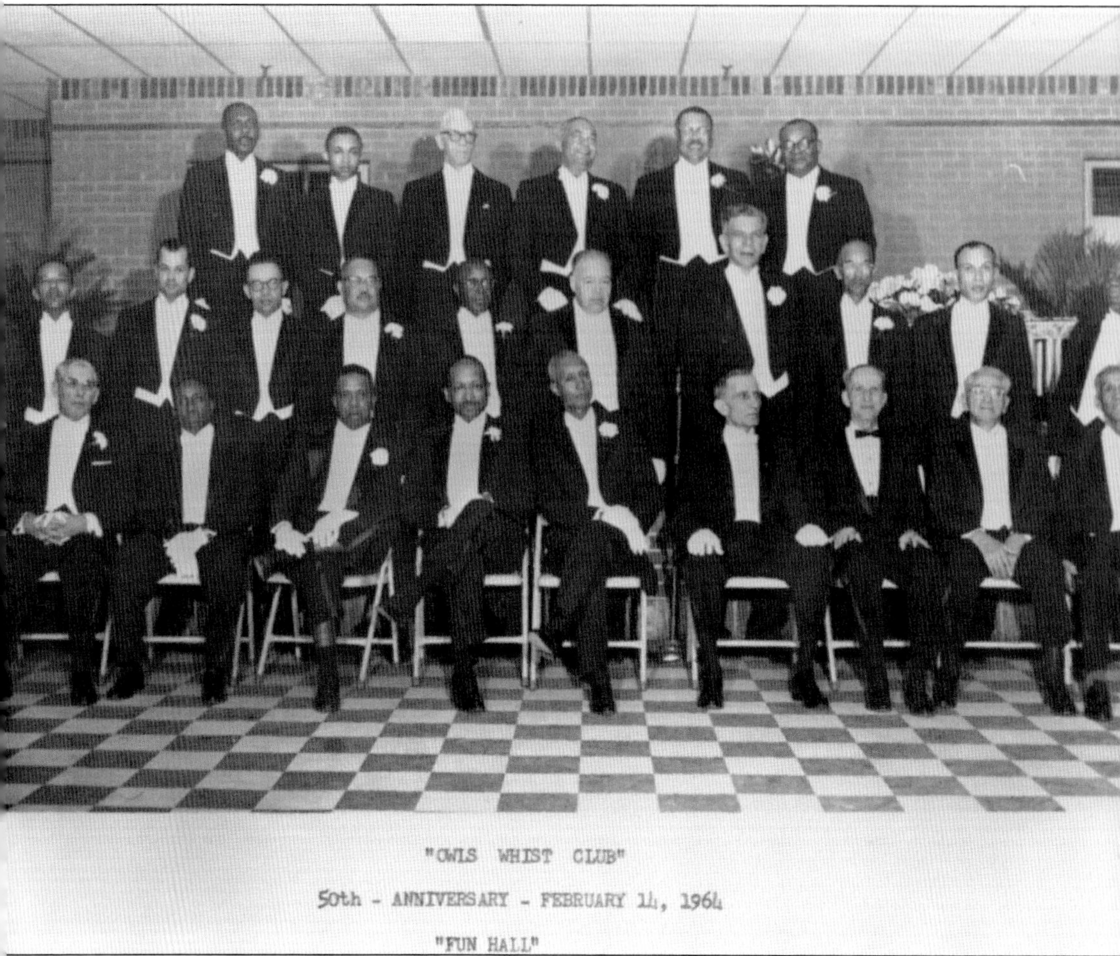

The Owls Whist Club first met at Frank Dawson's residence at 195 Smith Street in February 1914. The purpose of the club was social and initially limited to 16 members in order to make it convenient to play the card game Whist. In February 1964, members celebrated the 50th anniversary of the Owls Whist Club with a banquet and a ball. Dressed in the formal wear and ready for the event are, from left to right, (first row) Harold Mayzck, Eddie Jenkins, James Steward, Turner McCottry, J.R. Bonds, Paul Guenveur, Harry Guenveur, Granville Hurlong, and Joseph Miller; (second row) Crawford Huff, Bennett Caffey, H.A. DeCosta, J.T. Massey, W. Meriwether, J.I. Hoffman, Pinckney Ezekiel, Fred Brown, F. Hutchinson, and W. Frasier; (third row) James E. Brown, T.T. Carr III, A.T. Cornwell, W.W. Jones, T. C. McFall, and Luther Purvis. (Courtesy of the Avery Institute.)

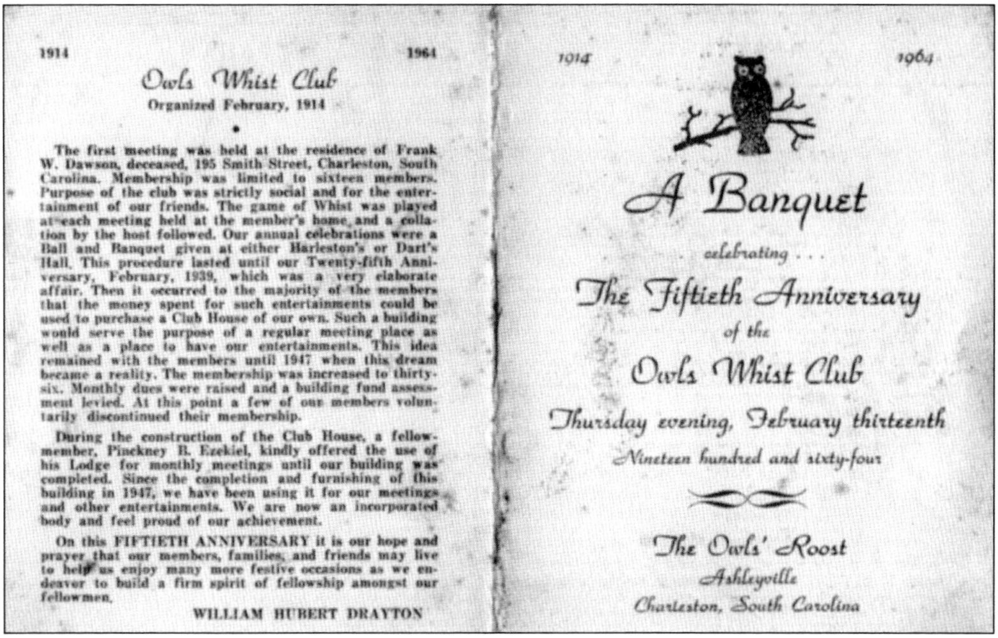

1914 1964

Owls Whist Club

Organized February, 1914

The first meeting was held at the residence of Frank W. Dawson, deceased, 195 Smith Street, Charleston, South Carolina. Membership was limited to sixteen members. Purpose of the club was strictly social and for the entertainment of our friends. The game of Whist was played at each meeting held at the member's home, and a collation by the host followed. Our annual celebrations were a Ball and Banquet given at either Harleston's or Dart's Hall. This procedure lasted until our Twenty-fifth Anniversary, February, 1939, which was a very elaborate affair. Then it occurred to the majority of the members that the money spent for such entertainments could be used to purchase a Club House of our own. Such a building would serve the purpose of a regular meeting place as well as a place to have our entertainments. This idea remained with the members until 1947 when this dream became a reality. The membership was increased to thirty-six. Monthly dues were raised and a building fund assessment levied. At this point a few of our members voluntarily discontinued their membership.

During the construction of the Club House, a fellow-member, Pinckney B. Ezekiel, kindly offered the use of his Lodge for monthly meetings until our building was completed. Since the completion and furnishing of this building in 1947, we have been using it for our meetings and other entertainments. We are now an incorporated body and feel proud of our achievement.

On this FIFTIETH ANNIVERSARY it is our hope and prayer that our members, families, and friends may live to help us enjoy many more festive occasions as we endeavor to build a firm spirit of fellowship amongst our fellowmen.

WILLIAM HUBERT DRAYTON

1914 1964

A Banquet

celebrating . . .

The Fiftieth Anniversary

of the

Owls Whist Club

Thursday evening, February thirteenth

Nineteen hundred and sixty-four

The Owls' Roost

Ashleyville

Charleston, South Carolina

The Owls Whist Club's 50th anniversary banquet was held at the Owls' Roost in Ashleyville. The program outlines the events for the evening, honors the members, and celebrates the history of the club. (Courtesy of the Avery Institute.)

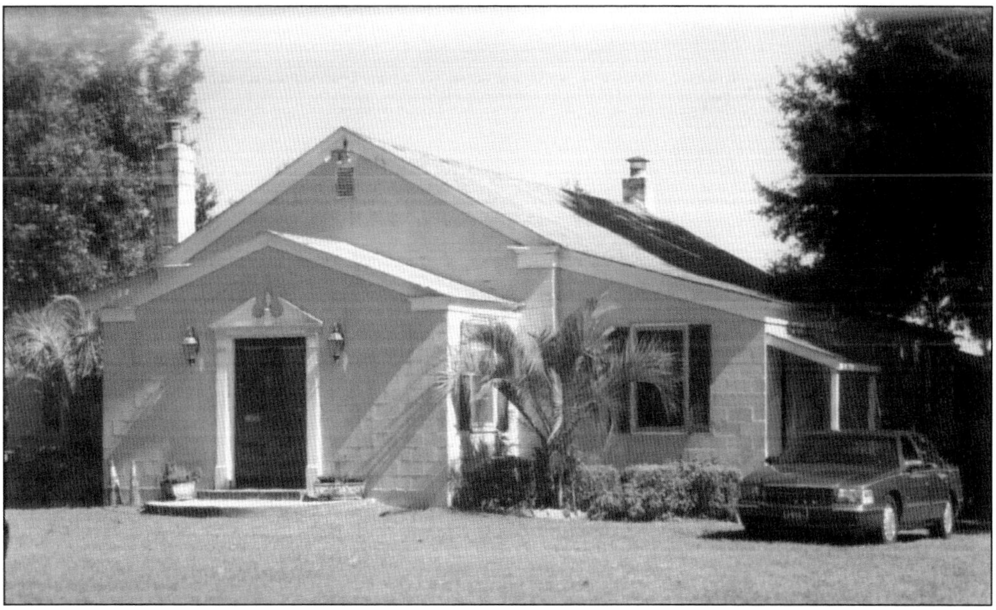

The Owls' Roost is located on Bender Street (previously East Bay Street) in Ashleyville with a splendid view of the Ashley River. The dream of a clubhouse began after the 25th anniversary celebration in 1939. In 1947, the dream became a reality; the club expanded to 36 members, increased dues, and levied a building fund assessment. The plat for the clubhouse was recorded in the Register of Mesne Conveyance Office in June 1947. It describes a one-story cinder block building on two lots "located between East Bay Street and the marshes of the Ashley River in Maryville." (Courtesy of Author.)

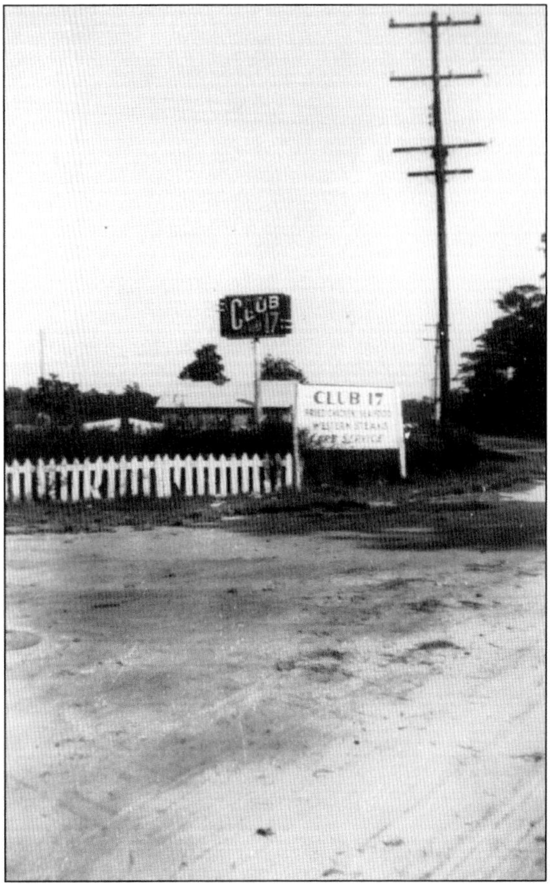

Who remembers Club 17 located adjacent to the Old Town Motor Court on Savannah Highway? Maybe the lady singing or the musicians in the band with the "BJ" logo are recognizable? Dan and Carnice Groves added Club 17 to the Old Town Motor Court property after they purchased it in the late 1940s. On occasion, Carnice's brother James Bernardo Jennings would play the drums at the club. The club featured Big Band music and was only opened on the weekends. The sign advertises fried chicken, seafood, Western steaks, and curb service. (Both, courtesy of Yvonne Groves Gilreath.)

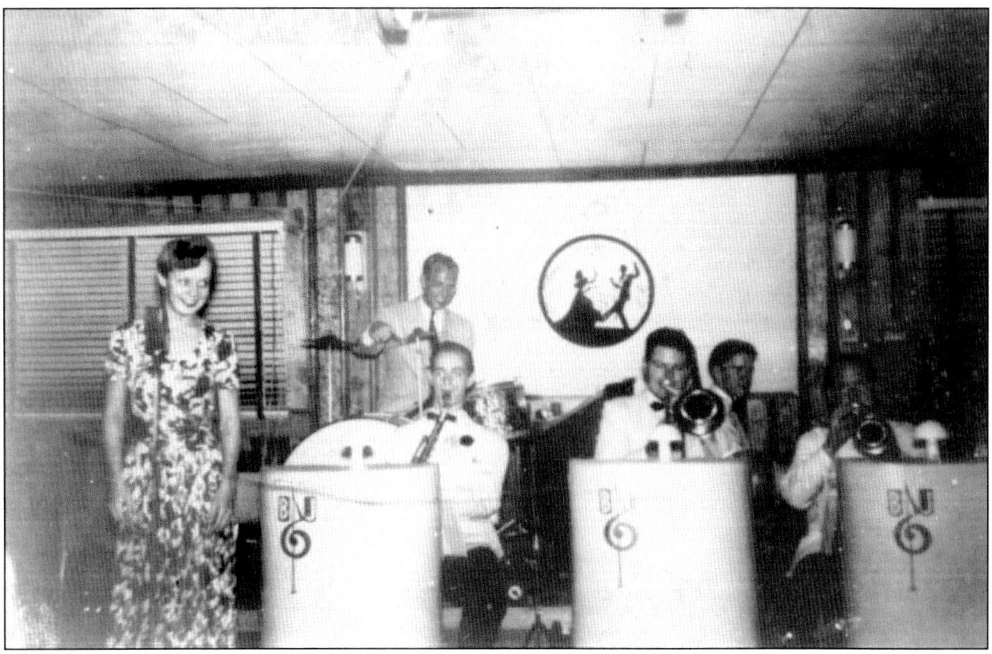

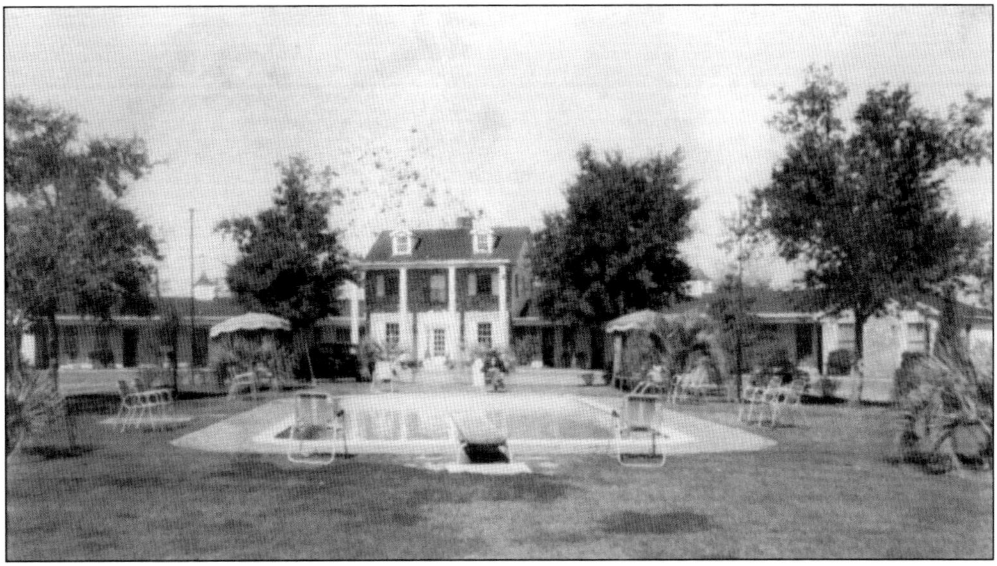

Dan Groves upgraded the Old Town Motor Court, tore down the cabins, and ultimately built the Camilla Motel on the corner of Savannah Highway and White Oak Drive in 1950. It was known for having the first motel pool on Highway 17 in South Carolina. Prior to the expansion into the hotel business in West Ashley, Dan operated a service station at the corner of Meeting Street and South Market, served in World War II, and was a partner in the Anchor located in downtown Charleston. (Courtesy of Yvonne Groves Gilreath.)

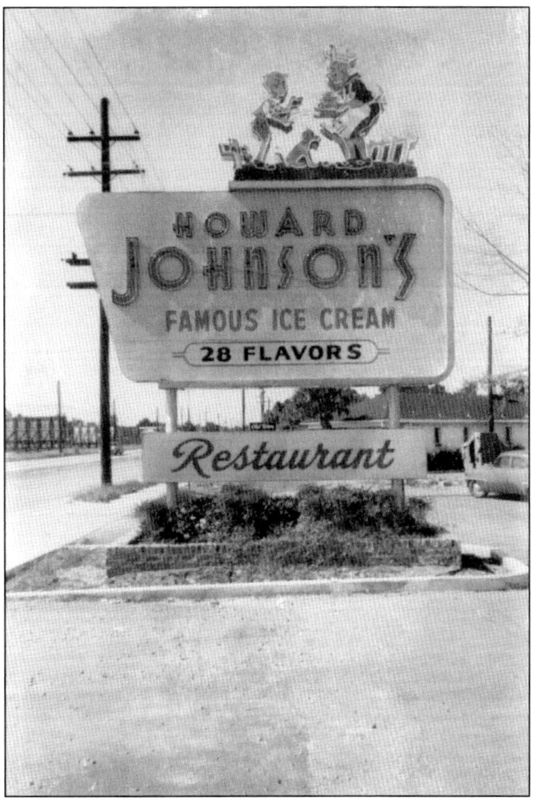

On the site where the Old Town Motor Court restaurant and cabins were located, Dan and Carnice constructed a lower profile building that would become Howard Johnson's. Their granddaughter Vonie Gilreath recalls sitting on the high dive board at the motel pool and watching the movies at the Magnolia Drive-in Theater. (Courtesy of Yvonne Groves Gilreath.)

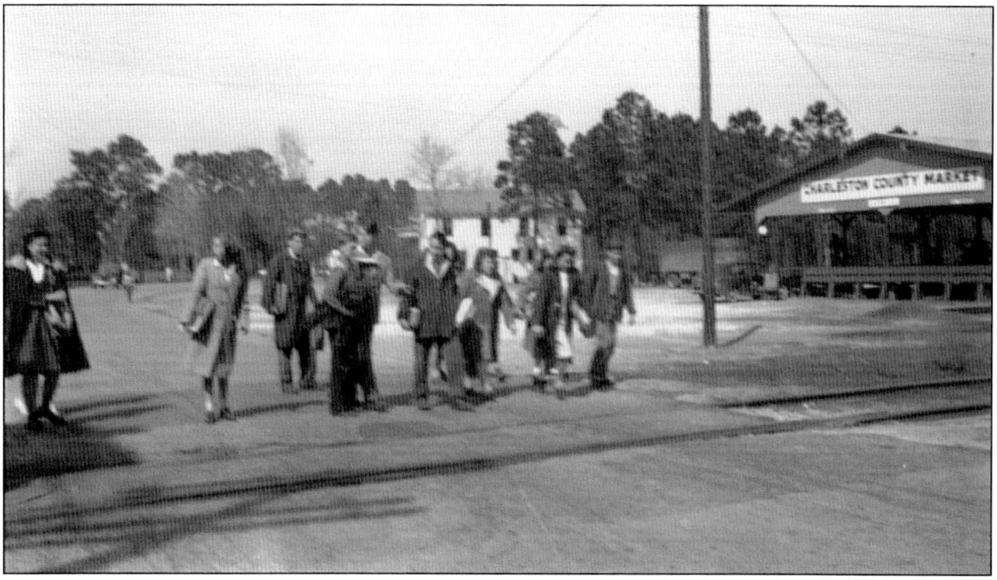

At the corner of Wappoo Road and Savannah Highway were several places to buy a soda and hang out. Students from St. Andrew's Parish High School would often take advantage of this fact and walk from the school. (Courtesy of P. Luther Bootle Jr., Ina Bootle.)

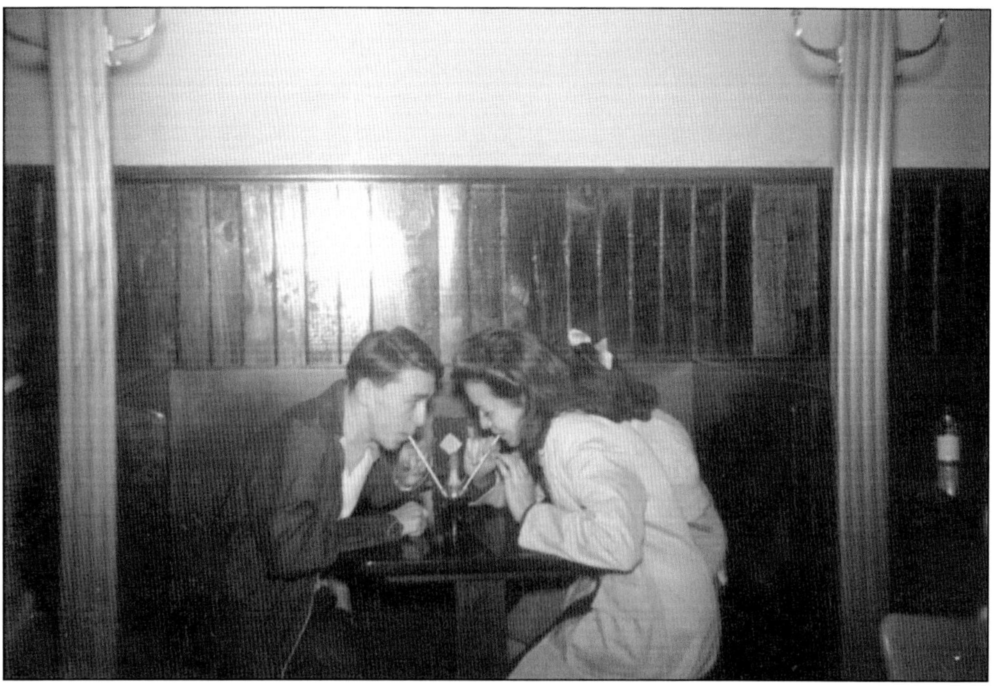

Luther Bootle shares a soda with a friend. Is this a timed photograph or did someone else take the photograph? Were they in one of the soda fountains in West Ashley or someplace in downtown Charleston? Luther photo-documented his senior year and yet only the negatives remain. (Courtesy of P. Luther Bootle Jr., Ina Bootle.)

Mr. Dotterer, owner of the County Store, and P. Luther Bootle share a moment at Bootle's Grocery. The Charleston County Market building can be seen out of the back door of the establishment. (Courtesy of P. Luther Bootle Jr., Ina Bootle.)

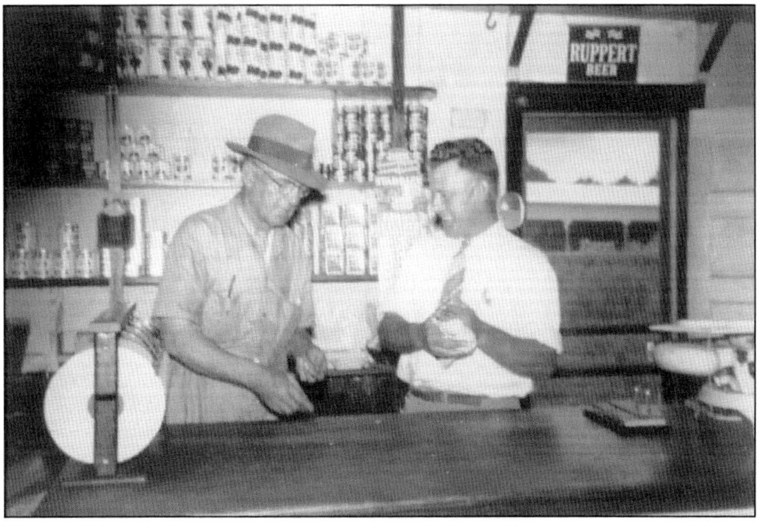

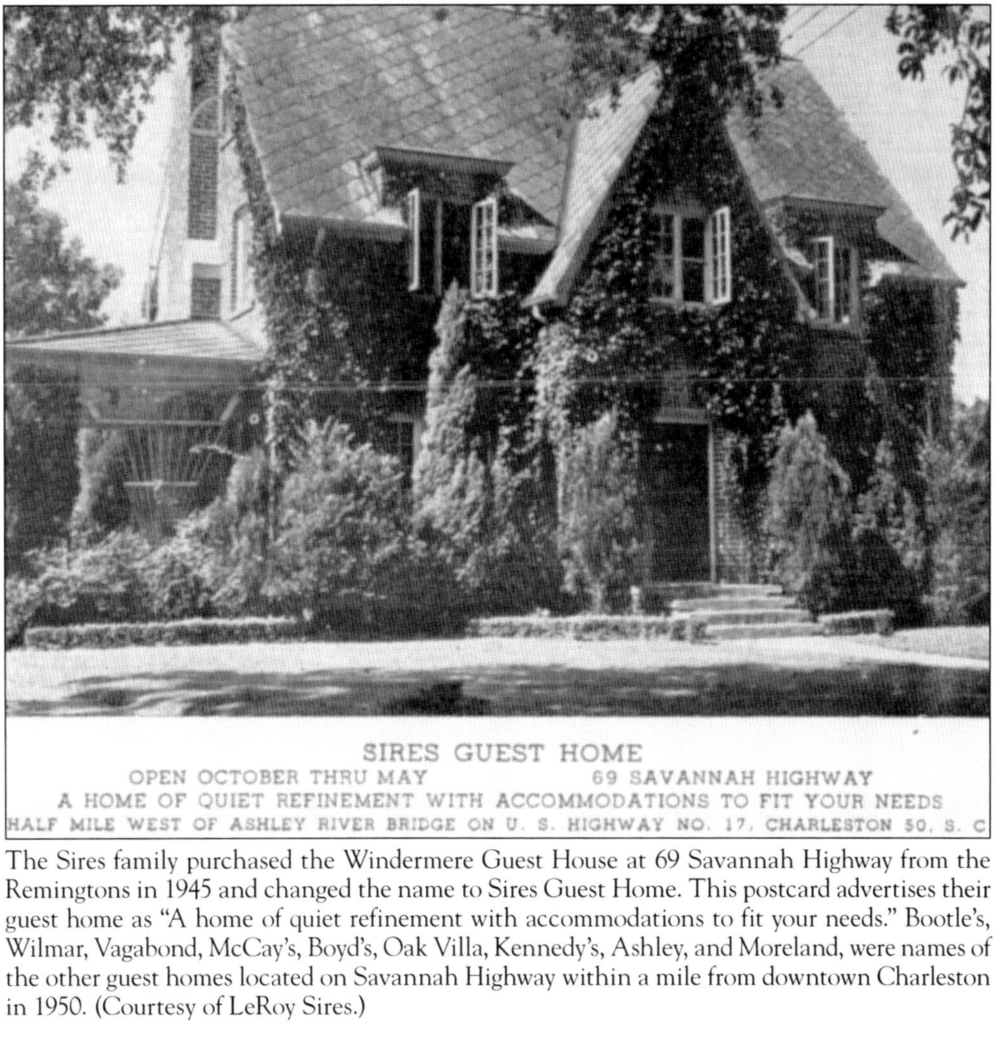

The Sires family purchased the Windermere Guest House at 69 Savannah Highway from the Remingtons in 1945 and changed the name to Sires Guest Home. This postcard advertises their guest home as "A home of quiet refinement with accommodations to fit your needs." Bootle's, Wilmar, Vagabond, McCay's, Boyd's, Oak Villa, Kennedy's, Ashley, and Moreland, were names of the other guest homes located on Savannah Highway within a mile from downtown Charleston in 1950. (Courtesy of LeRoy Sires.)

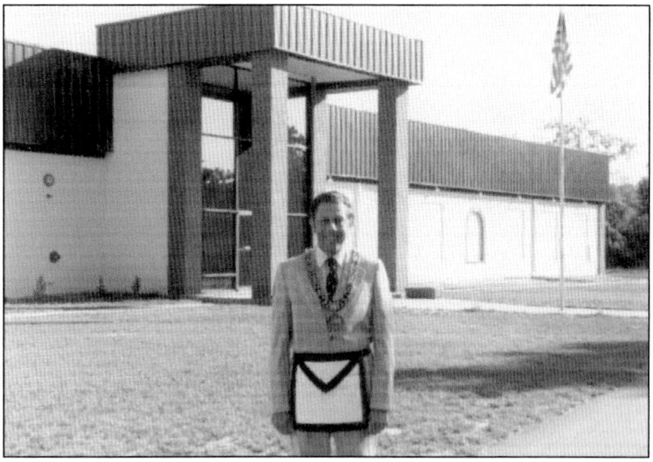

Herb Goldberg is a 33rd degree (honorary degree) Mason and a member of the Scottish Rite Masons that started in Charleston in 1801. Herb stands in front of the new Scottish Rite Building, west of the Ashley off Sam Rittenberg Boulevard. The Scottish Rite Foundation of South Carolina operates three Centers for Childhood Language Disorders throughout the state. (Courtesy of Herb Goldberg.)

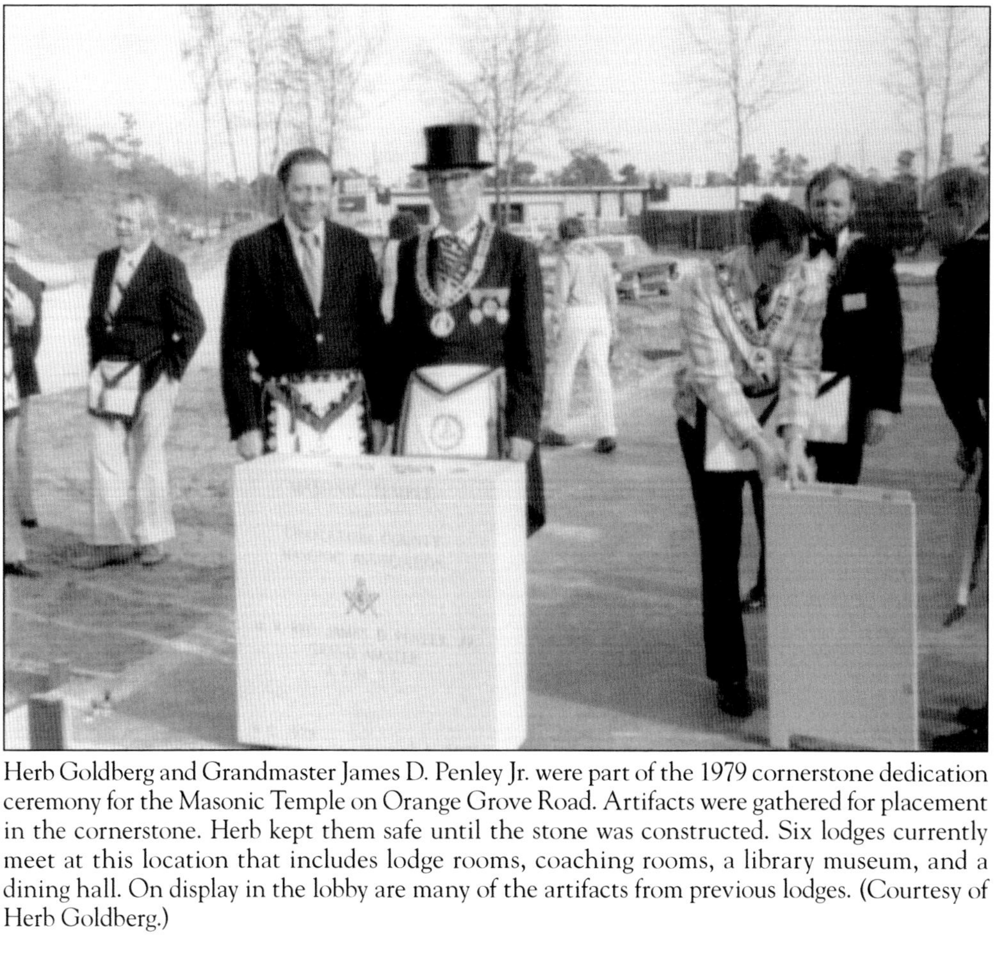

Herb Goldberg and Grandmaster James D. Penley Jr. were part of the 1979 cornerstone dedication ceremony for the Masonic Temple on Orange Grove Road. Artifacts were gathered for placement in the cornerstone. Herb kept them safe until the stone was constructed. Six lodges currently meet at this location that includes lodge rooms, coaching rooms, a library museum, and a dining hall. On display in the lobby are many of the artifacts from previous lodges. (Courtesy of Herb Goldberg.)

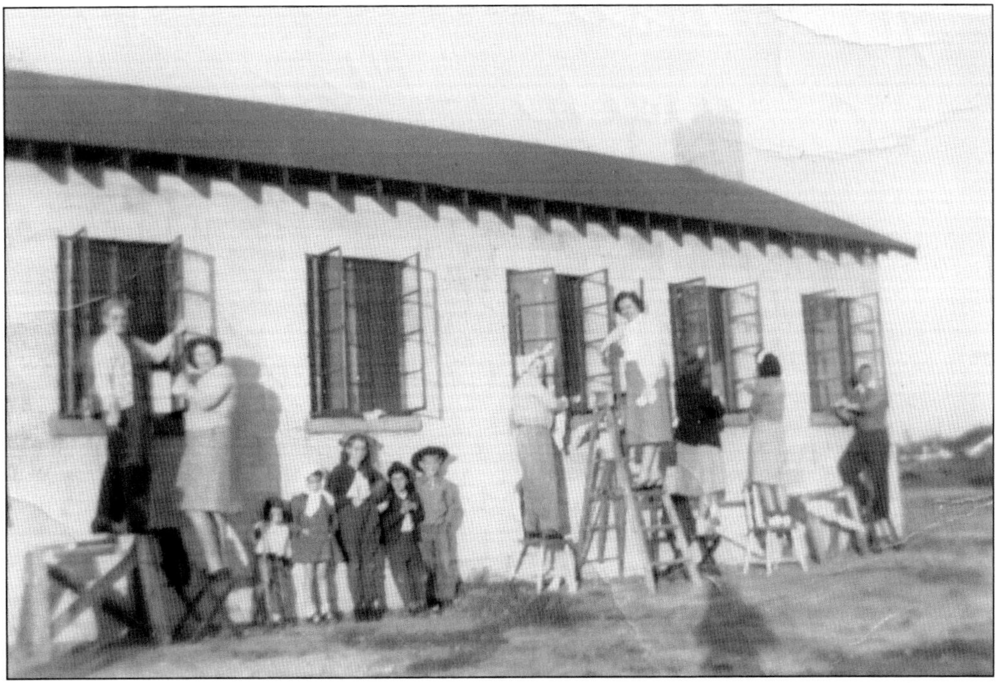

Many of the new neighborhoods formed civic clubs, neighborhood associations, or garden clubs soon after development. Stono Park was no exception. Members of the Stono Park Civic Club take a break from cleaning the windows at the Civic Club building to record the event on film. (Courtesy of Carole Clark Earhart.)

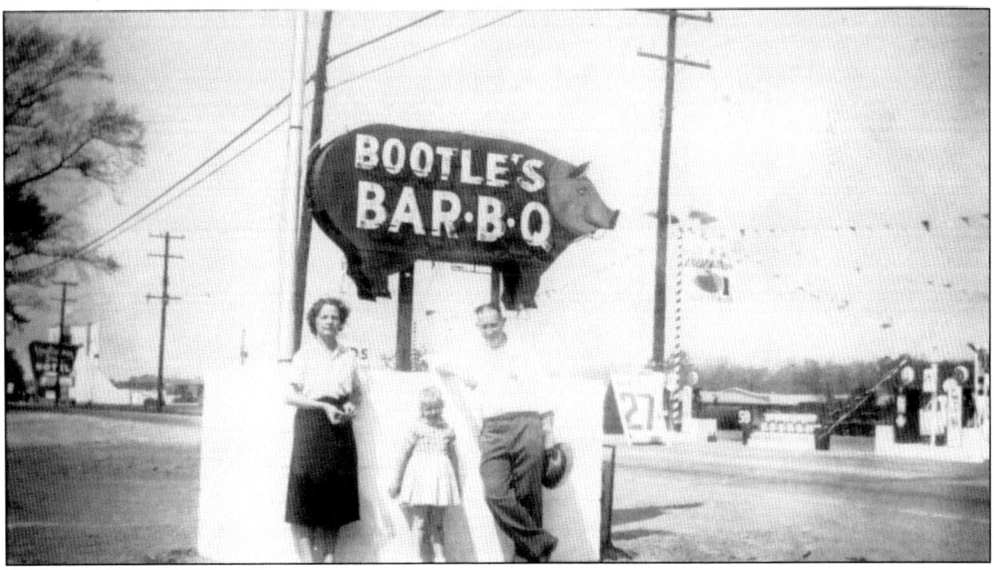

Sammie Bootle closed "the BBQ Stand" near the Ashley River Bridge on Sunday, February 20, 1955. At the grand opening of the new Bootle's Drive-In on April 20, 1955, free barbecue was served. Located two miles south of the original location, it was a popular hangout. Eugenia Price, the author of *St. Simons Memoir*, decided to move to St. Simons Island, Georgia, in the Bootle's parking lot after enjoying "those super barbecues." Eugenia would later write Sammie's daughter Ina and recount her life-changing experience in that parking lot. (Courtesy of Ina Bootle.)

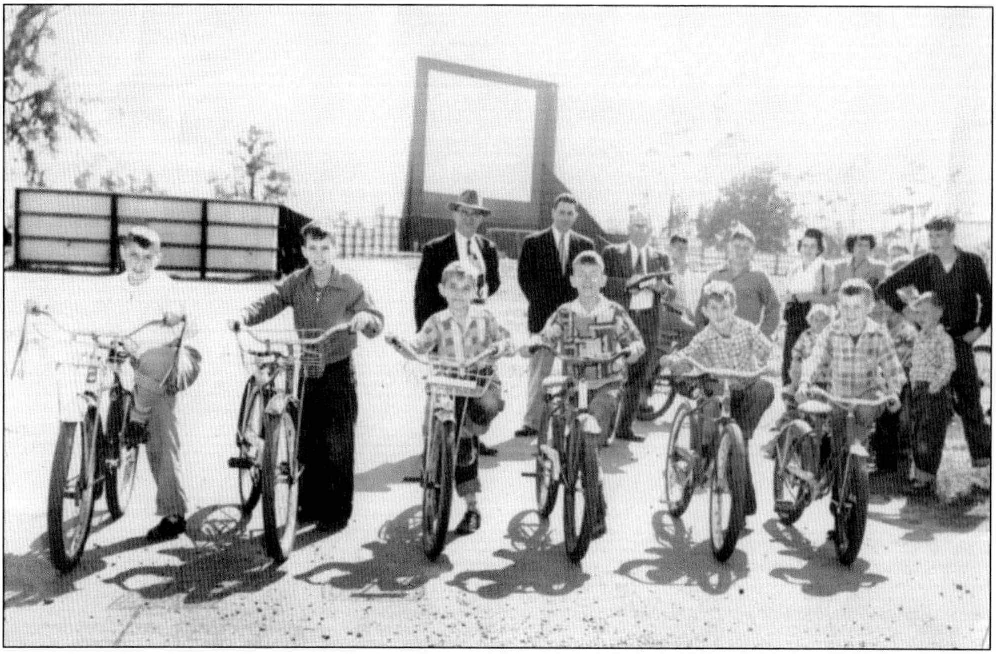

It is a bicycle rodeo at the Magnolia Drive-In Theater! The boys are lined up and ready to ride. The movie screen and speaker boxes provide the backdrop for the event. Bicycle Rodeos were one of many programs offered by the St. Andrew's Parks and Playground Commission. The South Carolina General Assembly formed this commission during the 1945 session. The commission grew out of a volunteer recreational council formed in the 1940s by area parents wanting to provide organized activities for the children. When the St. Andrew's Public Service District formed in 1949, one of its functions was assisting with finances for the commission. (Both, courtesy of St. Andrew's Parks and Playground Commission.)

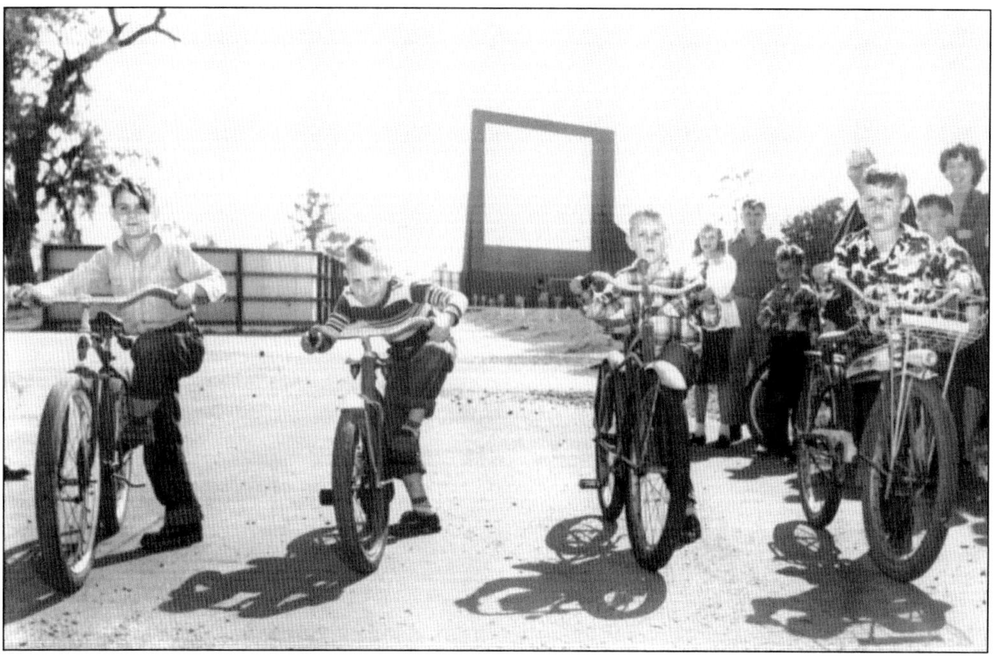

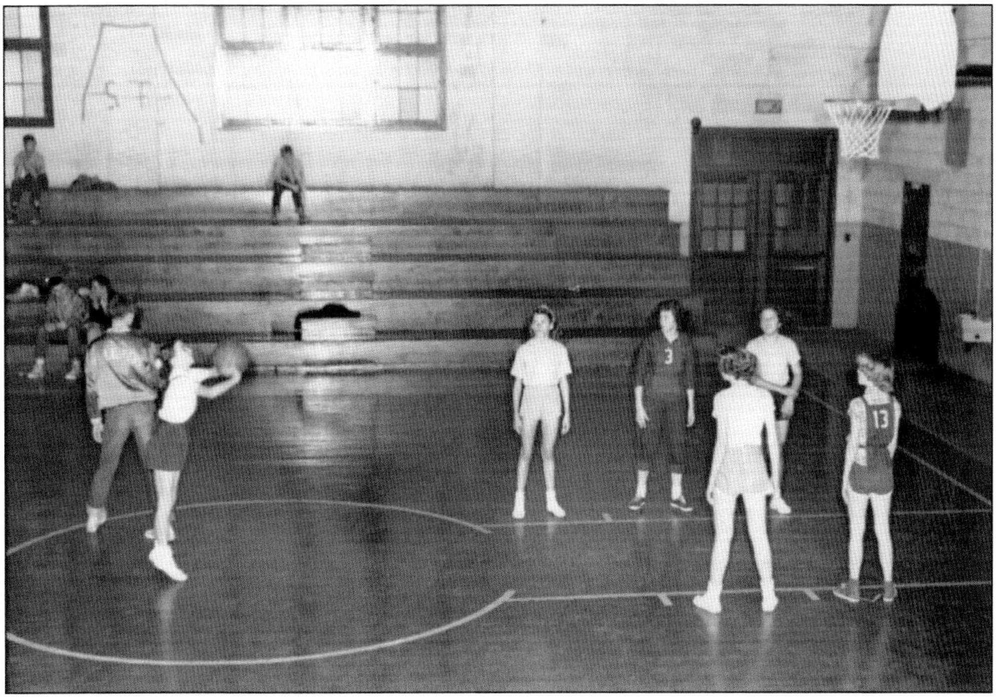

Basketball, football, softball, and baseball were some more of the organized activities provided by the St. Andrew's Parks and Playground Commission. The initial volunteer recreational council had raised private funds to acquire land for a ball field and recreation building on what will become Playground Road. In 1945, the 18.5 acres were deeded to the commission for $10. As the population of West Ashley grew, the commission developed additional recreational facilities throughout the Parish. Even though there was a formal organization to provide recreational opportunities, the volunteers and local leaders continued to play a vital role in the success of this organization. Charles M. Brinker was responsible for bringing the Little League program to the Parish, and the commission honored him by naming the community center's pony league and softball field the Charles M. Brinker Sr. Field. (Both, courtesy of St. Andrew's Parks and Playground Commission.)

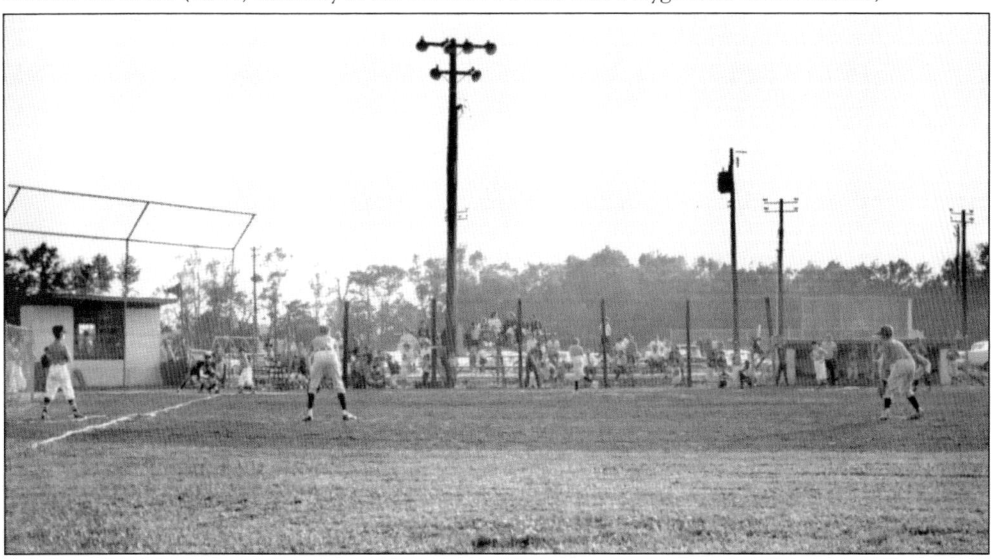

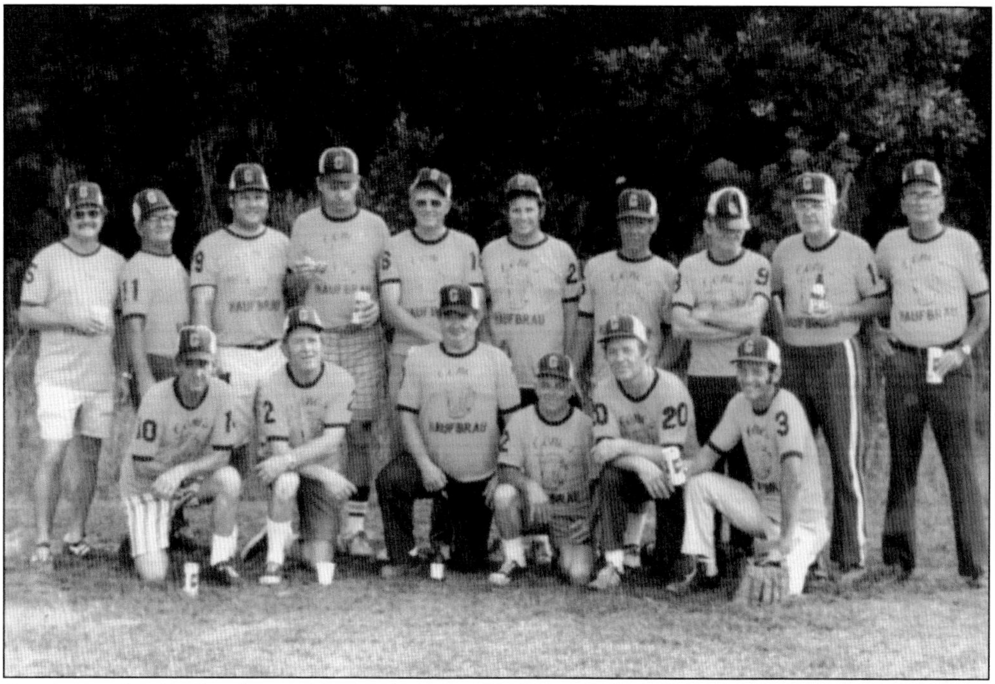

Summer and softball is the perfect combination for fun. Local establishments like Gene's Haufbrau and local businessmen like Richard M. Bunch and Bubba Weeks would sponsor teams during the season. (Above, courtesy of Anna Wireman McAllister; below, Richard E. Bunch.)

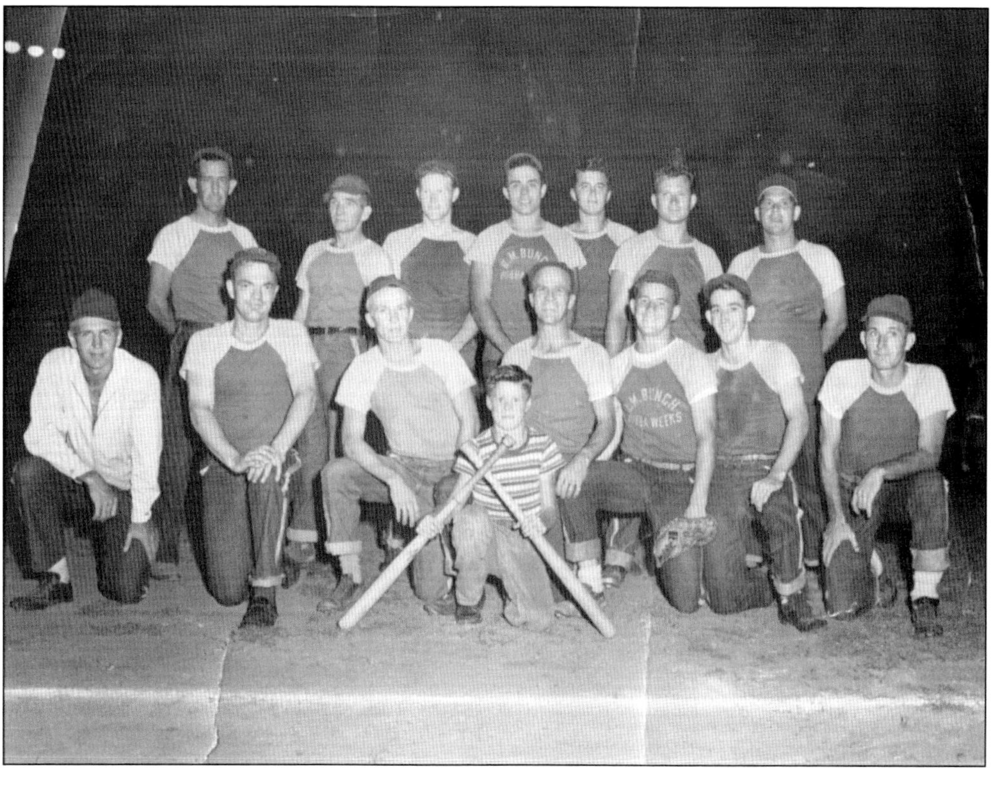

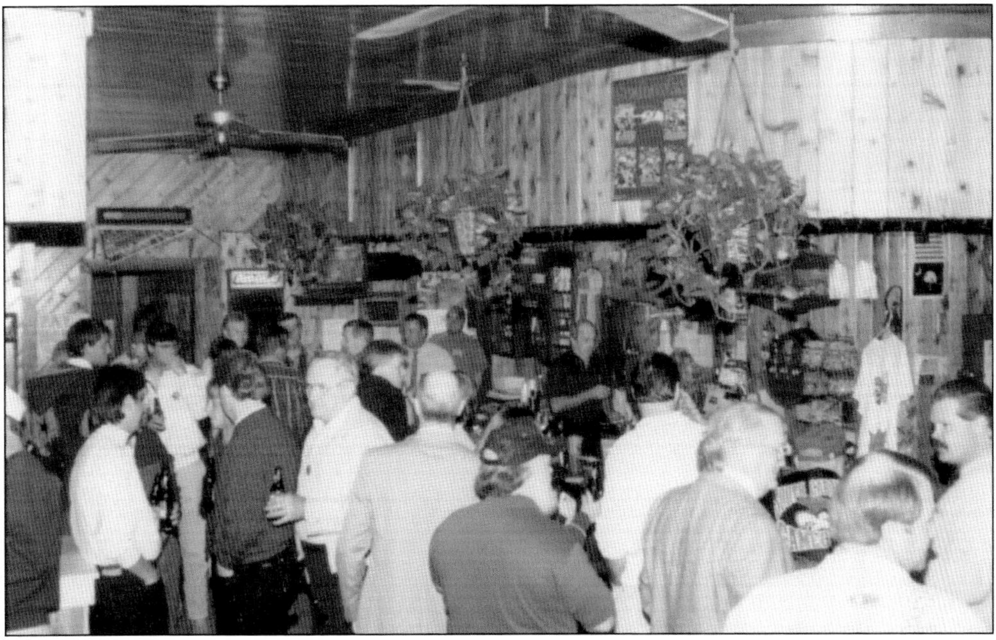

Gene's Haufbrau has been a popular hangout since the early 1950s. It was a place to go for a beer after work, watch a University of South Carolina Gamecocks football game, celebrate a local ball game victory, play shuffleboard, or compete in pool tournaments. Randy Mills, one of the previous owners of Gene's, stands in the far right of the above photograph during one of those game-day celebrations at Gene's. Samuel "Red" Blanton, second from left in the below photograph, discusses strategy during a pool game. Red and his wife, Camilla, lived in Byrnes Downs. (Both, courtesy of Randy Mills.)

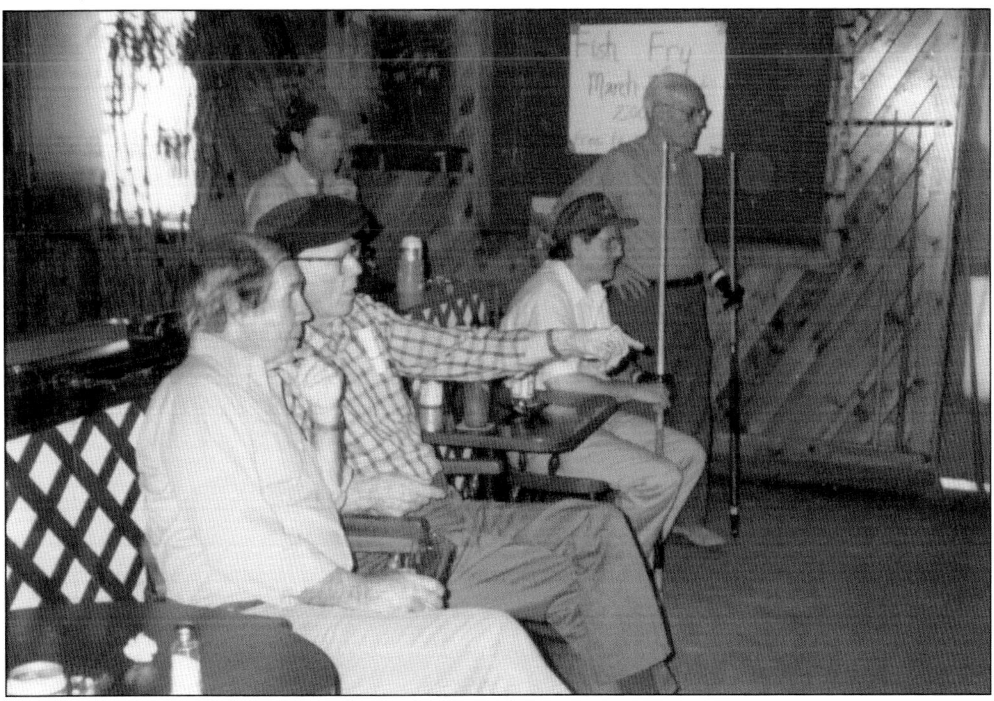

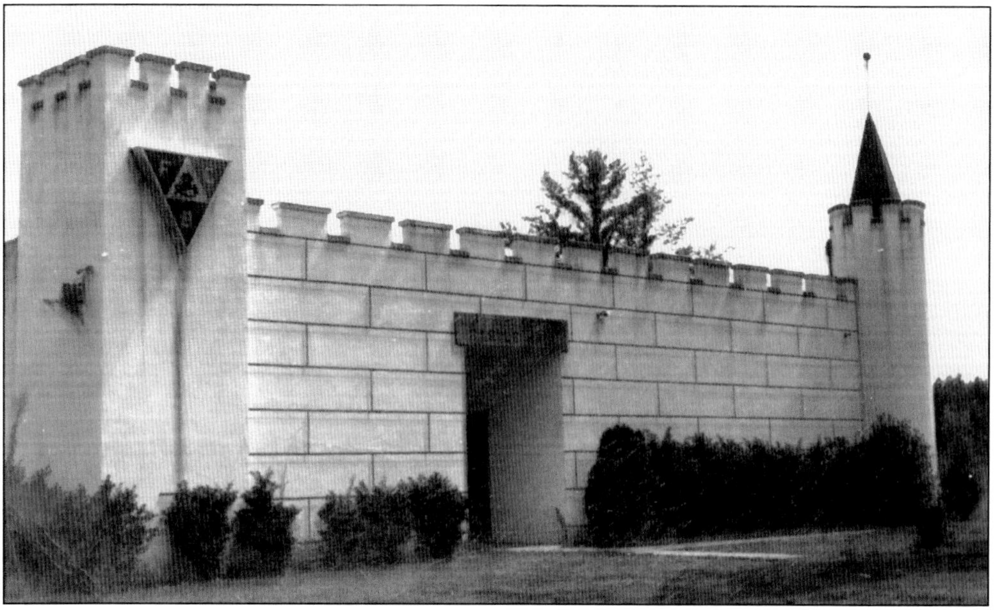

The Stonewall-Jasper Lodge No. 6 Knights of Pythias dedicated this new lodge hall in St. Andrew's Parish in April 1958. The Knights of Pythias is an international fraternal order established in 1864 in Washington, DC. The first Charleston lodge was organized in 1866 and was known as the "Stonewall Lodge No. 6." Three other lodges, Carolina Lodge No. 9, Calhoun Lodge No. 23, and Von Moltke Lodge No. 66 (later changed to Jasper Lodge) functioned in Charleston. In 1965, the Jasper and Stonewall Lodges merged to create the lodge that meets today. There are many memories past and present of social events held in this hall. (Courtesy of Yvonne Groves Gilreath.)

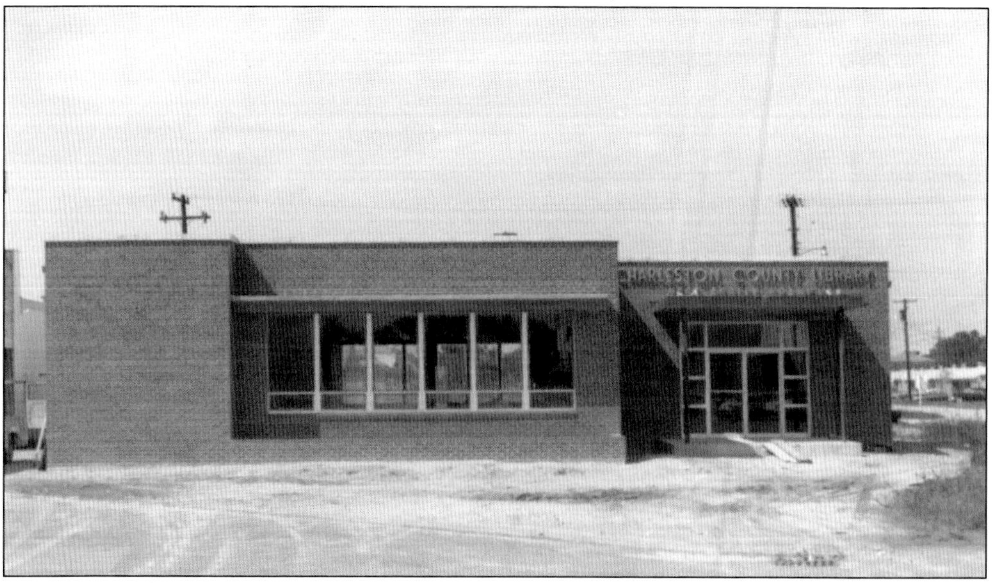

The West Ashley Branch of the Charleston County Library was constructed on property donated to Charleston County by South Windermere Realtors through William H. Ackerman. The branch opened on April 20, 1964, and has become one of the most popular in the area with the circulation reaching 279,000 in 2010. Sam Rittenberg was responsible for the legislation that created the county library system. (Courtesy of Yvonne Groves Gilreath.)

Six

Sapere Aude—Dare to Be Wise

Bernard Hester took it upon himself to design a ring for the graduating classes of St. Andrew's Parish High School. The design would also come to a more popular use as a symbol of the Parish. Mr. Hester was a history buff and carefully researched the symbols for the shield that would become the top of the ring. The shield is divided into four sections by an X-shaped cross. It is written that St. Andrew was crucified on an X-shaped cross. In the upper section is a magnolia blossom for the beautiful gardens of the Parish, on the left is a ship and "1670" representing the arrival of the colonists, on the bottom are tools, a pick, and a spade used in the mining of phosphate, and on the right is a pelican. Three pelicans adorn the base of the baptismal font at St. Andrew's Parish Church. The pelican is symbolic of atonement and fidelity. In the banner at the top of the shield is the Latin phrase *Sapere Aude*, which translates to "dare to be wise." This motto challenges the graduating senior at the commencement of life in the community. With the residential and commercial growth in St. Andrew's Parish over the first 60 years of the 20th century, this directive has become timely. The majority of St. Andrew's Parish voted to incorporate into the City of Charleston after much community debate over the possibility of incorporation. Mayor Palmar Gaillard brokered the deal. Today, St. Andrew's Parish has come to be known as West Ashley. Respecting heritage, understanding present day, and daring to be wise in the future are as important today as they were in 1963 when the Exchange Club's brochure described St. Andrew's Parish in an article titled, "Its Historic Past, Its Progressive Present, Its Glorious Future."

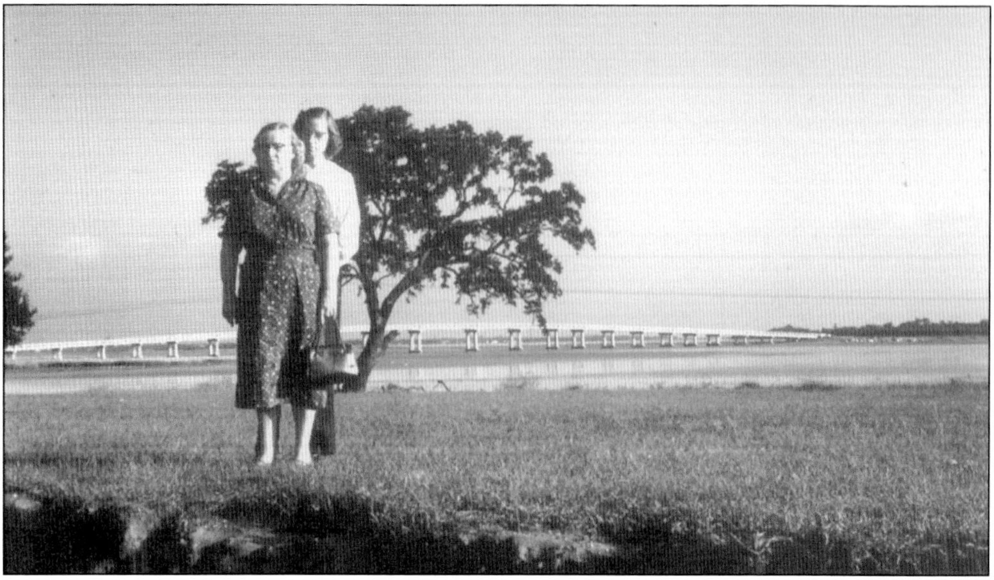

A 1955 newspaper article details the construction progress of the new World War II Memorial Bridge that will connect Charleston Heights with St. Andrew's Parish. The 2,291-foot structure cost $3 million and was another sign of the growth of St. Andrew's Parish. In typical Luther Bootle fashion, he photographed the new bridge with his mother, Grace E. (front) and his sister Grace standing with the North Bridge in the background. (Courtesy of P. Luther Bootle Jr., Ina Bootle.)

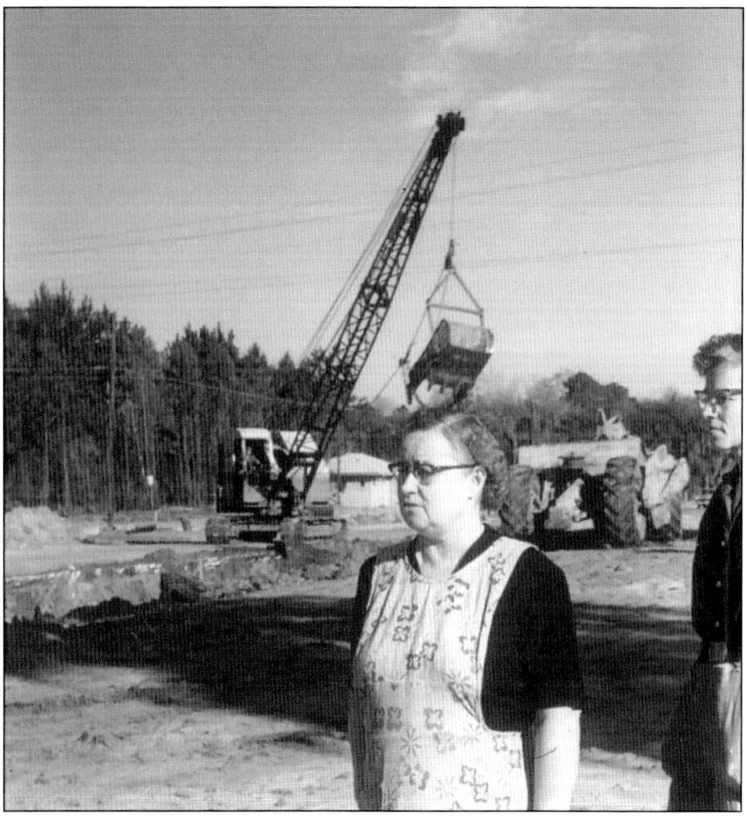

Grace E. (left) and her daughter Grace watch as US Highway North 17 is widened to four lanes near their store, Oak Lane Grocery. Considered a sign of progress for West Ashley, the impact on homes, businesses, and trees close to the highway was substantial. Many grand oaks were lost, storefronts were reconfigured, and front yards became smaller. A 1956 article in *Charleston Evening Post* described the nine-mile project from Charleston to Red Top. (Courtesy of P. Luther Bootle Jr., Ina Bootle.)

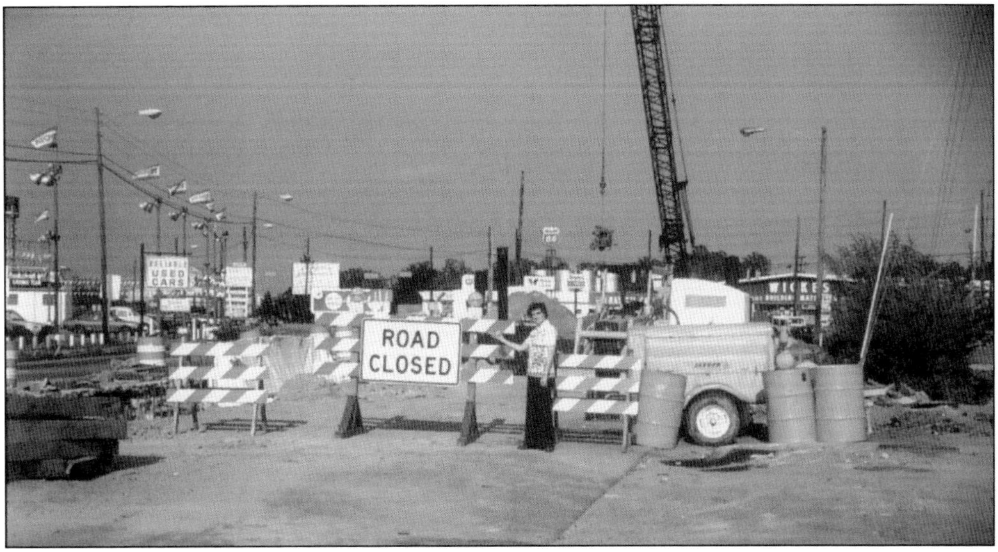

Another sign of progress was the construction of the Highway 17 overpass near Bootle's Guest House. The building of the new T. Allen Legare Bridge across the Ashley River ultimately required a reconfiguration of the roads along both sides of the river. Grace points out that the road is closed. The sign for Bill's Holly House can be seen on the left. (Courtesy of P. Luther Bootle Jr., Ina Bootle.)

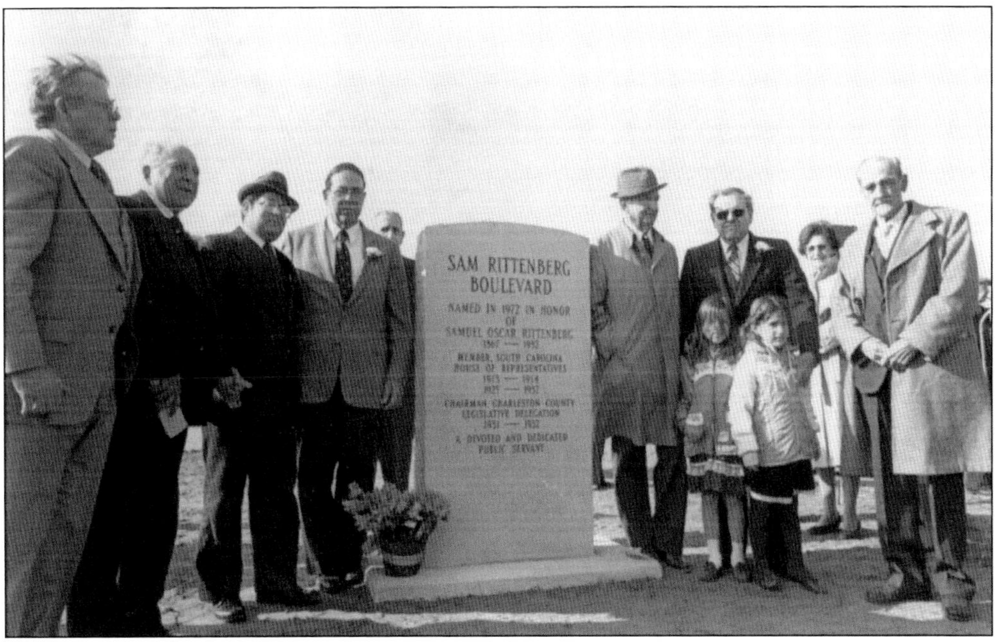

In 1972, the South Carolina Legislature played tribute to Sam Rittenberg when it adopted the resolution to name the section of South Carolina Route 7 between Highway 17 and the North Bridge in his honor. A Lithuanian immigrant, Sam was fluent in several languages, a student of Hebrew, and worked in the garment industry in New York before returning to Charleston to pursue real estate and insurance. He was first elected to the South Carolina House of Representatives in 1912, and at the time of his death, in 1932, he was the chairman of the Charleston County Legislative Delegation. (Courtesy of Special Collections, College of Charleston; gift of Henry Rittenberg.)

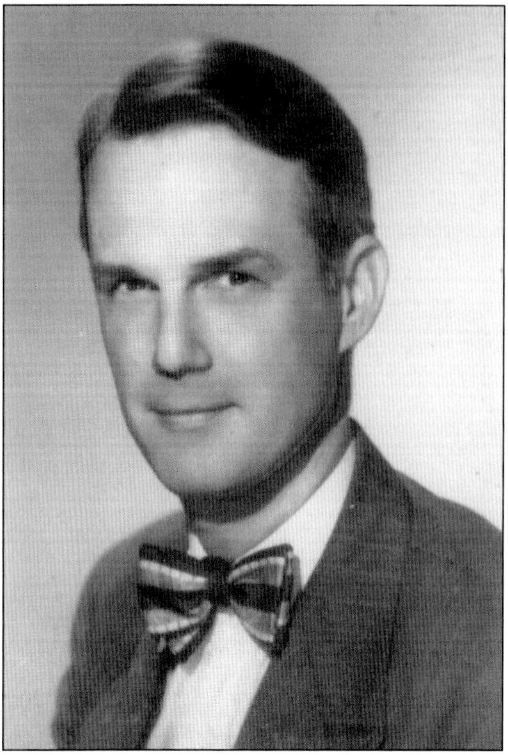

Joseph Kates Harris Sr. was in the insurance business with an office on Broad Street. He recognized that the opening of the World War II Memorial Bridge would create new opportunities in development. With another route to West Ashley, more people would be looking for homes. On land that was once considered out in the country and used for victory gardens during World War II, Joseph developed the subdivision of Melrose. (Courtesy of Joyce Harris Murray.)

Edward Kronsberg (far left) assists his grandson Avram Kronsberg Jr. with the ribbon-cutting at the Ashley Plaza opening of an Edward's store. "Mr. Ed," as the community called him, owned the popular Edward's 5 and 10 stores. (Courtesy of Ed Kronsberg.)

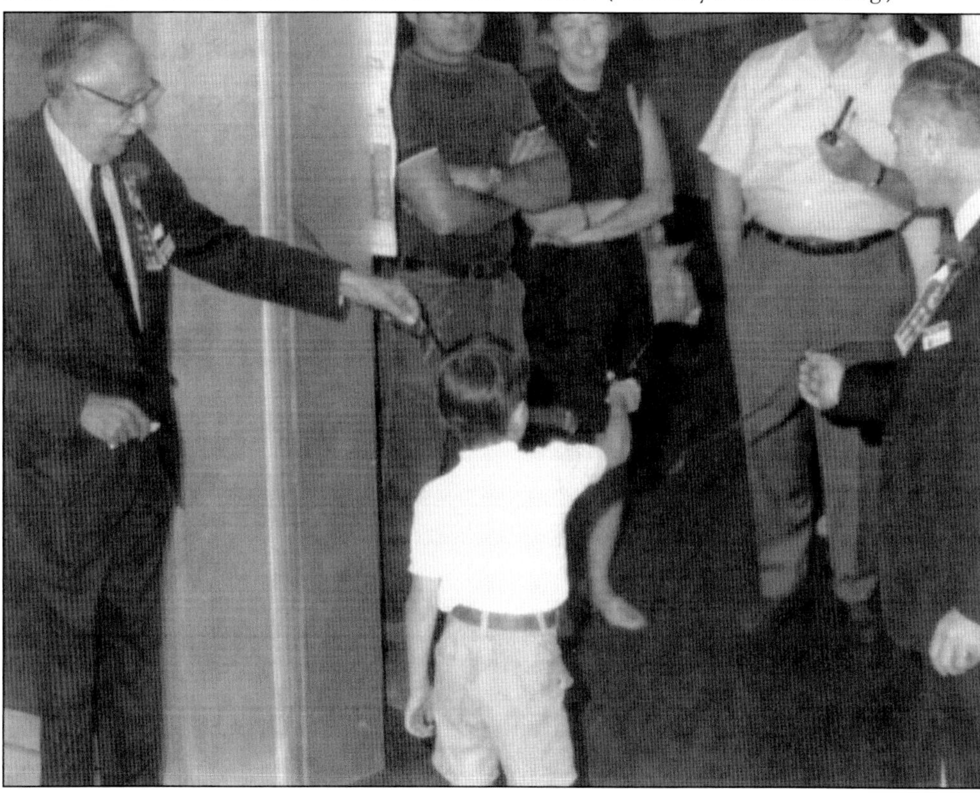

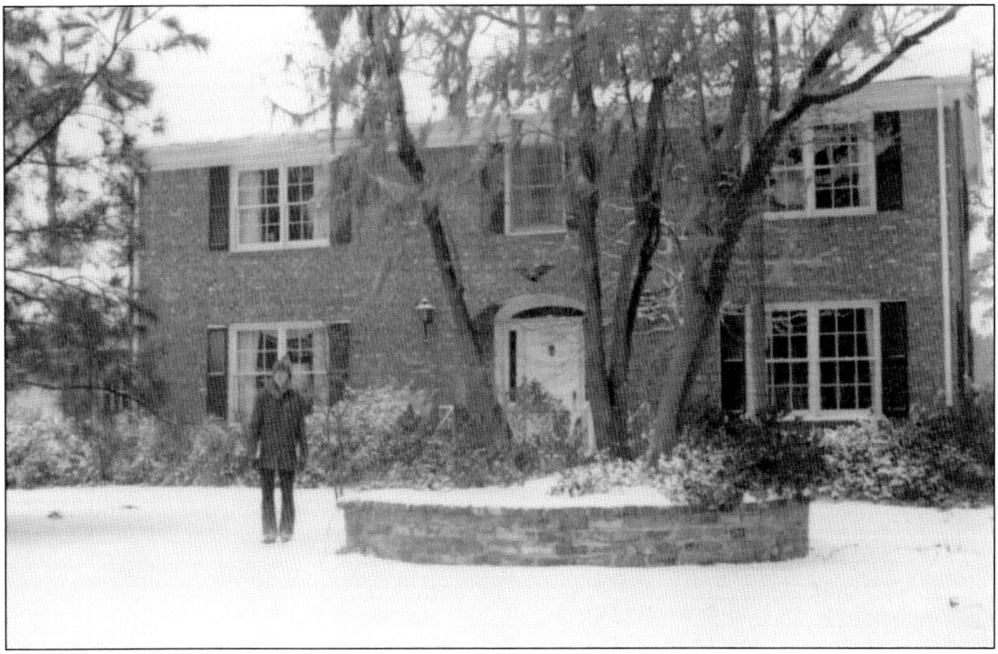

Francis (Frank) Edward Craven Jr. built 14 of the homes, including his own, in Sandhurst, a subdivision along the west bank of the Ashley River. Frank's father was a boat builder at the naval yard and Frank learned woodworking and building indirectly from him. Frank also worked at the naval yard but on submarines. He pursued a career in real estate and home construction after his retirement. On a rare snowy day, Mary Craven stands in the front yard of her home on Winchester Drive in Sandhurst. (Courtesy of Frank Craven.)

Cele Kearse casts a shadow while photographing (from left to right) Gail Fritz, Anna Wireman, Dolly Tisdale, and Diane Monroe in the parking lot of the JM Field's. The girls are in their senior year at St. Andrew's Parish High School. Gail, Anna, Diane, and Cele were affectionately known as the "Big Four." (Courtesy of Anna Wireman McAllister.)

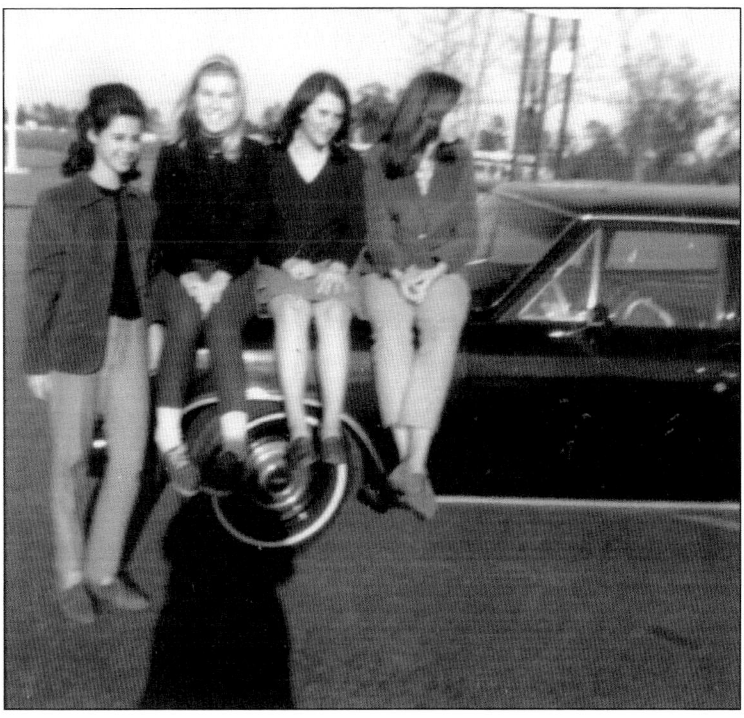

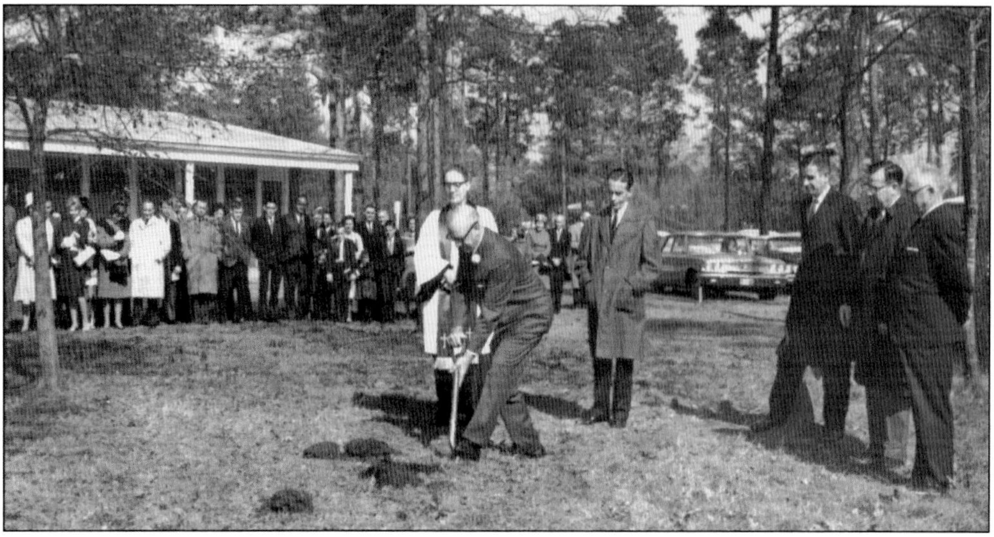

"In June of 1959 a seed was planted . . ." begins the history of Grace United Methodist Church written for the celebration of 50 years of ministry in 2010. Numerous references to planting seeds are made in recalling historical events of St. Andrew's Parish. In the above photograph, several of the parishioners watch as J.L. Griffin breaks the ground for the fellowship hall in 1961. Among the crowd are Wilfred Kearse and his wife, who were two of the first 100 members of Grace United Methodist Church. Shown in the below photograph is the 1966 view of the tree lot on Sam Rittenberg Boulevard, where the new sanctuary would be built in 1969 next to the Fellowship Hall, seen on the right. (Both, courtesy of Stella Milton Kearse.)

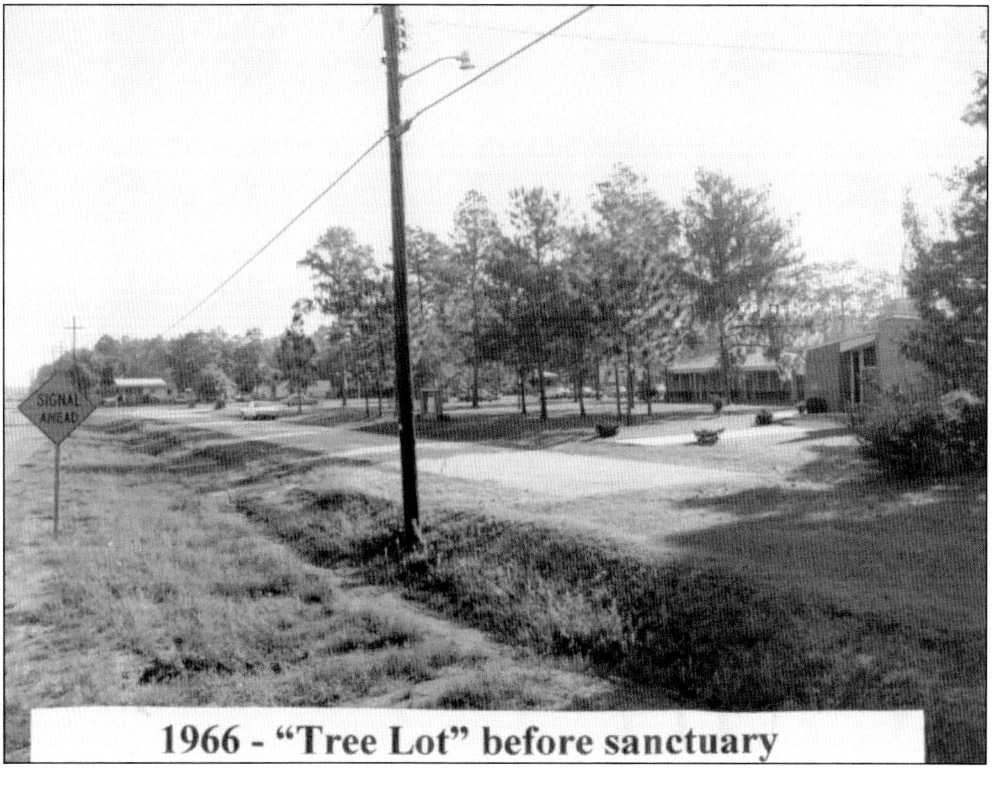

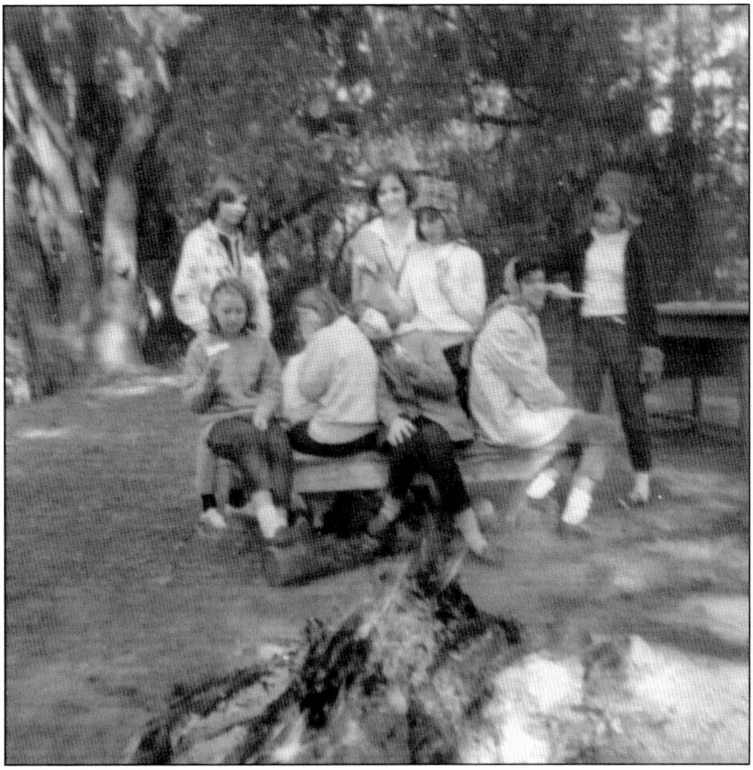

Girl Scout Troop No. 18 gathers around the campfire at the Waring Plantation, known today as Charles Towne Landing. Stella Kearse was the troop leader for this troop when it was invited to camp at the private Waring Plantation in 1965. The story goes that the invitation was extended after one of the girls saved one of Mrs. Waring's poodles that had escaped from the grounds. (Courtesy of Stella Milton Kearse.)

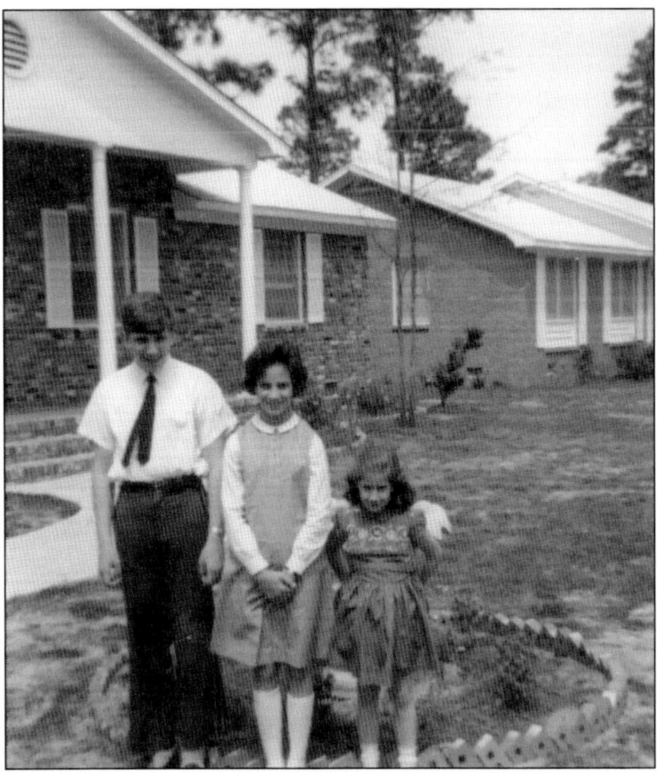

Herb and Helen Goldberg moved with their three children, Alan, Cheryl, and Susan to Coleridge Street in Charlestowne Estates III in 1965. Herb has been active in the Charlestowne Civic Club, serving as the vice president of Section III in 1967. The 1972 neighborhood directory was dedicated to him citing his many accomplishments. Charlestowne Estates was developed in three separate sections: I, II, and III. Section I abuts Charles Towne Landing on Old Towne Road. Section II is set between Sam Rittenberg Boulevard and Old Towne Road. Section III is set between Sam Rittenberg Boulevard and Orange Grove Road. (Courtesy of Herb and Helen Goldberg.)

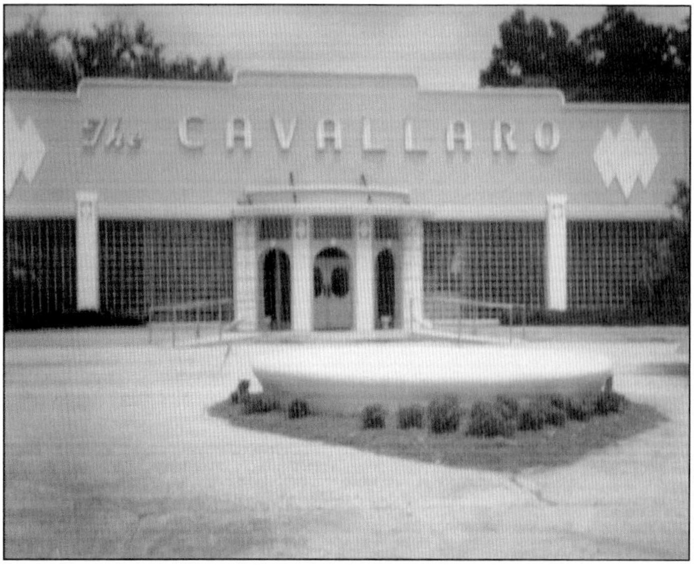

It was a sad day in West Ashley when the Cavallero closed its doors for good. There was a brief period when it was available for catered events before Rick Hendrick purchased the property to expand his automobile dealership. He responded to the outcry from the community to keep the building with its original facade. There was no more steaks, dancing, or live music but now a showroom for pre-owned Hondas. (Courtesy of Sears Saul.)

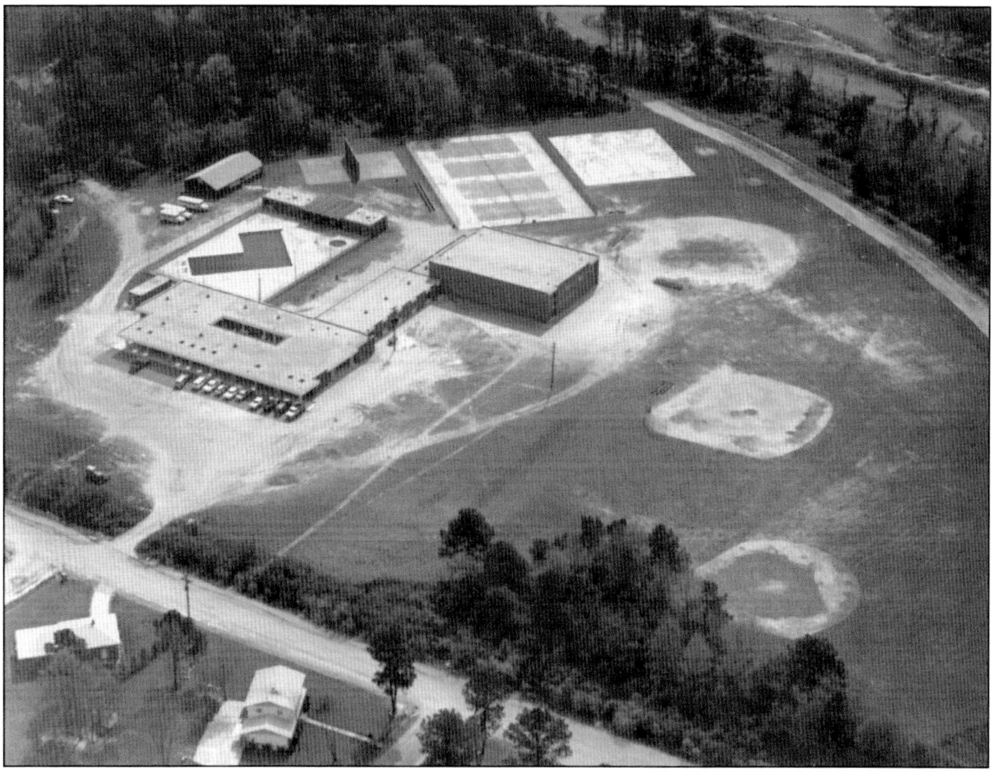

The Jewish Community Center has provided education, recreation, and social opportunities for the Jewish population of Charleston since 1923. The first center was located on George Street in downtown Charleston with Sam Rittenberg serving as president. There was a period of inactivity, but in 1945, the organization revived and incorporated. By 1959, it was decided to purchase land west of the Ashley River and build this complex on Millbrook Drive, now known as Raoul Wallenberg Road. (Courtesy of Special Collections, College of Charleston, the Jewish Community Center papers.)

Barrett Lawrimore was a dedicated public servant but his first love was horticulture. He graduated from Clemson and served in the Army before beginning a career with Clemson University Cooperative Extension Services. He not only worked diligently with area farmers, but he also served the community as a member and then chairman of Charleston County Council. Marilyn, his wife, recalls that his pet project was the Historic Charleston County Courthouse renovation. He is seen here at its dedication. (Courtesy of Marilyn Lawrimore.)

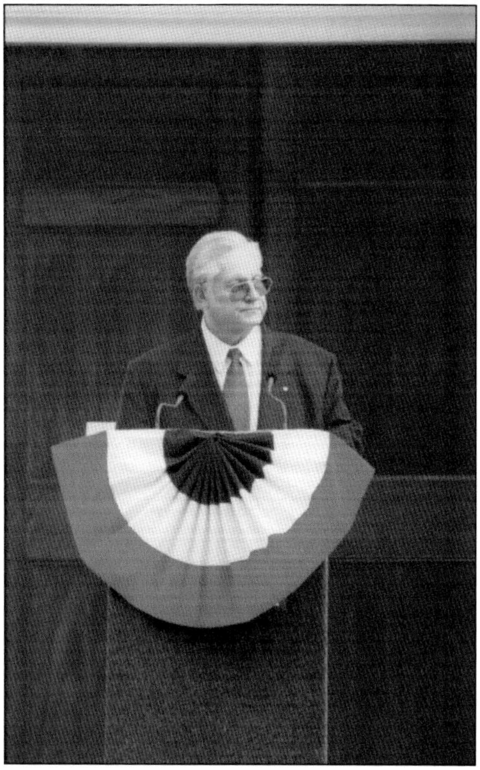

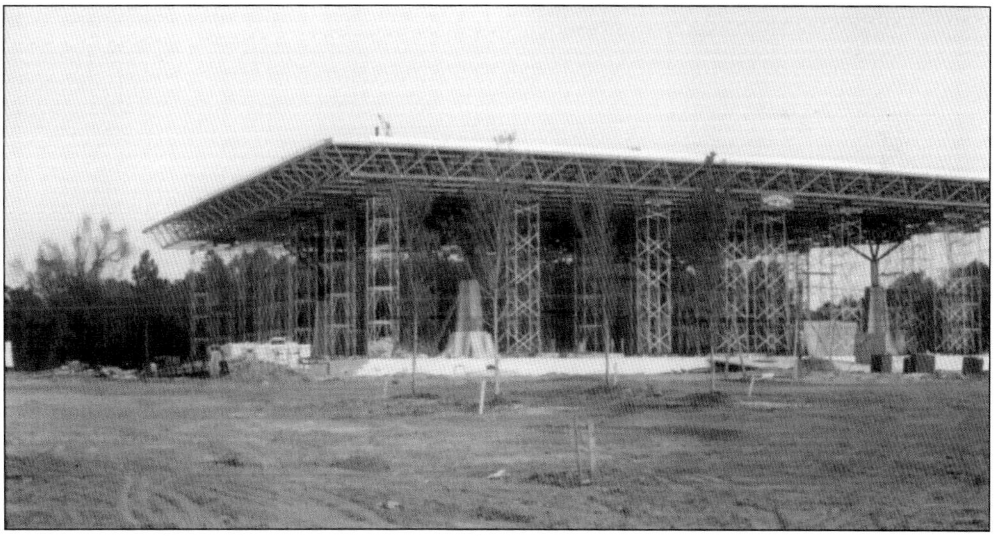

The image of the pavilion construction at Charles Towne Landing closes this preface of West Ashley's modern history. In 1930, Ferdinanda Izlar Legare Waring became the last of nine owners of Old Town Plantation. She established Old Town Gardens by growing flowers and marketing eggs. Ferdinanda and her husband, Joseph, realized the site's historic significance, transferring the property to the South Carolina Tricentennial Commission in 1968. In 1971, the property was transferred to the South Carolina Department of Parks, Recreation, and Tourism. Because they dared to be wise, the community can now embrace the history of South Carolina's birth at this magnificent state park. (Courtesy of P. Luther Bootle Jr., Ina Bootle.)